Lean Performance ERP Project Management

The St. Lucie Press/APICS Series on Resource Management

Titles in the Series

Applying Manufacturing Execution Systems
by Michael McClellan

Back to Basics: Your Guide to Manufacturing Excellence
by Steven A. Melnyk
and R.T. "Chris" Christensen

Enterprise Resources Planning and Beyond: Integrating Your Entire Organization
by Gary A. Langenwalter

ERP: Tools, Techniques, and Applications for Integrating the Supply Chain
by Carol A. Ptak
with Eli Schragenheim

Integrated Learning for ERP Success: A Learning Requirements Planning Approach
by Karl M. Kapp,
with William F. Latham
and Hester N. Ford-Latham

Integral Logistics Management: Planning and Control of Comprehensive Business Processes
by Paul Schönsleben

Inventory Classification Innovation: Paving the Way for Electronic Commerce and Vendor Managed Inventory
by Russell G. Broeckelmann

Lean Manufacturing: Tools, Techniques, and How To Use Them
by William M. Feld

Macrologistics Management: A Catalyst for Organizational Change
by Martin Stein
and Frank Voehl

Restructuring the Manufacturing Process: Applying the Matrix Method
by Gideon Halevi

Basics of Supply Chain Management
by Lawrence D. Fredendall
and Ed Hill

Supply Chain Management: The Basics and Beyond
by William C. Copacino

Handbook of Supply Chain Management
by Jim Ayers

Brian J. Carroll

Lean Performance ERP Project Management

Implementing the Virtual Supply Chain

ST. LUCIE PRESS

A CRC Press Company
Boca Raton   London   New York   Washington, D.C.

Library of Congress Cataloging-in-Publication Data

Carroll, Brian J.
    Lean performance ERP project management : implementing the virtual supply chain / Brian J. Carroll
       p. cm. — (The St. Lucie Press/APICS series on resource management)
       Includes bibliographical references and index.
       ISBN 1-57444-309-7 (alk. paper)
          1. Production control. 2. Production management. I. Title.
    II. Series
TS155.8 .C37 2001
685.5—dc21   2001048548

This book contains information obtained from authentic and highly regarded sources. Reprinted material is quoted with permission, and sources are indicated. A wide variety of references are listed. Reasonable efforts have been made to publish reliable data and information, but the author and the publisher cannot assume responsibility for the validity of all materials or for the consequences of their use.

Neither this book nor any part may be reproduced or transmitted in any form or by any means, electronic or mechanical, including photocopying, microfilming, and recording, or by any information storage or retrieval system, without prior permission in writing from the publisher.

The consent of St. Lucie Press does not extend to copying for general distribution, for promotion, for creating new works, or for resale. Specific permission must be obtained in writing from St. Lucie Press for such copying.

Direct all inquiries to St. Lucie Press, 2000 Corporate Blvd. N.W., Boca Raton, Florida 33431.

Trademark Notice: Product or corporate names may be trademarks or registered trademarks, and are used only for identification and explanation, without intent to infringe.

© 2002 by Performance Improvement Consulting, Inc.
St. Lucie Press is an imprint of CRC Press LLC

No claim to original U.S. Government works
International Standard Book Number 1-57444-309-7
Library of Congress Card Number 2001048548
Printed in the United States of America   2 3 4 5 6 7 8 9 0
Printed on acid-free paper

DEDICATION

For Kathryn,

who thinks I can do no wrong,

and Barbara,

who knows better

and loves me anyway

CONTENTS

Preface xiii
Acknowledgments xix
The Author xx
Figures xxi
About APICS xxv

I. Introduction to Lean Performance

1   Foundations of Lean Performance 3
     The Organizational Consequences of Mass Production 3
     The Origin of Lean Production 5
     What Is Lean Production? 7
     Why Aren't More Firms Lean? 9
     What Is Required to Become Lean? 12

2   Extending Lean Performance Foundations 15
     Implementing Lean Cross-Functional Processes 15
     Lean Quality Management 17
     Lean Maintenance 18
     Lean New Product Introduction 19
     Lean Design and Engineering 20

3   Lean Performance Methodology 23
     What Is the Lean Enterprise? 23
     Why Should Our Enterprise Be Lean? 24
     What Is Lean Performance? 25
     How Does Lean Performance Improve Processes? 28
     Why Lean Performance Is the Best Lean Methodology 29

4	**Lean Cross-Enterprise Processes** 41
	What Is Lean Commerce? 41
	Lean Customer Relationship Management 48
	Lean Supply Chain Management 50
	Lean Production Smoothing 51
	Supporting a Lean Factory Flow 53

5	**Lean Principles, Tools, and Practices** 55
	Lean Cultural Principles 55
	Process-Oriented Thinking Means What before How 55
	Product Quality Results from Process Quality 55
	Every Process Requires a Process Standard 56
	The Process Owner Is the Process Expert 56
	The Next Process Is Your Customer 56
	Loyalty to People Enables Continuous Improvement 56
	Process Data and Measurements Drive
	Process Continuous Improvement 57
	Lean Transformational Principles 57
	Precisely Specify Value by Product or Family 57
	Identify the Value Stream for Each Product 58
	Make Value Flow without Interruption 58
	Let the Customer Pull Value from the Process Owner 58
	Pursue Perfection 58
	Lean Diagnostic Tools 58
	3MUs 58
	5S 59
	5Ws–1H 59
	4Ms 59
	Lean Performance Practices 60
	Management Policy Deployment 60
	Lean Performance Teams 61
	Visual Management 62
	Lean Performance Analysis 63

6	**Steering a Lean Performance Project** 69
	Management in the Lean Performance Project 69
	Completing the Lean Performance Assessment 73
	Lean Performance Assessment 74
	Company Readiness 74
	Opportunity to Make Lean Applications 90
	Company Capability to Become Lean 92
	Lean Performance Project Constraints 94
	Analyzing Lean Performance Assessment Results 95
	Preparing for the Lean Performance Project 97

II. Lean Performance Planning Modules

7 Deploying Management Policy Module 101
   Management Tasks 101
      Organizing the Steering Committee 101
      Confirming the Lean Vision 102
      Identifying and Deploying Lean Business Policies 102
      Identifying and Deploying Lean Project Strategies 102
      Defining the Project Mission 105
      Defining the Project Scope 107
      Setting Up the Project Organization 107
      Identifying and Deploying the Project Objectives 110
      Conducting Steering Committee Meetings 114

8 Managing the Project Module 119
   Project Team Tasks 119
      Maintaining the Project Summary Bar Chart 119
      Maintaining Project Communications 119
      Maintaining the Project Plan 119
      Maintaining an Open Issue Resolution Process 121
      Maintaining the Project Organization 124
      Maintaining the Quality Assurance Process 127
      Reporting Progress to the Steering Committee 128

9 Developing Lean Performance Teams Module 129
   Project Team Tasks 129
      Finalizing Projects and Strategies 129
      Developing the Site Configuration 130
      Identifying All Processes 131
      Developing Site Teams 138
      Developing Lean Performance Team Training 138
      Reporting Progress to the Steering Committee 153
   What Follows Lean Performance Planning? 153

III. Lean Performance Improvement Modules

10 Improving Process Performance Module 165
   Management Tasks 165
      Maintaining Lean Performance Teams 165
      Conducting Steering Committee Meetings 166
   Project Team Tasks 167
      Lean Performance Team Education 167
      Finance Team Tasks 171
      Engineering Team Tasks 173
      Materials Team Tasks 177

Operations Team Tasks 179
Information Team Tasks 182
Lean Commerce Team Tasks 185
Performing Lean Performance Analysis 189
    Precisely Specify the Value by Product or Family 205
    Identify the Value Stream for Each Product 205
    Make Value Flow without Interruption 206
    Let the Customer Pull Value from the Process Owner 208
    Pursuit of Perfection 209
Completing Lean Performance Analysis 209
Producing Work Instructions 218

11   Integrating Systems Module 225

Project Team Tasks 225
    Installing Hardware and Software 225
    Initiating the System 226
    Setting Up System Security 226
    Creating Test and Training Environments 226
    Creating Production Databases 227
    Testing System Setup 227
    Managing the Data Conversion Process 227
    Evaluating Additional Software Packages and Interfaces 228
    Conducting Process-Oriented System Design 229
    Summarizing Proposed Modifications 231
    Completing Hardware and Communications Analysis 232
    Preparing Detailed Design Specifications 233
    Managing Outsourced Programming 234
    Defining Interface and Database Testing 235

12   Testing Improved Processes Module 237

Project Team Tasks 237
    Objectives of Testing 237
    Prototype and Pilot Test 238
    Establishing the Test Team 238
    Test Team Kick-Off Meeting 241
    Process Test 242
    Stress Test 248
    Process Workflow and Work Instruction Update 249
    Conducting the User Training Program 250
What Follows Lean Performance Improvement? 250

IV. Continuous Lean Performance Modules

13   Implementing Improved Processes Module 253

Management Tasks 253

Maintaining Lean Performance Teams 253
Implementing Lean Performance Management 256
Continuously Deploying Lean Policy and Strategy...................... 259
Auditing Lean Performance.. 260
Project Team Tasks... 262
Completing the Implementation Readiness Assessments............ 262
Verifying System Integration 263
Counting Down to Implementation.. 264
Implementing Improved Processes 264
Providing Additional Training... 264
Providing Production Startup Support... 265

14 Continuously Improving Lean Performance Module 267
Project Team Tasks... 267
Defining and Initiating Lean Performance Measurements 267
Continuously Improving Lean Performance 272

Index... 277

PREFACE

What Is Lean Performance?

Lean Performance is a project management methodology for lean implementation that starts with existing processes and develops process performance improvements and measurements. By developing process workflow standards of *what* work must be completed and then utilizing the process workflow standards to determine *how* to do the work, Lean Performance produces process work instructions for training to ensure continued process quality. Lean Performance also manages multisite projects by identifying common processes and prioritizing assignments. The methodology develops process performance measurements and continuous Lean Performance where information technology has already been implemented or as the implementation methodology for new projects.

Lean production is the philosophy and practice of eliminating all waste in all production processes continuously. Manufacturing workers may apply lean principles, tools, and practices successfully to continuously improve production processes, but usually information technologies do not readily enable continuous improvements in management decision processes, information/support processes, and linkages to lean physical processes. Methodologies for information technology installation, such as reengineering and process or system innovation, do not facilitate the use of lean thinking to improve management decision and information/support processes and their linkages to lean physical processes. Until now, lean thinking has been narrowly focused on physical processes, but this limited approach has several serious shortcomings:

- Process improvements driven by information technology are not always linked to management strategies and objectives.

- Management decision processes do not support lean physical processes.
- Physical process lean improvements are not supported by or linked to information systems.

The Lean Performance methodology presented in this book suggests a solution. Lean Performance uses lean principles, tools, and practices to improve and then *continuously* improve management decision and information/support processes and their linkages to the lean physical processes. The methodology trains and empowers the in-house experts, process owners, and customers, while employing the best of the process and system innovation and reengineering tools (from a lean perspective) to achieve system integration. Lean Performance develops or enhances a company culture of continuous improvement by recognizing the strength of the business: the people and processes. Lean Performance integrates strategy, people, processes, and information technology into a project management methodology that applies lean thinking to all processes, utilizing eight implementation and training modules.

Why Is Lean Performance Important?

Today's manager is faced with the dilemma of managing emerging cross-functional and cross-enterprise business processes such as e-commerce and the new supply chain management processes utilizing information technology in a business enterprise with an increasingly empowered team culture. All too often, traditional information system development based on methodologies such as reengineering and system or process innovation is woefully inadequate for use in an empowered team culture. Even in more traditional business environments, process analysis and system development projects run and performed by business or information technical "experts" often deliver miserable results, especially from a quality standpoint. Delivered systems either do not work technically or do not fit the process as the user performs it today or could best perform it tomorrow. In contrast, great results have been obtained by harnessing the power of all enterprise team members through methodologies that employ lean philosophy and thinking, such as Total Quality Management (TQM), *kaizen*, and continuous improvement. The Lean Performance project management methodology presented here incorporates lean philosophy and thinking in a task structure that, when executed, implements lean management decision processes, information/support processes, and information linkages that support lean physical processes and provides the structure to improve physical processes. The methodology performs best in the empowered team business environment, utilizing vendor-supplied, unmodified software packages for manufacturing such as enterprise resource planning (ERP), supply chain management (SCM), operations planning system (OPS), manufacturing execution system (MES), and customer relationship management (CRM).

A successful business process improvement or redesign approach considers inputs from the two hemispheres of management that typically are in conflict:

- Departmental, politically based management practices
- Emerging information-based management practices

In many companies, established politically based management practices rely on an individual, power-oriented management style that leverages power gained through controlling a "stovepipe" departmental structure and the flow of information (work) residing within that stovepipe. These structures are dependent on internal management alliances to manage the business through a process of negotiation, compromise, and accommodation. Emerging information-based management practices are fundamentally different in that the information that is held hostage in the stovepipes of an old-style organization is open in the empowered team workplace. In fact, opening up this information flow and designing work around it (workflow) is the real (and perhaps only) reason to consider information-technology-enabled process improvement or redesign. With open information, old alliances are not necessary, and team-based decision making can take place. Departmental structures are no longer efficient and are replaced by product- and process-based structures.

Obviously, these structural changes can be very threatening to old-line (stovepipe) managers, and they resist them. When an information technology specialist is introduced into the mix, numerous complications occur. The lack of a common language between power-style managers (who translate their information requirements into newer and better stovepipes) and technically adept information technology/data processing experts (who do not have the business process expertise of the people already performing the existing processes) leads to enough confusion to sink many business process improvement efforts. If the process owner is not the process designer, nonvalue-added tasks will dominate a new stovepipe at the end of the project. This collision of dysfunctional styles is a fundamental impediment to success in the information age, much as office-based manufacturing engineers of the mass industrial age were an impediment to success in the factory, leading to their removal by the originators and practitioners of lean production. Lean Performance defeats the nonvalue-added process constraints imposed on processes by well-intended, technologically adept but misguided individuals who presume they are experts in processes that they themselves do not perform.

Applying the Lean Performance methodology to a business process improvement or redesign project focuses the efforts on a common approach that uses common principles, tools, and practices. This approach promotes successful dialog among the managers, information technology specialists, and emerging computer-literate knowledge workers or team members, who in many cases are already in the workplace but generally not (yet) in a position of management. Lean Performance leverages the expertise of existing internal process owners and customers to design processes in terms of what needs to be done to produce value (product or service) for process customers immediately downstream. All methodology tasks are structured to "pull" process redesign/improvement activities from the point of view of the external customer so that optimum customer value is provided.

How Does Lean Performance Work?

Lean Performance identifies and deploys lean management business policies and strategies during software implementation, process improvement, and lean transformation projects by integrating lean thinking and process-oriented management at the management decision, information/support, information linkage, and physical process levels through the use of an integrative project and management practice: the Lean Performance Analysis. The methodology then utilizes business process reengineering techniques to design the process architecture. Lean Performance employs lean practices to develop Lean Performance teams of process owners and customers. These Lean Performance teams eliminate waste from existing management and information processes while developing value-added information linkages to support lean physical processes and improve the physical processes. Additionally, Lean Performance employs system innovation techniques from a lean perspective to provide a project management workplan and toolkit to integrate the information system (ERP, MES, SCM, OPS, CRM) and to provide an ongoing continuous improvement tool after implementation.

Who Is Lean Performance For?

This book is geared toward the 21st-century business manager, a new type of manager who is developing in the lean workplace and manages *with* technology, rather than simply managing technology. I propose that there is a critical difference. These new managers will have used information technology for most of their careers and will readily agree that most information technology projects fail or deliver poor results and require extensive after-project rework. These managers may already be chief executives or chief operating officers, engineering or operations or materials managers, or continuous improvement or lean coordinators. They have probably served as project managers at some point or now employ project management approaches to team management. Project managers who have been exposed to lean production are a ready audience for this book. These managers are or have been successful employing lean methodologies in their current or previous assignments.

Information technology professionals, on the other hand, may not see the relevance of the methodology. Many information technology professionals may be all too familiar with the failures of previous projects and methodologies; however, seasoned information technology professionals who are ready to try this more comprehensive approach will immediately hone in on the most obvious reason for information technology to support Lean Performance: Lean Performance puts the responsibility for a successful implementation or transformation squarely on the shoulders of the process owners and customers. The typically noninvolved system user of the past cannot function successfully in a Lean Performance environment.

Why Did I Write This Book?

I wrote this book in part because it expresses my theoretical interest in business process and performance improvement methodologies and incorporates what I have learned about them by trial and error. In my career in manufacturing management and consulting for a variety of domestic and international companies, I have had the opportunity to try out various approaches to business improvement and project management. Lean Performance is the result of my attempts to develop a methodology evolved from classical business consulting approaches but viewed through a lean-thinking lens. Perhaps most importantly, I have had the experience of being a project manager subject to Murphy's First Law of Project Management: about the time you know enough about the project to write a comprehensive project plan, you don't have time to stop managing the project and write it. For this reason, I wanted to develop a project template for myself and other project managers to apply to our projects before their weight becomes all we can carry.

As fond of information and other technologies as I am, I believe that the more complex and, therefore, more valuable (and costly) elements of business processes are tasks that are people based. When we deemphasize technology and introduce the concept of managing the office and linking the office to the factory with processes, in much the same way as we manage the factory, then introducing lean principles, tools, and practices to the management, information/support, and physical processes becomes possible. While my preference is to emphasize manufacturing, the broader methodological concepts are appropriate to computer-based process management and all business processes, regardless of service or industry. Also, the transition into the 21st century has revealed performance gaps in many new systems that will benefit greatly from applying Lean Performance.

In conclusion, management and information/support processes and information linkages to physical processes are not ineligible for continuous improvement. The Lean Performance methodology is a process-oriented approach that provides a project management structure for applying lean thinking to the entire enterprise, with an emphasis on the management, information/support, and physical processes.

Application of lean thinking in the factory has resulted in the elimination of some portion of direct labor while maintaining the same or greater productive output from fewer workers. The application of lean thinking to the office results in a reduction of management layers, with a corresponding higher output flowing from the same or fewer knowledge workers. The real challenge to the enterprise in applying these lean principles, tools, and practices is to recognize that, above all, lean is a growth strategy. Management cannot expect workers to continuously improve their way to the unemployment line. New challenges must continuously be presented to today's Lean Performance teams by modern managers who manage with technology.

Brian J. Carroll

ACKNOWLEDGMENTS

I owe a debt of thanks to many people who have helped me in the writing of this book, but I can name only some of them here. I would like to first thank my family, who has given me their consistent support. Roger Dykstra and Robert Montgomery of Manufacturing Management Associates gave me my first consulting experience and taught me much about the development and application of consulting methodology. John Toomey shared much of himself, and through the publication of his two fine texts[*] has been an inspiration to me by demonstrating the persistence necessary to write a book. John A. "Jack" Kalina explored many of the ideas in this book with me early on in our project collaborations. Gary Saunders allowed me to pursue my ideas on several critical projects. Guenter Leibold and Ron Spiers gave me an opportunity to try my ideas on their projects and added their creativity to the effort. Kevin Pastel and Fred Gruber were instrumental in pursuing these ideas while we collaborated on the behalf of clients. Ed Holmes, Chuck Morin, and especially Bob O'Shea of Engineering Systems had the patience to support my vision. Ed Allfrey of the Center for Enterprise Development stuck by me through the seemingly endless "startup." Dick Marshall listened to my ideas with incredible patience and provided a wise and informed perspective on the use of lean principles, tools, and practices in the team setting. I especially want to thank John Condon for his close counsel and friendship. Finally, Goto-San, here is the book. Thank you for your inspiration.

---

[*] Toomey, J., *MRPII Planning For Manufacturing Excellence* (Chapman & Hall, New York, 1996) and *Inventory Management Principles, Concepts and Techniques* (Kluwer Academic Publishers, Norwell, MA, 2000).

THE AUTHOR

Brian J. Carroll is the president of Performance Improvement Consulting, Inc., located in Downers Grove, IL. He has conducted numerous engagement in information technology and manufacturing management for domestic and international clients, including over 25 successful MRP/ERP implementation projects as a project manager or project director. He is also affiliated with Engineering Systems Associates (ESA), a management consulting firm specializing in Lean Performance services and located in Aurora, IL. The ESA website is www.esalean.com, or send inquiries to leancommerce@attbi.com.

FIGURES

I. Introduction to Lean Performance

Figure 3.1	Lean Performance Foundation Blocks	27
Figure 3.2	Comparison of Reengineering, Lean, and Lean Performance	27
Figure 3.3	General Methodology Comparison	32
Figure 3.4	Strategic Issues Comparison	32
Figure 3.5	Project Scope Comparison	33
Figure 3.6	Tactical Issues Comparison	33
Figure 3.7	Quality Issues Comparison	34
Figure 3.8	Results Comparison	34
Figure 3.9	Lean Progression	37
Figure 3.10	Future of Data Processing	38
Figure 4.1	Lean Commerce Manufacturing Model	43
Figure 5.1	Lean Performance Analysis: Lean Business Policy Deployed	61
Figure 5.2	Business Process Areas	63
Figure 5.3	Current Process Activity Overview (International)	64
Figure 5.4	Lean Performance Team (International)	65
Figure 5.5	Business Process Listing and Sequence	66
Figure 5.6	Lean Performance Analysis: Process and Team Identified	67
Figure 5.7	Workflow Diagram Template	67
Figure 5.8	Work Instruction Template	68

II. Lean Performance Planning Modules

Figure 7.1	Lean Business Policies	103
Figure 7.2	Lean Performance Analysis: Lean Business Policy Deployed	103
Figure 7.3	Lean Project Strategies	104

Figure 7.4	Lean Performance Analysis: Lean Project Strategy Deployed	105
Figure 7.5	Project Mission Statement	107
Figure 7.6	Project Scope Statement	107
Figure 7.7	Lean Performance Analysis: Project Objective Deployed	114
Figure 7.8	Policy Deployment and Measurements Summary	115–117
Figure 8.1	Lean Performance Methodology Project Summary Bar Chart	120
Figure 8.2	Project Work Plan	120
Figure 8.3	Open-Issue Form	122
Figure 8.4	Open-Issue Template	123
Figure 8.5	Business Process Areas Overview Diagram for Corporate Site of a Manufacturer	125
Figure 8.6	Business Process Areas Overview Diagram for Manufacturer of Products for the Aftermarket	125
Figure 8.7	Business Process Areas Overview Diagram for International Manufacturer	125
Figure 8.8	Project Organization Chart	126
Figure 9.1	Current Projects and Strategies Definition	130
Figure 9.2	Site Configuration	132
Figure 9.3	Information/Support Process Characteristics	133
Figure 9.4	Current Process Activity Overview Diagram (Corporate)	135
Figure 9.5	Current Process Activity Overview Diagram (Aftermarket)	136
Figure 9.6	Current Process Activity Overview Diagram (International)	137
Figure 9.7	Lean Performance Project Process Listing and Sequence	139–142
Figure 9.8	Lean Performance Team (Corporate)	143
Figure 9.9	Lean Performance Team (Aftermarket)	143
Figure 9.10	Lean Performance Team (International)	143
Figure 9.11	Process Workflow Example	148–150
Figure 9.12	Work Instruction How-To Example	151–152
Figure 9.13	Project Control Spreadsheet	153–158
Figure 9.14	Process Workflow Diagram: Status for All Business Areas for Aftermarket Site	159
Figure 9.15	Progress by Major Business Areas for Aftermarket Site	159
Figure 9.16	Progress by Primary Business Areas for Aftermarket Site	160
Figure 9.17	Progress by Secondary Business Areas for Aftermarket Site	160

III. Lean Performance Improvement Modules

Figure 10.1	Workflow Diagram Template	169
Figure 10.2	Work Instruction Template	170
Figure 10.3	Training Assignments Spreadsheet	171
Figure 10.4	Overhead Cost Accumulation Model	172
Figure 10.5	General Ledger Accounts	174–175
Figure 10.6	Database Financial Entities	176
Figure 10.7	Material Flow Diagram	180
Figure 10.8	Material Flow Transactions	181
Figure 10.9	Lean Performance Analysis: Technology Deployed	184
Figure 10.10	Policy Deployment and Measurements Summary — Technology Deployed	186–188
Figure 10.11	Lean Performance Analysis: Process and Team Identified	190
Figure 10.12	Policy Deployment and Measurements Summary — Process and Team Identified	191–193
Figure 10.13	Process Requirements Definition: Interview and Status Listing	196–203
Figure 10.14	Process Requirements Definition: Order Entry	204
Figure 10.15	Fuel Pump Returns Process Workflow Standard	211–213
Figure 10.16	Lean Performance Analysis: GAP Solution and Benefit	218
Figure 10.17	Online Return Credit Work Instruction	219
Figure 10.18	Process Master Index	220–223
Figure 11.1	Process/System Overview Diagram	230
Figure 12.1	Pilot Prototype Test Roadmap	239–244

IV. Continuous Lean Performance Modules

Figure 13.1	Implementation Readiness Assessment for International Site	263
Figure 14.1	Lean Performance Analysis: Process Measurement Identified	268
Figure 14.2	Policy Deployment and Measurements Summary — Performance Measurement Identified	269–271

ABOUT APICS

APICS, The Educational Society for Resource Management, is an international, not-for-profit organization offering a full range of programs and materials focusing on individual and organizational education, standards of excellence, and integrated resource management topics. These resources, developed under the direction of integrated resource management experts, are available at local, regional, and national levels. Since 1957, hundreds of thousands of professionals have relied on APICS as a source for educational products and services.

- **APICS Certification Programs** — APICS offers two internationally recognized certification programs, Certified in Production and Inventory Management (CPIM) and Certified in Integrated Resource Management (CIRM), known around the world as standards of professional competence in business and manufacturing.
- *APICS Educational Materials Catalog* — This catalog contains books, courseware, proceedings, reprints, training materials, and videos developed by industry experts and available to members at a discount.
- *APICS — The Performance Advantage* — This monthly, four-color magazine addresses the educational and resource management needs of manufacturing professionals.
- *APICS Business Outlook Index* — Designed to take economic analysis a step beyond current surveys, the index is a monthly manufacturing-based survey report based on confidential production, sales, and inventory data from APICS-related companies.
- **Chapters** — APICS' more than 270 chapters provide leadership, learning, and networking opportunities at the local level.

- **Educational Opportunities** — Held around the country, APICS' International Conference and Exhibition, workshops, and symposia offer you numerous opportunities to learn from your peers and management experts.
- **Employment Referral Program** — A cost-effective way to reach a targeted network of resource management professionals, this program pairs qualified job candidates with interested companies.
- **SIGs** — These member groups develop specialized educational programs and resources for seven specific industry and interest areas.
- **Web Site** — The APICS web site at http://www.apics.org enables you to explore the wide range of information available on APICS' membership, certification, and educational offerings.
- **Member Services** — Members enjoy a dedicated inquiry service, insurance, a retirement plan, and more.

For more information on APICS programs, services, or membership, call APICS Customer Service at (800) 444-2742 or (703) 237-8344 or visit http://www.apics.org on the World Wide Web.

I

INTRODUCTION TO LEAN PERFORMANCE

1

FOUNDATIONS OF LEAN PERFORMANCE

THE ORGANIZATIONAL CONSEQUENCES OF MASS PRODUCTION

A rigid mass production system leads to a highly structured, centralized, and inflexible command and control management system. The management hierarchy in a mass production environment is generally several levels deep. Approvals for changes have to flow up and down this chain of command. Departmental boundaries, not process requirements, determine where processes initiate and terminate, resulting in processes being chopped into inefficient subprocesses. Examples of this phenomenon found in most mass production environments include the processes of maintenance, quality, procurement, design and engineering, customer service, scheduling, shipping, and invoicing, all of which snake their way through department after department, in-basket after in-basket, paper queue after paper queue, until they are handed off to completion. While all of this is going on, orders, projects, purchases, and deliveries are being expedited, requiring various search missions for papers, negotiations for priority, and the occasional compromise. Managers in the mass production environment are usually more concerned with their departmental objectives than with organizational objectives which results in the dissipation of energy and resources as departmental objectives are achieved at the expense of organizational objectives.

When rigid production systems in the mass environment grow into static organization structures and management systems, the resulting emphasis placed on maintaining the status quo chokes off innovation. Competitive, low-bid purchasing systems lead to adversarial relations with suppliers that virtually eliminate the incentive to improve anything, except cost. Customer service is a secondary consideration, limited to fulfilling contracts and warranties. Customer service usually does not employ any mechanism beyond the stated goal of desiring or seeking customer feedback on their needs, product improvement, effective new product development, ongoing customer relationships, or effective linkage to production. Customer relations management is technology driven and often is only a vehicle for pursuing customers, not for retaining them through better service. Innovation is focused on product development, not process development. This results in the introduction of products that cannot be efficiently or effectively manufactured with existing production and/or information systems.

In the mass environment, systematic improvement is a staff activity, not a worker responsibility, and is generally performed by industrial and systems engineering technologists which results in elimination of a major source of process improvement: the process owners. Quality standards that are set to be readily achievable and are not continuously improved lead to low standards that are easy to attain and maintain, thus perpetuating the process conditions that caused such low standards to be set initially. Functional areas have little or no incentive to work together to establish cross-functional processes, eliminate delays, improve work flows, balance and synchronize operations, or treat departments receiving products or services as customers.

Operating systems and reporting structures follow departmental lines of authority. This makes interdepartmental cross-functional processes difficult, if not impossible, to design and operate effectively. Systems and operating procedures are not well documented because of the inherent advantages of not documenting (e.g., job security). If systems and procedures are viewed as not changing, why write them up? We can just do it the way we always have. Without a documented, standard way of operating, not being held accountable becomes easier. In many cases, standard ways of operating have not been established because the transition from craft industry to mass production was evolutionary and not explicitly designed on a company-wide basis. In many companies existing at the time of transition, it was more a matter of introducing an assembly line in the production area and adjusting to its impact. In other words, an explicit process design never existed, and generations of emulation and stagnation have devolved the processes in the mass production workplace even farther from optimum.

Interestingly, the lack of standard operating procedures may be the ultimate impediment to the one seemingly successful mass production strategy: the cost mechanics of volume achieved through interminable mergers, acquisitions, and takeovers. Without standard processes being understood and documented, the apparent cost savings of eliminating personnel in the target company are often negated by the elimination of expertise, followed by reductions of the very profitable results predicted by the takeover financial strategists.

Many of the mass production practices developed during the transitional period of early adopters of the Ford and Taylor schools of mass thinking are still predominant today. The absence of standard ways of operating leaves the workers in charge and seems to empower them, but is not in the best interests of the company. Management's failure to facilitate change derives from the desire to project the idea that the way we have always done it is the standard.

Performance measures in the mass production environment primarily reflect departmental and individual outputs, not process performance (except as part of departmental performance). Performance measures are generally focused on outputs, not inputs or throughputs; on cost, not quality (except in meeting minimum standards); and after-the-fact activities (rework), not preventive measures (supplier quality). Management controls are set to maintain operations within preset limits (i.e., achieving what we have already demonstrated we can achieve). In this way, the need to improve by looking for root causes is eliminated, as is the need to train workers in problem-solving techniques.

Mass production systems incorporate management decision and information/support processes that operate within departmental stovepipe boundaries, not as cross-functional and cross-enterprise processes operating across departmental and company boundaries. Cross-functional processes requiring lean improvement in most mass production environments include quality management, maintenance, new product introduction, and design and engineering. Cross-enterprise processes are just beginning to be recognized as the information technologies necessary for their execution emerge. The need for effective design of these processes is apparent in the early meltdown of many of the dot.com pioneers and the continuing struggles of the "click-and-mortars" that are reinventing themselves for the digital age.

Finally, the negative characteristics of mass production are mutually reinforcing and interlocking. Owners and top managers in these firms have a vested interest in maintaining the status quo. Middle managers and employees follow suit. They are not given the support, training, or motivation to improve or "lean" operations. Relentlessly, the global competitive beast pursues and, increasingly, leaner is swifter to market and stronger in profit and growth.

THE ORIGIN OF LEAN PRODUCTION

The Industrial Revolution (beginning roughly in 1750) marked the emergence of the foundations of lean thinking in operational practices, such as standardization of methods and materials, interchangeability of parts, specialization of labor, large batch operations, and dedicated machinery.

However, these operational practices were used only in manufacturing processes for high-volume products (e.g., rifles manufactured by Eli Whitney). The lean practices were in a very rudimentary state, and craft-based manufacturing practices dominated industry. The now-recognized cultural and transformational principles of lean were not codified. The lean enterprise was still a long way off — in fact, about 200 years into the future.

Henry Ford provided the first industrial firm that can be accurately called lean: his 1913 automobile assembly plant, which was a very limited case of lean operations and retained many mass characteristics. For 12 years no product changes occurred (e.g., the Model T from 1915 to 1927). Only the main assembly line and key subassemblies were lean, and then only with respect to some of the eventually defined lean transformational principles of value, value-added, and flow. Other operations (e.g., parts machining and fabrication) were still job shops. Cohorts of middle management and emerging staff positions (e.g., industrial engineers, tooling engineering, maintenance) plus a large clerical staff controlled operations. Nonmanufacturing operations, such as accounting, were grudgingly considered necessary by Ford and received very little attention. Limited as the lean operational practices were, the Ford Model T plant was a value-added flow process that revolutionized manufacturing. Ford later expanded upon his lean achievement by developing the Rouge River plant, long considered the inspiration for the Japanese lean manufacturers, who toured it extensively. Perhaps most critically, Ford did not incorporate the essential lean cultural principles of process orientation and ownership later adopted by the lean manufacturers. Ford workers were primarily unskilled and uninvolved, reduced to "a pair of hands." For all that, Ford's mass production methods were widely emulated and viewed as the crowning achievement of U.S. industry in 1955, the peak of their dominance and success.

After the 1950s, the limitations of mass production practices became increasingly evident. Mass economics dictated that mass production practices include long production runs. Expensive tooling requiring longer and longer setup support and dedicated machines were economically feasible from a return-on-investment (ROI) perspective only by utilizing ever-expanding economic order quantity (EOQ) production lots. Large finished-goods inventory resulted from pushing product (be it automobiles, televisions, or refrigerators) down the pipeline and could be found at several stages of distribution, including at the dealers. Mass production inventory management practices were not responsive to changing customer demand, and inventory build-and-drain cycles did not respond well to fluctuating or shrinking customer order patterns. Low quality standards and large equipment sunk costs and reduced incentive to adopt new technology. High wages and rigid work rules began to dominate increasingly contentious labor/management relationships.

In contrast to the operational practices of Ford and other mass producers, lean emerged as a new way of organizing and operating industrial firms. Lean was pioneered at Toyota in Japan by Eiji Toyoda and his production genius, Taiichi Ohno, primarily after World War II. They began a series of experiments and innovations that has sparked nothing less than a global transformation in manufacturing that accelerates each year. The success of Toyota and other lean automotive assemblers did not go unnoticed in North America and Europe, although unshakable faith in U.S. mass manufacturing practices made it difficult, if not impossible, for some mass producers to learn from the lean pioneers and survive. By the early 1980s, it became clear that something had to be done.

One key response in 1984 was formation of the Massachusetts Institute of Technology (MIT) International Motor Vehicle Program at its then newly formed Center for Technology, Policy, and Industrial Development. A broad study of emerging manufacturing practices was undertaken (Womack et al.*):

> We [the authors] felt that the most constructive step ... would be to undertake a detailed study of the new Japanese techniques, which we subsequently named "Lean Production" compared with older Western mass-production techniques, and to do so in partnership with all the world's motor vehicle manufacturers.

In all, 90 automobile assembly plants worldwide were included in this study. Table 1.1 provides some results of making a successful lean transformation.

WHAT IS LEAN PRODUCTION?

Lean production is the name given to the management theory comprising the assorted lean practices documented by MIT during a 5-year study of automotive assemblers and suppliers worldwide (documented in the book *The Machine That Changed the World* by Womack et al.). Even before their groundbreaking study, literature about the emerging Japanese manufacturing practices had begun to observe that lean producers had superior manufacturing methods, especially in the overriding lean manufacturing phenomenon of continual or continuous improvement in the physical process workplace driven by the production workers themselves. Some felt that such worker involvement in the continuous suggestion and implementation of cost-saving and quality-improving practices was something that should

---

* Womack, J., Jones, D., and Roos, D., *The Machine That Changed the World: The Story of Lean Production,* HarperCollins, New York, 1990, p. 4.

Table 1.1 Lean vs. Mass[a] Production

	General Motors/Framingham	Toyota/Takaoka
Gross assembly hours per car	40.7	18
Adjusted assembly hours per car	31	16
Assembly defects per 100 cars	130	45
Assembly space per car (ft^2)	8.1	4.8
Inventories of parts (average)	2 wk	2 hr

[a] Lean vs. mass rather than Japanese vs. U.S., as both systems have spread globally.

Source: Womack, J., Jones, D., and Roos, D., *The Machine That Changed the World: The Story of Lean Production,* HarperCollins, New York, 1990, p. 81. With permission.

be copied, and one of the several useful ideas adopted as a result was Total Quality Management. Others felt that involvement of the workers was a cultural phenomenon that could not be implemented in the U.S.

In essence, lean production is the philosophy of eliminating all waste in all system processes continuously. The system is the complete set of processes required to produce the product. In lean production, every action taken to improve processes is planned, implemented, and evaluated in terms of the overall goals of the system. To be lean in production is to eliminate waste in all its forms, including, but not limited to:

- Operator time
- Materials
- Techniques
- Inventory
- Methods/time/motion (MTM)
- Space required
- Facilities required
- Cycle time
- Equipment
- Rework/rejects/scrap
- Tooling and fixtures
- Setup
- Waiting time
- Downtime
- Distance traveled by a part

Most lean firms have already implemented any number of lean operational practices, including:

- Cellular production
- U-shaped cells
- Cell design and layout for flow
- Single-minute exchange of die (SMED)
- Internal vs. external setup
- Work group/team error proofing
- Zero defects (ZD)
- Station and operation process control
- Sending only what is needed
- Error proofing (poke–yoke)
- Part conveyance between stations
- Takt time
- Kanbans
- Level loading
- Small lot production
- One-piece flow
- Balanced flow
- Synchronous flow
- Mixed flow lines

Lean firms have also implemented lean human resource practices, designed to eliminate the conflicts that emerged between mass production wage systems and lean operational practices, such as:

- Pay-for-performance wage systems
- Productivity group bonus systems
- Payment for ability
- Developing and rewarding multiple-skill operators
- Multifunction operations and skills matrices
- No-layoff job sharing and hours-available practices (work sharing)

Any number of terrific books have been published on these topics and on applying lean principles, tools, and practices to the physical processes. It is not our purpose to reinvestigate these topics. Rather, we are going to discuss the use of the principles, tools, and practices of lean to implement processes enabled by information technology and examine a lean methodology designed to enable the virtual lean enterprise.

WHY AREN'T MORE FIRMS LEAN?

After over 40 years, many of us still do not believe that Japanese industry developed a production system superior to our mass production system; however, we have become willing to grant that Japanese quality, until recent U.S. industry improvement, was superior to that of the U.S. Unfortunately, many of us also believe that rigorous applications of lean quality practices have passed the point of diminishing returns, but quality remains an expensive obsession for some. Others of us believe that quality is always improved at the expense of productivity and that we can keep our mass production system and still improve quality. To some degree, even in the emerging lean U.S. operations, we have.

Some of us have tried to meet ISO 9000 requirements, even though we feel that it is just more bureaucratic red tape — the latest flavor-of-the-month gimmick of top management — and we have treated it that way, expensively documenting procedures that most of us would agree represent only how we would *like* to do things, not how we *actually* do them. We have felt that quality is an option, not a necessity, and that "making production" is the ruling motto of our production world. As a result, we have often pursued superficial improvements in quality without a thorough and critical review of our production systems.

The way we have received and used information from Japan has not helped the situation. We are picking up such information in bits and pieces, a lean tool or lean practice at a time. We hear about the results, not the process, of using these tools and practices in various circumstances and cultures. Then, to make matters worse, U.S. consultants often give the Japanese approach their own spin, thus losing the key ideas in the translation. U.S. management and engineering schools continue to focus on U.S. mass production practices, with only a passing reference to the lean approach. In some instances, lean practices such as flow or cellular production or Kanban signaling have been implemented by industrial or manufacturing engineers, who see these practices as the harvest of lean thinking. What they are not seeing is that the origin of these practices (and their effective application in any environment) is found in the underlying power of the cultural principles of process ownership and respect for the knowledge of the worker. As a result, we pursue superficial improvements in production or expensive investments in technology innovation, again without a thorough and critical review of our production systems, including our management decision and information/support processes.

Prior to the MIT International Motor Vehicle Program study referred to previously, we did not have a comprehensive, in-depth understanding of the lean production system. In fact, Womack et al. did not publish *The Machine That Changed the World* until 1990, over 40 years after Toyota began its journey toward becoming lean. As a result, many firms have taken a superficial approach to becoming lean, primarily by applying lean practices such as statistical process control (SPC), just-in-time (JIT), etc., again without a thorough and critical review of their production systems.

But now this tactical approach to lean is inexcusable, as we know what it really takes to become lean.

Formidable barriers to lean thinking in most U.S. firms include a not-invented-here attitude that asks how lean firms could have better production systems than what is being used now. Many of us still believe that the lean principles, tools, and practices are gimmicks that cannot possibly yield such great results. Our management performance measures retain a fixation on mass production, volume-cost thinking that includes results-centered analysis and decision making without process awareness or understanding. We revert to a quick-fix attitude at a moment's notice, especially when that notice is a layoff slip. We retain an emphasis on machine utilization, only sporadically focusing on zero inventory, pull, JIT, or any number of other lean practices that rarely work when implemented in isolation from the principles and tools of lean. We cling to the belief that other countries use low-cost labor, government aid, sweatshops, or exploitation, anything but superior lean production systems. Occasionally, we express a widespread feeling that management has the answers, not the employees. In the recent low-unemployment labor market, we decided that no good people were out there anymore to hire. Many of us share the belief that loyalty is a thing of the past. Following are some other self-defeating beliefs:

- Lean may be good, but I know of some fat firms that are making tons of money.
- Computers are the real answer.
- We want to get lean but our union won't let us.
- I would only be eliminating my own job.
- What I know is my job security.
- All these improvements add up to zilch; our real problem is [fill in the blank].
- We have always done it this way, why change now?
- Relax; this is just another one of management's flavors-of-the-month.
- What we are doing is good enough.
- It never hurts to have a cushion.

The main philosophical points that we hope to make in this book are these:

- Lean principles, tools, and practices can and should be applied to all processes.
- Utilizing the tools and practices of lean production without adopting the lean cultural and transformational principles is analogous to painting over rust — you really haven't changed anything; things just look nicer (for now).

WHAT IS REQUIRED TO BECOME LEAN?

It is an appropriate baseline to assume that many manufacturing firms are familiar with the principles, tools, and practices of lean production. Many firms have some lean physical processes, but getting lean requires that everyone participate. Most lean firms are struggling to transform both their information-based processes and the physical processes supported by information into lean processes. At the same time, other companies are learning to use lean principles, tools, and practices to transform themselves into lean enterprises. They are learning that getting lean requires fundamental adjustments in thinking, attitudes, and behavior; it is not simply a matter of acquiring another set of tools and practices. Getting lean also requires the adoption of a new set of transformational and cultural principles. The lean transformation is a continuous, neverending, incremental process. The project approach presented here is no more than a good start.

First, here are some standard but often ignored factors necessary for a successful lean transformation:

- Management commitment to becoming lean
- Involvement and participation by *all* employees
- Team approach
- Long-range view (a year or more, for starters)
- Assigning responsibilities and tasks to teams on a project basis
- Incorporating lean assignments in each employee's job on a daily basis
- Education and training at all levels

Second, a major change in attitude is necessary to realize that the lean approach embodies utilizing a set of diagnostic tools as well as an integrated and systematic approach to using those tools to operate a business built on the foundation of cultural and transformational principles. Last, but not least, the company's lean vision, mission, strategies, and policy deployment, as well as the processes, systems, and standards, must incorporate lean principles and practices.

Because they receive the initial focus, the physical operations processes generally become leaner in emerging lean production systems and lean companies than do the management and information/support processes. From a Lean Performance perspective, a company can be considered lean when it is designed, organized, and operated according to the cultural and transformational lean principles.

The lean cultural principles presented here are derived from the lean literature that is the foundation of Lean Performance, especially Imai, M., *Kaizen: The Key to Japan's Competitive Success* (McGraw-Hill, New York, 1986) and *Gemba Kaizen: A Commonsense, Low-Cost Approach to Management* (McGraw-Hill, New York, 1997) and include:

- Process-oriented thinking means putting what before how.
- Product quality results from process quality.
- Every process requires a process standard.
- The process owner is the process expert.
- The next process is your customer.
- Loyalty to people enables continuous improvement.
- Process data and measurements drive process continuous improvement.

The lean transformational principles presented here are an adaptation of those presented by Womack and Jones in the follow-up to *The Machine That Changed The World*, the 1996 publication *Lean Thinking: Banish Waste and Create Wealth in Your Corporation* (Simon & Schuster, New York, pp. 15–26):

- Precisely specify value by product or family.
- Identify the value stream for each product.
- Make value flow without interruption.
- Let customer pull value from process owner.
- Pursue perfection.

The Lean Performance methodology is primarily directed at those organizations that are well along the path to lean in the physical processes and perhaps in some cross-functional processes as well. Changing a mass production system to a lean production enterprise requires three things:

1. A comprehensive leaning of processes based on recognition of processes within process areas
2. Leaning of the cross-functional *process organization* of the manufacturing enterprise
3. Leaning of the cross-enterprise *process partnerships* of the extended or virtual enterprise, the lean supply chain

In order to get started on the journey toward a lean enterprise, you must know where you are now. If your firm embarks on a Lean Performance project, the key tasks of the planning phase are to identify all company process areas, all processes within those process areas, all process owners and customers, cross-functional processes and linkages, and cross-enterprise processes and linkages. We will provide a comprehensive structure for performing these tasks and the tasks that follow in the remainder of this book.

2

EXTENDING LEAN PERFORMANCE FOUNDATIONS

IMPLEMENTING LEAN CROSS-FUNCTIONAL PROCESSES

Early adopters who applied lean principles, tools, and practices primarily to production/operations physical processes were successful in large part because the barriers to lean improvements in these process areas are contained within only one or possibly two "stovepipe" bureaucracies. The cross-functional processes that have undergone lean improvements in some companies implementing lean production systems include:

- Quality management
- Maintenance
- New product introduction
- Design and engineering

Employing lean principles, tools, and practices in these processes has provided an opportunity to apply lean principles within processes as well as link several processes in a lean flow. Often, however, even companies that experience success in transforming these first four cross-functional processes to lean may not be providing effective support of information systems, or the information systems supporting the lean processes are not based on integrated systems and control data. We will discuss these processes further in this section, defining the requirements for these processes from a lean perspective. We will eventually assign the task of improving these processes to specific cross-functional teams.

In a lean system, the focus is on transforming the organization into a set of interlocking, interdependent lean processes. Without an organization-wide lean process perspective, any lean process can be rendered inefficient and ineffective by being linked to or constrained by upstream or downstream processes operating with traditional mass production (non-lean) design. The next challenge on the path to achieving a truly lean enterprise, then, is attaining lean linkage and flow between *all* organization processes, including management, information/support, and physical processes. Implementing such lean cross-functional processes is essential to completing the lean transformation at the organizational level in a manufacturing firm and points the way to developing lean processes across the supply chain — the cross-enterprise lean processes.

Two important objectives are accomplished by developing and implementing lean cross-functional processes. First, this activity leads to an understanding of how mass production principles impact organizations, and, second, such an activity helps the manufacturing organization develop a perception of the organization as a set of *lean-able* processes contained in definable process areas, such as design, engineering, etc. Advocates of continuous improvement may ask at this point why we need to move to these other levels of analysis. Why can't we just continue at the individual process level that seems to be working well so far?

There are three major reasons for a broader approach to the leaning of cross-functional and cross-enterprise processes, especially those enabled by information technology. The first reason is that the design and operation principles of mass production are so deeply imbedded in our manufacturing firms at all levels that they preclude a successful lean transformation unless eliminated. Second, lean processes do not and will not automatically link themselves in a lean production system operating on a company-wide basis. These cross-functional linkages, operating systems, organization structures, and external relationships all must be improved from a lean perspective. Finally, lean processes do not easily link themselves in a lean production system operating on an enterprise-wide basis. These cross-enterprise linkages, operating systems, organization structures, and external relationships are the final frontier of the lean transformation.

To identify the primary lean requirements of cross-functional processes, several problems must be overcome. These processes span organizational units (divisions, departments, sections, companies) but require improvements that reinforce lean principles and practices unfettered by organizational units. Leaning these processes requires changes in operating systems and organization structures. Cross-functional processes pose several other design problems for firms attempting a lean transformation in that they require a new approach to external relationships (primarily suppliers and customers) and realignments of managers, staff, and workforce.

In order to expand the application of lean principles, tools, and practices more widely in an organization, cross-functional processes require explicit elimination of two barriers that are much easier to overcome in the narrow stovepipe of production operations (not that the obstacles encountered here are necessarily easy to overcome). The first barrier includes the impediments to a lean operation caused by organizational boundaries (divisional, departmental, or company). Examples of this barrier include interruption of flow (paper, data, information), administrative "turf battles," waiting for authorization, nonconformance to standards, bottlenecks, scheduling problems, lack of training, and lack of feedback among and between processes. The second barrier incorporates the process "linkage" issues — that is, how processes are linked through a set of operating policies and reinforcing mechanisms, such as transfer of personnel, cross-training, location, information flows, and physical equipment such as tote boxes or flat trucks.

LEAN QUALITY MANAGEMENT

As mentioned earlier, in spite of the barriers several cross-functional and cross-enterprise processes have been "leaned" in emerging lean enterprises. Chief among these processes is quality management. *Quality* is often defined as the meeting of standards (specifications or tolerances) at an acceptable level of conformance. This acceptable level is variously defined — for example, as zero defects, according to the six sigma, or as the number of defective parts per million. Quality management, not quality control or quality assurance, is the appropriate term to convey that the goal of achieving and improving quality is an area of management concern and responsibility. Most companies with lean production systems have developed quality management systems by following three lean business policies:

- Pursuit of quality is a strategic company goal.
- Top management is committed to and actively involved in achieving quality objectives.
- A permanent, organized, company-wide effort to continuously improve product process quality, including training and measurements, is maintained.

An essential component of lean quality management is an understanding and acceptance of quality as a central tenet of the organization's lean business policies and strategies. Managers, staff, and workers in a lean organization are trained in lean quality management tools and practices, including the lean diagnostic tools of the 3MUs (*muda, mura, muri*), 4Ms (man, machine, material, and method), 5Ss (sort, straighten, scrub, systemize, sustain), and 5Ws–1H (who, what, where, when, why, and how). Workers are considered process owners, and the cultural principles of lean have been adopted, at least as they relate to quality.

In a lean production system, both the standard and acceptable levels of conformance are continually improved. In a lean enterprise, lean quality management practices are implemented across the entire supply chain to continually improve the standard and acceptable levels of conformance to quality standards. In a lean supply chain, quality applies to inputs, throughputs, and outputs of all processes. *Incoming* goods are certified by the supplier, not inspected at the receiving dock. Essentially, the quality of these goods becomes the supplier's responsibility. *During* the production processes (throughput), interim outputs are operator monitored for quality (for both machine and manual processes), not just after completion. *Output* is always monitored for quality to determine if and how a process produced defective product, not merely to identify acceptable product and weed out or rework defective products. In the Lean Performance project, leaning the quality management process is assigned to the Operations Team.

LEAN MAINTENANCE

In many lean production systems already functioning in Western companies, maintenance processes are designed, organized, and managed according to lean principles and practices, and empowered physical process workers use lean diagnostic tools to continuously improve the maintenance of their own process and process enablers. In concert with engineers, supervisors, and machine experts, these cross-functional maintenance processes (including operator-oriented preventative maintenance practices) eliminate production problems such as unscheduled machine downtime, process failure to meet quality standards, and machine failure or other mechanical trouble that causes an operation to fail to meet process capabilities and requirements.

In a lean production system, maintenance processes are also considered in equipment, new product, and process design decisions to ensure that maintenance problems do not contribute to inefficient and ineffective operations during later production operations. It is not enough to simply regard maintenance as being necessary for the smooth functioning of production. Maintenance is a major cost center in manufacturing firms and has a major impact on quality, cost, and delivery. So, why wouldn't we concentrate on the quality of these processes? In a lean production system, maintenance processes are identified and standardized and are the responsibility of production personnel. As an extension of the lean diagnostic tool of 5S, machine operators are trained in how to use their machines properly and how to clean, oil, paint, and otherwise maintain the equipment according to maintenance, operating, and quality standards.

Lean maintenance processes allow maintenance problems to be detected and addressed as quickly as possible through preventive maintenance as well as operator inspections based on cumulative run time or a periodic schedule. In lean maintenance processes, maintenance and performance records are kept on all major pieces of equipment. These records are used routinely and cross-functionally by maintenance and production management and periodically by top management to ensure lean operations. Records maintained include Lean Performance standards, such as lost time, defects caused by maintenance issues, safety, delays, and breakdowns. In lean maintenance processes, all maintenance activities are scheduled, whether they involve routine maintenance or major equipment overhaul. Schedules are observed to ensure minimal unplanned, emergency, and reactive maintenance (all more costly and disruptive to customer delivery than scheduled downtime). These lean practices result in a smooth flow of production that incorporates planned downtime coordinated with production schedules. One challenge for the Lean Performance Information Team will be to examine the information system maintenance responsibilities from a lean perspective. In the Lean Performance project, responsibility for leaning the maintenance process is assigned to the Operations Team.

LEAN NEW PRODUCT INTRODUCTION

A lean new product introduction process includes all activities that contribute to new product development: marketing, research, development, design, product engineering, process engineering, procurement, and operations, as well as suppliers, distributors, and customers. This process is the lean cross-functional and cross-enterprise frontier in many emerging lean environments, because the use of enabling information technologies has driven a corresponding need for the establishment of standard protocols of data transfer, interface, and management.

Benefits of a lean new product introduction process include increased communication, better teamwork, and concurrent vs. sequential ("over the transom") development of products. These lean practices result in reductions in costly reengineering, limit off-target product development, and discourage process disconnects and turf battles during the development of products for increasingly brief product life cycles. Other benefits include increased productivity and improved quality through better manufacturability of products that have been designed through an inclusive approach that incorporates the knowledge of all team members, with both production capabilities as well as production constraints factored in. One of the important tasks for the Lean Performance Engineering Team will be to examine the opportunities present to apply concurrent practices within information support processes based in the project information technology enablers, as they are assigned the responsibility for learning the new product introduction process.

A lean new product introduction process generally requires assignment of personnel to the product development project for as long as development of that product continues. A lean new product introduction process requires a career ladder based on new product development and performance evaluations that use specific development tasks to evaluate and assign personnel. These tasks relate to factors beyond the responsibility of individual departments or functions and rely upon an individual's contribution to the product development projects. A lean new product introduction process is not ultimately controlled through a coordinator, committee, departmental manager, or matrix management (although these organization techniques may prove useful as support mechanisms); rather, the lean new product introduction process is generally "owned" by a new product development manager who has full authority and responsibility over the life of the project. Lean Performance steering committee responsibilities during the project and Lean Performance management responsibilities after the project include the definition and administration of human resource policies and structures that recognize and support the requirements of lean process management.

LEAN DESIGN AND ENGINEERING

A lean design and engineering process maintains products that have been designed and engineered for the processes that produce them. It should be obvious (but is not always accepted) that products designed and maintained without attention to manufacturing capabilities cannot be produced efficiently or effectively. Product and manufacturing engineers must be cross-trained in their respective capabilities. Rather than being a sequential linking of discrete processes, a lean design and engineering process consists of concurrent (overlapping) discrete or subordinate processes in research and design, product engineering, manufacturing engineering, and manufacturing operations management.

A concurrently linked lean design and engineering process provides a vast number of benefits. First, the usual errors based on faulty assumptions or misinformation about downstream capabilities are detected as the product design progresses. Downstream processes are empowered to prepare for new demands on their capabilities in a timely fashion, because they are included in the planning early on. Necessary changes, including equipment or tooling, can be incorporated in subordinate processes before production deadlines prevent an effective deployment of new capabilities, many of which are factored into the cost justification for the product introduction itself. Intended operations efficiencies that are not realized when the product is manufactured can cause profit targets to be missed.

Mass production design and engineering processes often lead to an approach of "we'll learn how to make it as we go, and then we'll make our money back." Of course, this does not work very well in a global competitive marketplace where product life cycles are short. A penalty of relying upon mass processes in a short-cycle world is that if your design and engineering process has a mass, "throw it over the wall to production and we'll figure out how to make it there" cost dynamic, even with a successful product, the product life may not be long enough to make your money back.

Implementing a lean design and engineering process demands that all tasks be examined from a team-based lean perspective, because design and engineering staff traditionally operate with a degree of autonomy. The full range of processes necessary to fulfill the customer order (including cost, quality, and delivery realities) are not always uppermost in their minds. Lean principles and practices viewed as good for the plant are not necessarily viewed as applicable to engineering. Professional objectives may take precedence over company objectives. The introduction of information technology into these processes and the need for these process owners to support an enterprise system can also be problematic. Engineers may prefer to build their own systems, in isolation from the processes and data relied upon by the rest of the enterprise. Not only does this cause difficulty in maintaining data integrity, but these separate systems are forever on a different and often highly modified or customized development and support path.

A lean design and engineering process effectively links design and engineering to other process areas. This linkage ensures that problems with communication, information transfer, and coordination of schedules are minimized or avoided altogether. A lack of cross-functional inputs for maintenance and operations processes and equipment purchase planning and installation can be avoided altogether with great benefit.

When design and engineering processes are monitored by top management from a lean perspective to anticipate and avoid delays in production, the primary benefits are the detection of product specifications that cannot be met by production processes, elimination of product features that are not required by customers, and avoidance of the corresponding time delays necessary to incorporate those specifications or features. The design and engineering processes are assigned to the Lean Performance Engineering Team for lean improvement in the project.

3
LEAN PERFORMANCE METHODOLOGY

WHAT IS THE LEAN ENTERPRISE?

Where can lean thinking be used? It is the premise of this book that it can be used on any job, in any process, in any manufacturer or service sector firm, in any economy, regardless of the size of a firm, level of technology, operator skill, or professional staff employed. In lean production, the system is the complete set of processes required to produce the product in the producing company. A company is lean when lean principles, tools, and practices are applied to all processes in the company.

In their 1996 publication, *Lean Thinking*, Womack and Jones (two of the authors of the original Massachusetts Institute of Technology study discussed in Chapter 1) describe the phenomenon of applying lean production principles to all processes in a company and to all processes in the chain of companies involved in producing a product. The concept of lean enterprise extends the process definition to include all processes required to produce the product in all the companies that play a role in producing the materials, components, supplies, etc., for that product. We are reminded in *Lean Thinking* (p. 239) that "the machine that changed the world" relies upon "Toyota's interconnected ideas about Product Development, Production, Supply Chain Management, and Customer Relations *systems* [italics added]."

When lean companies are linked in a business activity to produce product together, they are a lean enterprise. When lean companies are linked in a business activity to produce product together and are enabled by the Internet and other information technologies, they are a virtual lean enterprise. Lean Performance project methodology is designed to enable a virtual lean enterprise to draw upon the proliferation of information technologies that are stabilizing in the e-commerce marketplace right now.

The computer is a processor of data and supports other system processes (in the lean enterprise sense, not just the information sense) by providing information. These system processes include the management decision and information/support processes (including the cross-functional and cross-enterprise), as well as the physical processes themselves. Notice the minimized role assigned to the computer. The computer is not the process, and the processes are not in the computer. At best, the computer is a central processing unit (CPU) of data that supports and enables lean processes across the virtual enterprise. First and foremost in achieving the lean virtual enterprise must be the recognition that the technology is only the enabler of lean processes.

The lean enterprise has a number of recognizable characteristics. It is process managed or product team managed, not department or hierarchically managed. The lean enterprise utilizes teams and empowerment. All three types of processes (management decision, information/support, and physical) are identified and continuously improved. All cross-functional and cross-enterprise processes are subject to lean principles, tools, and practices. Continuous improvement activities identify and eliminate waste in all processes, continuously.

WHY SHOULD OUR ENTERPRISE BE LEAN?

Why get lean? The four important reasons for doing so are:

1. To survive among lean competitors
2. To gain a strategic advantage
3. To meet customer expectations
4. To respond quickly to opportunities and threats

Recent studies show that lean production is the primary strategy used by U.S. manufacturing firms to improve their global competitiveness. This is generally so because lean manufacturing focuses on the entire business of production, resulting in inventory reductions, productivity gains, and greater product introduction and customer order fulfillment flexibility (TBM Consulting Group, *APICS Performance Advantage,* April 1999).

Does lean have a payoff? The stock prices of companies that had effective lean programs outperformed control groups by 44% in a recently completed 5-year study by the Georgia Tech School of Management (*APICS Performance Advantage,* April 1999). This study included 600 publicly traded companies that had won such awards as the Shingo and Baldrige prizes. A control group by size and industry was also constructed. The award winners experienced not only 44% higher stock price returns, but also 37% higher sales growth. They also outperformed the control group in operating margins, employee growth, and asset growth.

It is safe to assume that "business processes are almost always in need of improvement or redesign" because "processes evolve over their lifetimes. When initially created ... they are usually quite simple and straightforward. ...As time goes by ... changes become more complex [and] begin to erode the effectiveness of the process" (C.B. Adair and B.A. Murray, *Breakthrough Process Redesign*, AMACOM, New York, 1994, p. 6).

In the early reengineering days, it was recognized that "a process' inputs, outputs, and goals must be easily understood by anyone in the organization," but, unfortunately, reengineering was also built on the premise that "each process should focus on goals and measurable outputs, not on activities and methods" (M. Hammer, *The Reengineering Revolution*, Harper Business, New York, 1995, pp. 18–19). This approach is fundamentally shallow (or arrogant) and is one source of the reengineering "problem." How can you possibly improve the flow of work when all you concentrate on is the output and not the processes that produce the output? Doing so is analogous to focusing on the cake and forgetting that the ingredients have to be mixed properly or, in the case of deploying information technology to support a reengineering effort, like focusing on the oven and not the cake itself. No wonder so many reengineering efforts have spent a lot of money on newer and better "ovens" but have failed to improve the cake. Focusing on process results (goals and measurable outputs) is exactly the opposite of what lean theory espouses.

In lean theory, improved processes equal improved results. You cannot manage the result, but you can manage the process, and this is best done at a task level by the process owner in consultation with the process customer. The best time to redesign processes for Lean Performance is when processes have acquired extra steps (such as redundant and check steps), especially at barrier handoffs. Another good time is when processes have responsibility divided among multiple owners or co-owners and no one is identifiably responsible for process outputs and quality. In a process in need of Lean Performance, downstream processes are not supported fully; approval steps are numerous, and specialists have emerged in functional silos (departments). No one has the authority to correct his or her own process and restore it to effectiveness. Queues are lengthening at various tasks, and process time is increasing.

WHAT IS LEAN PERFORMANCE?

Lean Performance is a management strategy that recognizes and leverages the fundamental strengths of any business: the people and processes. The goal of Lean Performance is to produce lean processes by determining the value-added process tasks in the process and then defining the use of vendor-supported, unmodified software as the process enabler. In Lean Performance methodology, management policy deployment aligns lean policies and strategies with the decision and action processes that execute tasks, including those enabled by information technology. Lean policies and strategies regarding the company's mission, markets, products, and services are deployed to a process level. These decision and action processes include all primary processes, as well as discrete processes at a task level. When information technology is involved as the process enabler for a task or group of tasks, such subordinate, data-level processes are also improved.

Lean Performance is a synthesis of the three dominant business improvement methodologies being utilized by business consultants today:

1. Business process reengineering
2. System innovation
3. Lean

Lean Performance is a *business process reengineering* methodology in that it utilizes the best techniques of business process reengineering to identify and implement lean business strategies. Lean Performance is also a *system innovation* methodology in that it provides an information technology project management workplan and toolkit with the task list necessary to implement information technology projects. Finally, Lean Performance is a proven *lean* methodology that develops Lean Performance teams of process owners and customers. These teams perform value-added lean process improvement and eliminate waste from existing management decision, information/support, and physical processes, as well as facilitating development of information processes that support lean physical processes (Figure 3.1).

The final result of the Lean Performance project is an ongoing, continuous improvement process resident in the enterprise that manages the process of managing processes after the initial project is successful. Above all, Lean Performance is a methodology of lean business process improvement and system implementation that integrates information technology innovation with lean principles, tools, and practices to improve the performance of information/support, management decision, and physical processes. The philosophical inspiration for Lean Performance is found in this comment from one of the giants of lean management, Masaaki Imai: "When western management combines *Kaizen*® with its innovative ingenuity, it will greatly increase its competitive strength" (M. Imai, *Gemba Kaizen*, 1997) (Figure 3.2). The Lean Performance methodology develops process

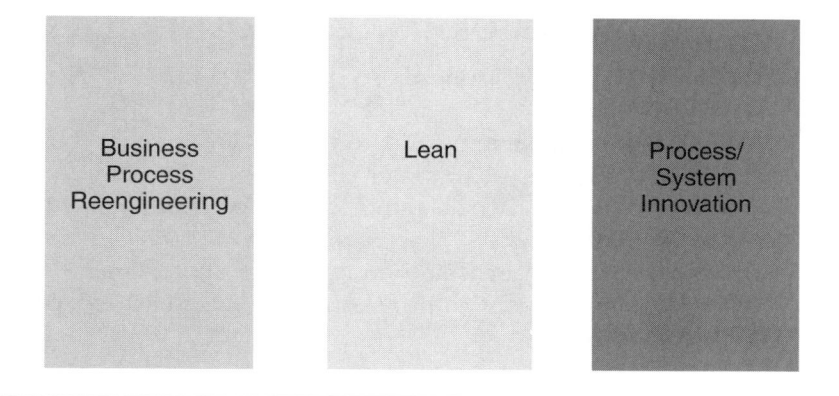

Figure 3.1 Lean Performance Foundation Blocks

Business Process Reengineering | Lean | Process/System Innovation

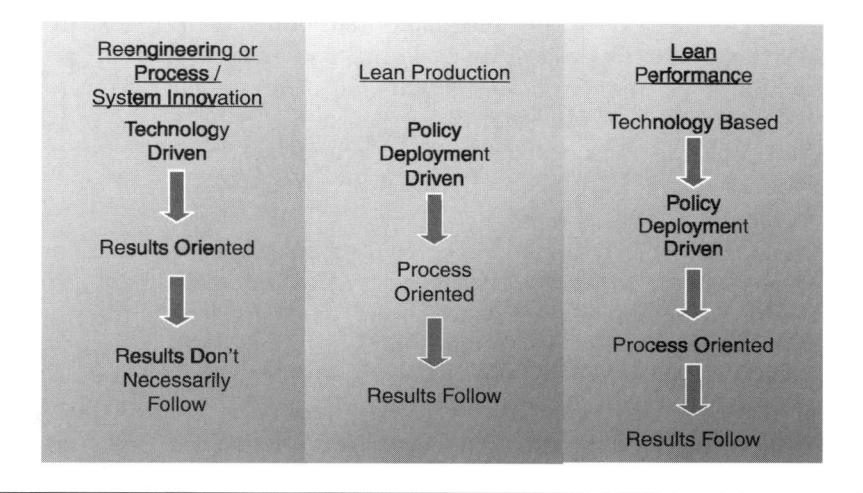

Figure 3.2 Comparison of Reengineering, Lean, and Lean Performance

Reengineering or Process / System Innovation
Technology Driven
⇩
Results Oriented
⇩
Results Don't Necessarily Follow

Lean Production
Policy Deployment Driven
⇩
Process Oriented
⇩
Results Follow

Lean Performance
Technology Based
⇩
Policy Deployment Driven
⇩
Process Oriented
⇩
Results Follow

performance measurements and continuous Lean Performance where information technology has already been implemented or acts as the implementation methodology for new information technology initiatives, including enterprise resource planning (ERP), manufacturing execution system (MES), operations planning system (OPS), customer relationship management (CRM), and supply chain management (SCM) systems implementation. The output of Lean Performance is lean processes that deliver added customer value, have no waste remaining to eliminate (until next time), can be measured, and can be continuously improved.

HOW DOES LEAN PERFORMANCE IMPROVE PROCESSES?

Lean Performance begins by asking these questions:

- What constitutes maximum value to the customer, either the external product customer or the internal process customer?
- How can the process owners and customers be effective in a project of process improvement?
- How can we identify areas and processes for improvement?
- How do we implement information-technology-enabled process changes successfully?

Lean Performance works with existing processes and develops process improvements that adapt the enabling information technology to the business, not the business to the information technology. The Lean Performance team begins by deploying lean business policies and strategies to the management decision, information/support, and physical process levels. Next we identify process owners and customers — all of the process owners and all of their processes. Following development of the project plan, we complete lean value-added process analyses for all the processes identified, utilizing a lean standardize/do/check/act (SDCA) process for each, followed by a plan/do/check/act process (PDCA) of continual improvement.

During the project, teams produce process standards that include process workflow and work instruction standards and document information/support and management decision processes, as well as the physical processes they manage, inform, and support. Lean Performance teams will learn and utilize practices that apply unmodified vendor-supported software to leverage standard software packages such as ERP, MES, SCM, or OPS, also following the project workplan task definition. Teams analyze and close process and system gaps and establish process-oriented performance measurements to verify the changes necessary to improve process measurements of cost, quality, and speed. Finally, the team introduces a practice that continually deploys management policy to identify and implement new opportunities.

During the project, management decision, information/support, and physical processes are improved by integrating "disconnects" and by eliminating non-value-added tasks at process boundaries (checking, counting, verifying). The enabling software is applied so that it provides greater information visibility, availability, accuracy, and timeliness throughout all the processes. The objective is to develop flow in all processes by eliminating batches and queues, with particular emphasis on developing information/support processes that support lean physical processes, including "pull" information for one-piece flow. The goal is not to execute a "perfect" implementation, where every process is supported at a 100% optimum level by the software; rather, the team is constrained by the capability of the software employed and is moving so quickly that it does not have time to wait for modifications. Solutions to "missing" features are developed over time and may include manual work-around where necessary.

WHY LEAN PERFORMANCE IS THE BEST LEAN METHODOLOGY

Before we begin, let's back up a bit and compare the lean methodology to previously existing methodologies. Process redesign is the activity that changes processes by changing process enablers. Some examples of process redesign methodologies mentioned earlier are business process reengineering, process innovation, and system innovation. In experience, process redesign methodologies often fail or deliver poor results that negatively impact customer quality. Internal customers lack critical information, and external customers encounter undesirable impacts on cost, quality, and delivery performance. Often, a process redesign may turn out not to be a process performance improvement at all. To be considered a process improvement, an improved process must be capable of being implemented where the firm is today, not where the firm proposes to be after a reorganization, merger, acquisition, return of the dot.coms, or [your situation here].

Often, process redesign is driven by the desire or perceived need to add a feature to a process. The addition of a feature to a process that does not add value from the customer perspective is a process redesign but is not a performance improvement. This phenomenon often results from an approach of having technology solutions in search of problems to solve. Such an approach generally creates more problems than it solves, and any problem solving occurs later and more expensively than planned. This partially explains the dot.com meltdown. There were not enough paying customers who needed all that neat stuff. When there were enough customers, the lack of product to ship drove them away, often never to return.

The impact of information technology methodologies now in use was reported by 16,000 corporate computer executives surveyed by the Cutter Information Corporation (*APICS Performing Advantage,* April 1999). The results showed that information technology workers spend their time as follows:

- 31% developing improvements to existing programs
- 34.6% developing new programs
- 34.4% fixing bugs in existing programs

As reported by Grant Thornton LLP in 1998, of U.S. manufacturers with annual sales between $20 million and $500 million, only 36% described their information technology infrastructure as being well integrated and only 11% had an ERP system (*APICS Performance Advantage*, April 1999). Of those with ERP systems, many reported positive results:

- 50% had reduced inventory
- 43% had reduced order cycle times
- 36% had increased production capacity

Grant Thornton LLP also reported that of U.S. manufacturers with annual sales between $501 million and $1 billion, only 29% had an ERP system. The fact that 1997 revenues for ERP, SCM, and PO or MES application software companies exceeded $14 billion (*AMR Research,* April 1998) indicates that there is a lot of software out there, and most companies are not overwhelmed with its performance (*APICS Performance Advantage,* April 1999).

Let's return to our discussion of methodology, especially the methodologies that underlie the less-than-optimum deployment of all the software referenced above. The evolution of traditional business management theory coupled with the emergence of information technology resulted in *business process reengineering*. In this methodology, process redesign is performed from the top down in the organization, based on recognition of four core processes. As has been demonstrated at numerous sites, this approach can work on management processes but generally requires extensive custom software development for use in manufacturing.

The evolution of information management theory resulted in a *process innovation* and *systems innovation* (RAD-JAD) approach based on recognition of 9 to 18 core processes and relying on a process where system design takes place before process design. Generally, this deployment methodology requires extensive custom software development, and, again, its success has not been widely demonstrated (.com, anyone?). Neither of these methodologies develop lean processes or culture, and they are difficult to utilize in an enterprise that is getting lean.

Each of these approaches is supported by a number of methodologies, many of which mix terminology, tasks, and steps freely. The common assumption that reengineering and process or system innovation share is that by changing the process enablers you can change the process. Lean Performance is the only process redesign methodology that proceeds from the assumption that a process redesign can be successful using new systems enablers only after we know what the value-added process is, according to the process owner. The process redesign (*what* needs to be done) must precede the system design (*how* to do what needs to be done).

Process and system innovation are not really business process redesign methodologies, because they redesign underlying data processes, not the management decision and information/support business processes themselves. The data processes redesigned by these methodologies are not utilized to perform the operations that produce products or services, although they may enable them. For example, a grinding process is utilized in a boilerplate company to prepare their product — boilerplates in various shapes and sizes — for shipment. The enabler of the process is a grinding machine utilized by the grinding process owner to grind the individual boilerplates. The enabling process performed by the grinding machine is to rotate the spindle of a shaft to produce a circular motion on a wheel attached to a holder on that shaft that is held against the boilerplate by the process owner. This is analogous to a data process performed by computer that provides data to the customer order entry process. The process of grinding itself includes the tasks performed by the operator: select which boilerplate to work on next, lift and position that boilerplate, place or move the boilerplate against the grinding wheel, and turn and shift the boilerplate against the wheel in whatever series of movements the process owner (who performs this task several hundreds of times each day) has determined to be the sequence that best grinds the boilerplates.

The customer order process is similar in that a process owner (who performs the process multiple times each day) utilizes an enabling data processor to "grind" the data. The process owner's tasks for completing the customer order entry process include selecting the orders to be entered and in what sequence, as well as addressing the specifics of each order according to the vagaries of each customer. The process owner performs these duties according to experience picked up over days, weeks, months, or years of experience.

The data processes support the discrete management decision and information/support processes of the company but should not be mistaken for them. Process and system innovation work well on the data processes, but not so well on the actual processes of the business, where the value-added work really happens. An ERP, MES, OPS, CRM, or other system installation project masquerading as a process or system (innovation) redesign is likely to be a failure. This recipe for disaster can be identified by the project investment emphasis. The project budget will emphasize hardware, systems technical consultants, and business experts rather than team-based value-added analysis training and activities.

Reengineering has a different problem. Properly executed, reengineering assumes that we can write as much software as we need. The sometimes complex business process redesign is almost always completed by experts from outside of the affected business, and only then are ideal data processes programmed with enabling code (but who can afford that?)

32 ■ Lean Performance ERP Project Management

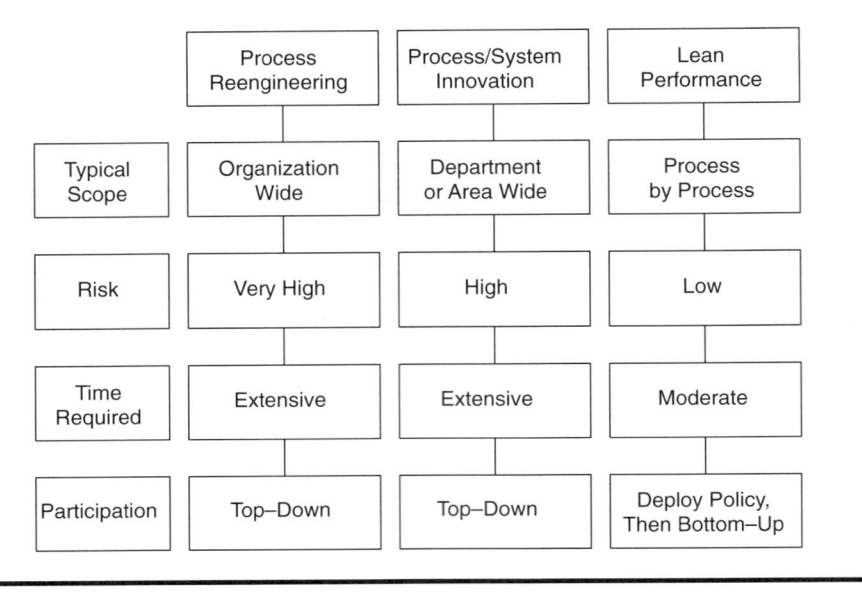

	Process Reengineering	Process/System Innovation	Lean Performance
Typical Scope	Organization Wide	Department or Area Wide	Process by Process
Risk	Very High	High	Low
Time Required	Extensive	Extensive	Moderate
Participation	Top–Down	Top–Down	Deploy Policy, Then Bottom–Up

Figure 3.3 General Methodology Comparison

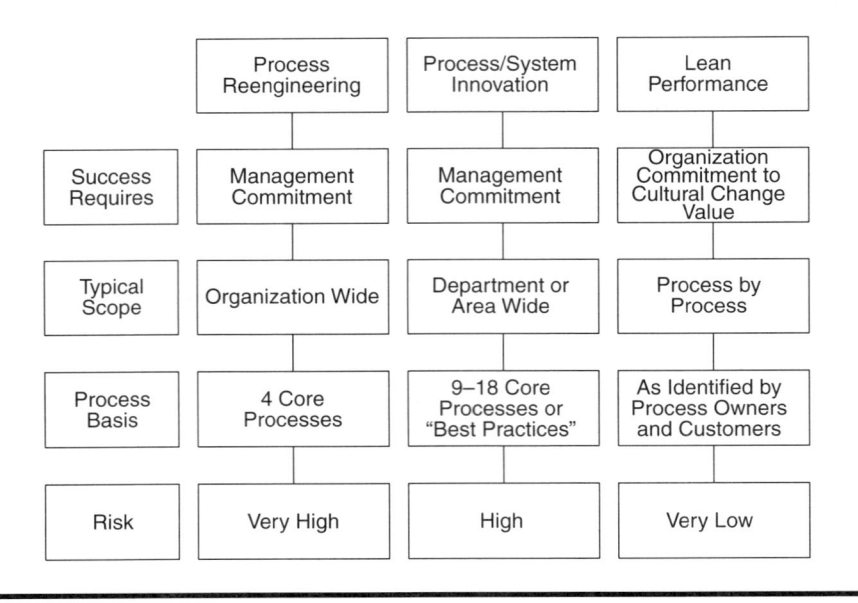

	Process Reengineering	Process/System Innovation	Lean Performance
Success Requires	Management Commitment	Management Commitment	Organization Commitment to Cultural Change Value
Typical Scope	Organization Wide	Department or Area Wide	Process by Process
Process Basis	4 Core Processes	9–18 Core Processes or "Best Practices"	As Identified by Process Owners and Customers
Risk	Very High	High	Very Low

Figure 3.4 Strategic Issues Comparison

(Figures 3.3 to 3.8). Because lean manufacturing is so successful, and technology-driven improvement and implementation methodologies are

Lean Performance Methodology

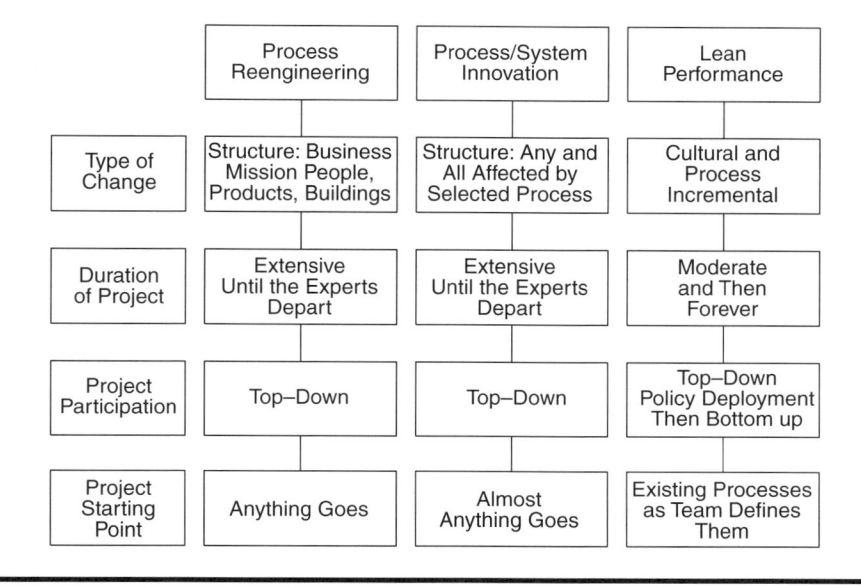

Category	Process Reengineering	Process/System Innovation	Lean Performance
Type of Change	Structure: Business Mission People, Products, Buildings	Structure: Any and All Affected by Selected Process	Cultural and Process Incremental
Duration of Project	Extensive Until the Experts Depart	Extensive Until the Experts Depart	Moderate and Then Forever
Project Participation	Top–Down	Top–Down	Top–Down Policy Deployment Then Bottom up
Project Starting Point	Anything Goes	Almost Anything Goes	Existing Processes as Team Defines Them

Figure 3.5 Project Scope Comparison

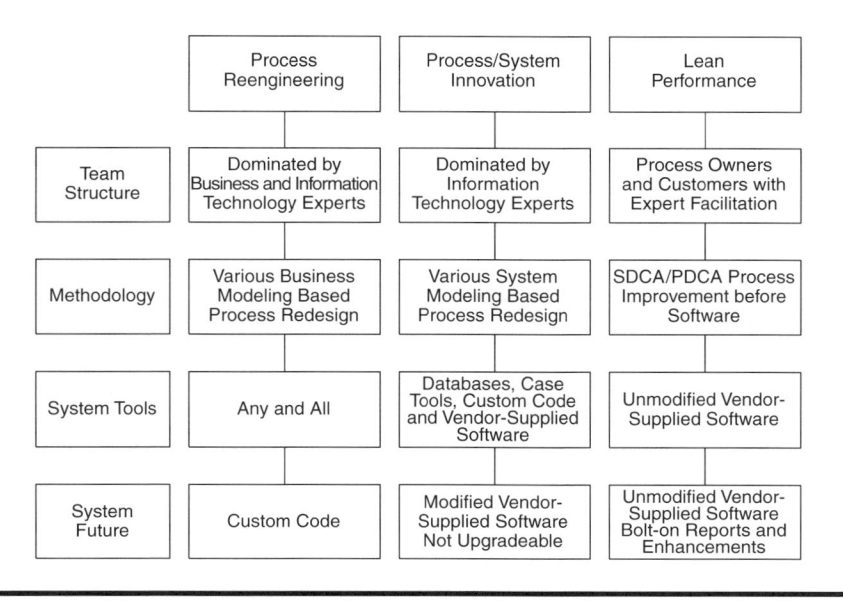

Category	Process Reengineering	Process/System Innovation	Lean Performance
Team Structure	Dominated by Business and Information Technology Experts	Dominated by Information Technology Experts	Process Owners and Customers with Expert Facilitation
Methodology	Various Business Modeling Based Process Redesign	Various System Modeling Based Process Redesign	SDCA/PDCA Process Improvement before Software
System Tools	Any and All	Databases, Case Tools, Custom Code and Vendor-Supplied Software	Unmodified Vendor-Supplied Software
System Future	Custom Code	Modified Vendor-Supplied Software Not Upgradeable	Unmodified Vendor-Supplied Software Bolt-on Reports and Enhancements

Figure 3.6 Tactical Issues Comparison

not, it is about time we started to apply lean thinking to all processes in the enterprise.

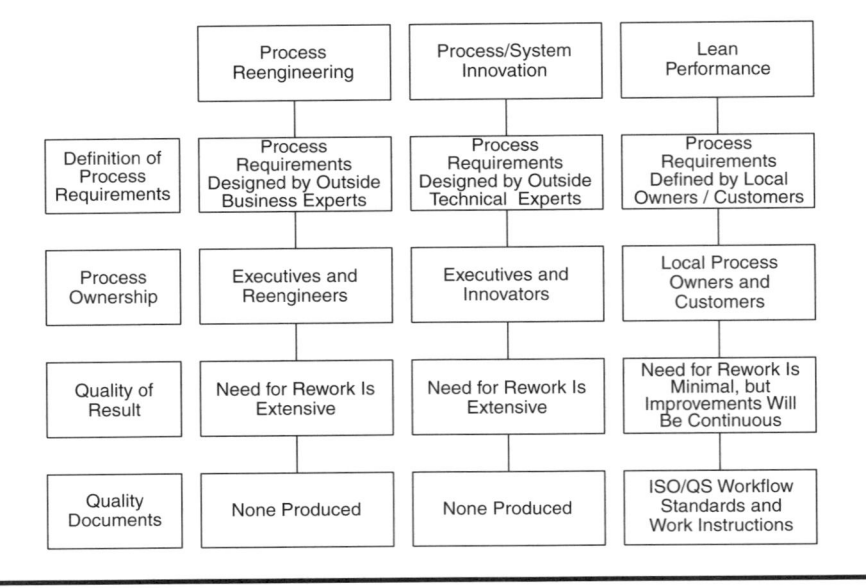

Figure 3.7 Quality Issues Comparison

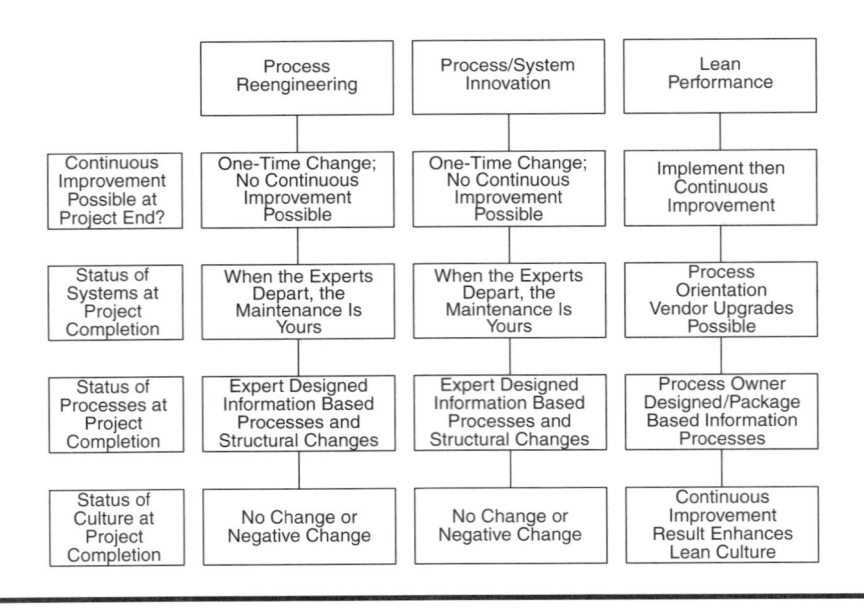

	Process Reengineering	Process/System Innovation	Lean Performance
Definition of Process Requirements	Process Requirements Designed by Outside Business Experts	Process Requirements Designed by Outside Technical Experts	Process Requirements Defined by Local Owners / Customers
Process Ownership	Executives and Reengineers	Executives and Innovators	Local Process Owners and Customers
Quality of Result	Need for Rework Is Extensive	Need for Rework Is Extensive	Need for Rework Is Minimal, but Improvements Will Be Continuous
Quality Documents	None Produced	None Produced	ISO/QS Workflow Standards and Work Instructions

Figure 3.8 Results Comparison

	Process Reengineering	Process/System Innovation	Lean Performance
Continuous Improvement Possible at Project End?	One-Time Change; No Continuous Improvement Possible	One-Time Change; No Continuous Improvement Possible	Implement then Continuous Improvement
Status of Systems at Project Completion	When the Experts Depart, the Maintenance Is Yours	When the Experts Depart, the Maintenance Is Yours	Process Orientation Vendor Upgrades Possible
Status of Processes at Project Completion	Expert Designed Information Based Processes and Structural Changes	Expert Designed Information Based Processes and Structural Changes	Process Owner Designed/Package Based Information Processes
Status of Culture at Project Completion	No Change or Negative Change	No Change or Negative Change	Continuous Improvement Result Enhances Lean Culture

Lean thinking is value-added thinking from the perspective of the process owner or customer. The evolution of Total Quality Management has resulted in lean theory and lean thinking. Lean thinking uses process orientation and team development as the bases of change. Lean thinking is usually employed today on physical processes, but Lean Performance assumes any process is eligible. Lean thinking develops lean processes and culture. Lean thinking is not often applied to management decision and information/support processes, primarily because of the difficulty in identifying the processes to be improved (as opposed to physical processes, which can be readily observed and are obvious). A process architecture is prerequisite to applying lean thinking to information/support and management decision processes, as is an information technology infrastructure.

To be competitive, today's successful business must have timely and accurate information about customer demand and internal supply. It must increase capability to service customers with a quality response at a competitive price and must rapidly improve processes to meet or exceed changing customer requirements. The processes that any organization uses to meet customer requirements must be visible and readily adaptable to customer changes, including information-based processes and physical processes dependent on or linked downstream from information-based processes. Increasingly, processes are tightly linked to both customers and suppliers.

Many companies successfully apply lean principles, tools, and practices to continuously improve production processes; however, information technology does not readily enable improvements in information/support and management processes. Information technologies do not readily or easily allow for process focus or orientation. As a result, many information technology projects and the information systems that result from them have two recurring problems: Business strategies are not implemented by the system installation, and the resulting processes cannot be readily adapted to changing customer requirements.

Business strategies may be defined at the beginning of information technology innovation projects, but they are usually forgotten in the maze of project details for two reasons: They are not deployed through the project methodology, and they become secondary to deadline and budget pressure. Today, businesses are being organized around business processes, but information technology projects often install technologies focused on data processes. This introduces a "disconnect" between the actual business processes and the information system and produces a data system and processes that do not adequately support the actual business processes that are the customers of that data. As already mentioned, these data processes usually cannot be readily modified to keep up with a customer's changing needs. The data processes and the management decision and information/support processes they enable are usually not documented, and no standards exist. Information systems are heavily customized, and it can be difficult, time consuming, and costly to improve them. Standard vendor-supplied and -supported software is not leveraged to the best benefit over the long term.

Many business process reengineering, system innovation or process innovation, and other process redesign and process improvement projects fail due to poor project methodology. Methodologies are not really redesigning the process as the process owner understands it. Experienced project managers often are thrown at a project without a complete task list (workplan). New project managers are also fed to the lions and are susceptible to repeating old mistakes in new, creative, and faster ways. Other process redesign methodologies are technology driven, not process oriented. They put the technology first, then discover that the data processes do not fit the business processes. Ideally, process workflows (standards) should be documented by process owners and customers to identify the work that must be completed, and then this work should be mapped to the software to determine how best to do the work. Major software modifications to vendor-supported software often result and complicate later support when these tasks are reversed. In summary, then, information technology projects must implement business policies and strategies. Information technology systems must be business process oriented, and information technology improvement projects must utilize a project workplan with a complete project task list. All business processes that result (management decision as well as information/support) must be documented and have process standards. Unmodified vendor-supplied software must be leveraged to the long-term benefit of the business.

The Lean Performance methodology provides a solution to the usual project chaos. The methodology we are about to discuss here implements business strategies and is business-process oriented, not data-process oriented. The methodology utilizes a project workplan with a complete task list. It produces and uses process standards (workflows/value-added process analyses) to identify the work tasks that must be completed. It relies on the 95% principle; that is, standard software should accomplish 95% of our process requirements. The methodology value-maps workflows to the software to determine how to do the work and produces process standards for all process redesigns using unmodified software packages. The Lean Performance methodology demonstrates that lean principles, tools, and practices can be utilized to improve existing management decision and information/support processes and to provide support to the lean physical processes. The Lean Performance process approach empowers process owners and customers while developing process workflow standards of what work or tasks must be completed in the process. Finally, by value-mapping the process workflow standards to determine how to

Lean Progression

	Executive	Management Decision Processes	Lean Performance
	Office	Information Processes	Lean Performance
	Shop Floor	Physical Processes	Total Quality Management

The Old Enterprise → ... → *The Lean Enterprise*

Organization Commitment →

Figure 3.9 Lean Progression

perform the work or tasks utilizing the enabling information technology, this approach produces work instruction standards to provide for training and to audit continued process quality. The implementing lean enterprise can then utilize these process standards to enable ongoing, continuous improvement (Figure 3.9).

The output of the Lean Performance methodology is lean processes that deliver added customer value and can be measured and continuously improved. Lean Performance completes the journey begun by Total Quality Management: "...delivering customer value in everything a company does ... not just through products and markets, but through business processes: the integration of functions, departments, and even suppliers, customers, and competitors into a company's strategy" (C.B. Adair and B.A. Murray, *Breakthrough Process Redesign*, AMACOM, New York, 1994, p. 6).

Why is the Lean Performance methodology readily applicable to management decision processes? Because of the widening scope of standard vendor-supplied software, these processes are becoming further enabled by information technology. The term *information/support process* will disappear as management decision processes become supported by information technology to a greater extent. Only decision and action processes will remain, and they will be enabled by information technology, not defined by information technology (Figure 3.10). Process design will drive

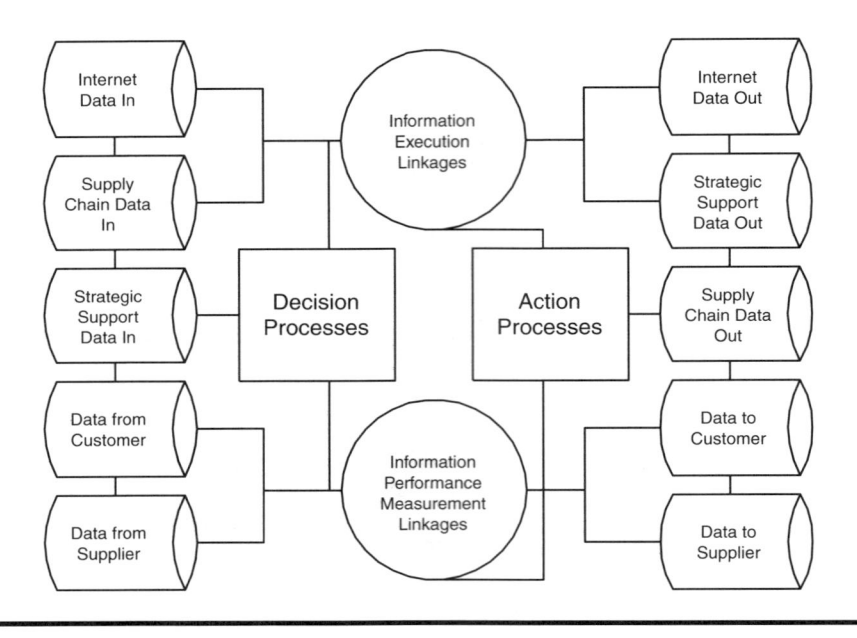

Figure 3.10 Future of Data Processing

object-oriented computing when (and if) case tools and software objects replace software packages. In this scenario, the better the software object, the better the software functionality. The better the software functionality, the better the enabling of the process. The better the enabling of the process, the better the process. The better the process, the better the software object. (Repeat as needed.) Building a new information technology system before improving the management decision and information/support processes is like building a new production facility before improving the flow of the physical processes. You could end up with walls where you need doors. Lean Performance performs bottleneck engineering on management decision and information/support processes.

Lean Performance supports an overall strategy to attain a lean enterprise. It builds from the same attitudes and disciplines as lean production, with management preparing the organization and demonstrating commitment. Lean Performance is also a growth strategy, just like lean production. Because people never get fired for improving their processes, we need to grow into our "leaned" capacity by utilizing resources freed up by lean improvements. Finally, Lean Performance is necessary because management decision and information/support processes often are not value added, are not integrated with other processes or process data, and do not adequately support lean physical processes already continuously improving in the workplace. The output of Lean Performance is lean information/support, management decision, and physical processes because these processes:

- Deliver added customer value
- Have no waste remaining to eliminate (until next time)
- Can be measured and continuously improved

Proposed: Following the Lean Performance methodology is necessary in order to provide the framework, initiative, culture change, and process focus that are prerequisite to transforming a manufacturing company into a continuously improving lean enterprise.

4

LEAN CROSS-ENTERPRISE PROCESSES

WHAT IS LEAN COMMERCE?

The emerging characteristics of time-based competition in manufacturing include a heavy emphasis on information integration and sharing, especially across the Intranet and Internet. Manufacturing companies striving to reduce cycle time are flattening organizational layers and leaning processes to take out non-value-added tasks and to minimize queues and inventories wherever possible. Information technology is becoming the enabler of quick response and supply chain management (SCM) by providing rapid communication of material requirements and current information about these requirements wherever and whenever that information is needed, as well as computing planned component availability using just-in-time (JIT)-triggered pull mechanisms in the production processes. The accuracy and timeliness of information are measurable quality attributes. The turn-around time from initial data gathering or input until the information is available to be acted upon is a key factor in determining the ability to respond quickly to customer requirements.

The top priorities for time-based competition involve learning processes for which any improvement will be noticed and appreciated by customers. Important among these priorities are customer relationship management and production scheduling processes. Highest on the list, however, is the shipping process. Getting positive feedback from your customer is always possible when you are able to ship *what* the customer wants *when* the customer wants it (and it is also nice to ship it *where* the customer wants it shipped). The lean commerce model presented here links selling and distribution as fully integrated parts of the entire production system that provide accurate information to all processes in the lean supply chain. This integration synchronizes the entire virtual lean enterprise, creating significant benefit and competitive advantage for all the virtual partners. The lean commerce model also addresses the implications of web retail and B2B markets by integrating information systems in the management of the lean supply chain. Management decision support systems are included if they are employed in management decision processes tied to central enterprise resource planning (ERP) system data. The lean commerce model deployed through the Lean Performance methodology merges lean process improvement with lean supply chain integration.

The foundation of the lean commerce model is lean production, a manufacturing system that has reduced throughput times and improved product quality. These improvements are achieved through the use of focused product-oriented manufacturing cells, volume paced to customer demands, and flow of production sequentially mixed (scheduled) to provide a smoothed demand on internal and supplier resources. Lean production is characterized by an extraordinary flexibility to shift the mix of products manufactured. This capability is supported by forecast and production smoothing processes to provide for smooth material and production flow.

Lean commerce builds from this foundation by improving the information flow in the enterprise process to include the direct (Internet, EDI, XML, or manual) input of customer forecast and order data into a master production schedule (MPS) process that utilizes a central database and shared information access to present a dynamic flow of customer requirements. The lean commerce model (Figure 4.1) as designed will allow open access to the sales and operations plans as well as daily changes in customer requirements, along with the ability to input MPS agreements into appropriate periods to facilitate capacity and material planning.

The transition to lean production requires a commitment to change as well as a strategy to accomplish change. Extending the use of lean principles, tools, and practices across the lean enterprise and into the virtual lean enterprise requires no less. Lean production systems have been implemented in many Western companies based on the Toyota production system (TPS) model. These companies have proven that lean principles, tools, and practices are transferable to any manufacturer who chooses to employ them in pursuit of a continuously improving enterprise. Many emerging lean companies and their supply chains are successfully employing a majority of the practices of lean production, but they are still being whipsawed by previous mass-production thinking in their order entry, scheduling, and production processes, especially the information/support processes that are dependent on accurate customer demand

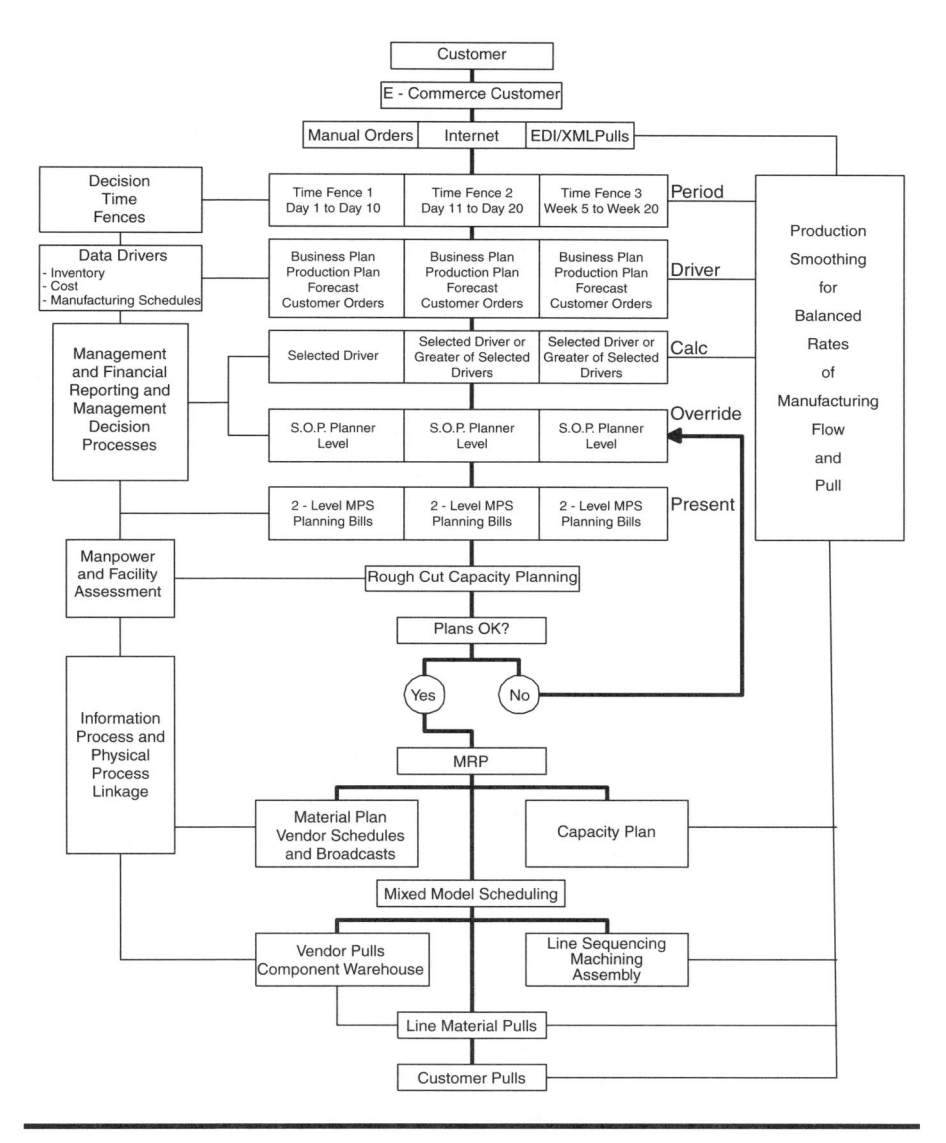

Figure 4.1 Lean Commerce Manufacturing Model

data. While many production facilities have become lean, the ERP-based planning and ordering processes of customers continue to be highly cyclical, including periods of classical mass-production inventory build and drain. Rapid short-term shifts in the mix of products are still required, even when total demand is predictable.

The lean commerce strategy is to use the characteristics of *pull* and *push* whenever appropriate. Prior to applying or developing applications in the planning, forecasting, and scheduling processes, companies striving to achieve a lean enterprise should consider the characteristics of lean production in their own manufacturing processes. We have learned, the hard way, that you cannot produce to the plan and too often you cannot ship to the schedule. Material requirements planning (MRP), MRPII, and ERP notwithstanding, the customer never pulls to the plan, and the customer's customer doesn't either. As a consequence, the manufacturing processes struggle with an ever-changing schedule, especially in regard to changes within lead time. Until there is a fundamental shift in the approach to selling and distribution to one that incorporates a lean pull of customer-order-driven requirements planning, these cycles will remain and our planning and scheduling processes must accommodate them.

Lean commerce is designed to extend the advantages of lean manufacturing forward through customer relationship management and back through the entire material requirements and production scheduling processes. The fundamental purpose of lean commerce is to understand and respond to customers' time-based demand expectations. The lean commerce model is designed to provide a rate-based flow of customer-focused requirements to facilitate the overall lean production system.

A lean manufacturing enterprise requires lean process improvement of processes within all process areas (i.e., marketing, production, etc.) and across process area functional boundaries, in addition to lean process improvements across enterprise boundaries. An emerging lean enterprise model that extends the use of lean practices across the supply chain is demonstrating that companies can work together in a virtual lean enterprise if they all adopt lean principles and tools to develop lean practices in their processes. Transformation to a lean enterprise in the e-commerce and e-business supply chain must not only include aspects of Internet-driven customer relationship management but it must also do so in a lean model. Either the emerging lean enterprise model must leverage existing ERP systems, which have come to dominate planning, forecasting, and scheduling, or new software enablers must be created and implemented.

The lean commerce model utilizes a direct Internet and EDI link to customer orders and forecasts, as well as production smoothing (leveling), and provides information to assist mixed production scheduling techniques to facilitate a balanced flow of production. This capability is developed by the overall model, where customer orders are the primary demand source. In lean commerce, the MRP module of existing ERP software packages is used to develop production and supplier schedules, with mixed-model scheduling utilized to balance or smooth the final assembly schedule and upstream production flow.

The primary design objective for the model has been to meet today's customer requirements while supporting a company transition to lean production and participation in the emerging virtual lean enterprise. The model is not perfectly lean, however. Elements of push or mass production remain in the lean commerce model as a result of the continuing demand fluctuations and short order-delivery requirements of some customers. This mass production push can be observed at several points in the model, wherever inventory is bought, manufactured, moved, or stored at an earlier time or in larger quantity than is actually demanded (pulled) by the customer. Lean environments, even the TPS, utilize production smoothing (*heijunka*) to forecast production of parts for which the production cycle (which includes suppliers) is longer than the order lead time from the customer. In the context of production planning and scheduling, a perfectly lean system would be one in which customer demand pulls (via order and forecast) the system at a balanced rate, so that a flow of customer orders would replace the planning forecasts, with no significant unplanned fluctuations. To continue the production analogy, when an imbalance exists in a production process, either a queue of components waiting to be processed or an excess supply of component inventory will exist somewhere in the process to provide a steady production. It is these imbalances that we strive to eliminate through the continuous improvement process on the factory floor. Correspondingly, when an imbalance exists in the planning and scheduling processes, an excess (or inadequate) supply of planned purchase or production orders will exist. These orders require management and data manipulation continuously. The balance between this planned order flow and the wasteful work and cost necessary to juggle them is improved using the lean commerce model.

The lean commerce model is based on lean principles but with a clear recognition of information technology systems development and operations and financial considerations that must be made in the cross-functional and cross-enterprise process areas of customer relationship management, supply chain management, and production and operations management. The model can be used with the capabilities of most elite ERP suites, or as part of a strategy embracing the best of breed in CRM, APS, SCM, MES, etc. The lean commerce model supports the overall transition to the lean enterprise while still accommodating today's customer, who is not always providing a lean order pull. The lean commerce model as it is designed, however, will support a company transition to lean. As customers become lean producers, with a correspondingly smoother and more balanced flow of delivery requirements, the model will accommodate them by enabling a customer order/forecast (smoothed) pull on production and material requirements. The lean commerce model will accommodate today's mass production customers and, as they become lean producers, the processes will already be there to accommodate them. At the same time, customers who are already lean producers, who provide a stable flow of planning forecasts, and who pull their deliveries JIT are also provided for in the lean commerce model. This is especially important during this era of transition to lean production, as quality and delivery performance are the measurements that will ensure future orders from these customers. When lean customers are lost, companies are left with the remaining mass producers as their only customers, and these customers are looking more and more like endangered species in the (lean) global production base. If they become extinct, so do you.

In seasonal markets, consideration must also be given to the classical ideas of inventory build and drain. Unless an enterprise is willing (and able) to pay for the short-term capacity needed to service shipments in a seasonal consumption market (think Christmas sales), inventory will remain in any e-commerce model. Developing information/support processes based on the lean commerce model supports the overall transition to lean production by developing material and production schedules from the customer demand pull while supporting production smoothing techniques to level production. A primary characteristic of the lean commerce model is the pull of demand from the downstream process to the upstream supply process. A truly lean production system is balanced so that no unneeded materials exist in production. A truly lean supply chain would contain no unneeded materials. The primary assumption of the lean commerce model is "You can't get a schedule from an ERP system, but you can get a pull-able plan if you do it right." Delivering in small lots directly from a supplier process to a consuming process, with no buffer inventories to account for quality or planning imbalances, is rare. Buffer inventories continue to be required in the supply chain, and the lean commerce model accommodates them. Also, under the lean production model truly lean information/support processes of planning and scheduling would contain no unneeded manufacturing or supplier orders. In this context, successful management occurs in MRPII when supply is resolved with demand, aggregate planning is translated into detailed planning, and planning and execution are linked together via a two-way flow of information (the closed loop). A vendor partnership is required to provide support to pull customer requirements, and a vendor-supported MPS module is utilized for production smoothing. While the lean commerce model approach supports these activities, it is primarily an enabler of customer-focused planning and scheduling activities and in this way adds value to the lean production system. Leveraging the information/support process architecture through the application of continuous improvement techniques can and should produce continued information/support process improvements as the lean enterprise evolves.

Lean commerce processes span two or more organizational units (divisions, departments, sections, companies) but rely upon process designs that reinforce lean principles and practices unfettered by organizational units. These processes require changes in operating systems and organization structures (including realignments of managers, staff, and workforce), as well as a new approach to external relationships (primarily suppliers and customers). Lean commerce processes require explicit elimination of barriers to lean operations created by organizational departmental, corporate, divisional, and enterprise boundaries. Such barriers might include interruptions of workflow caused by management decision making, circuitous information flow, and administrative "turf battles" that result in waiting for authorization, bottlenecks, and a lack of feedback/feed forward and communication in general.

The lean commerce model is being proposed because level customer demand pull is not the norm. Internet-based customer relationship management processes are driving the transition to e-commerce and e-business, so lean enterprise transformation is not possible without an Internet-based production smoothing approach that allows existing ERP technologies to be leveraged. As illustrated in Figure 4.1, the lean commerce system is driven entirely by customer requirements. Customer requirements are loaded into the planning or push cycle at the top of the model and are used to pull the manufacturing processes at the bottom of the model.

These customer requirements consist of customer orders obtained from a variety of sources, and perhaps managed by a variety of system enablers in most information technology environments, although the elite ERP systems suites including or integrated with best of breed CRM, APS, SCM, and MES can accommodate this design. As the model illustrates, the requirements are delivered via EDI/XML order sets, by EDI/XML release or planned order sets, and via manual order entry, necessary for orders or plans received by fax, snail mail, phone, or otherwise. The production smoothing process that is possible with lean commerce is simple. Rather than continuously manipulating the planned, firm planned, and released orders in the typical system, it is proposed that the mechanics of MRP, driven by the push of customer orders, forecasts, and internal SOP demand smoothing, be allowed to function as designed by the MPS/MRP designers. Loading and smoothing the demand data on a daily or more frequent basis provides an invaluable resource to the entire lean chain. The planned order output shows all eligible viewers exactly what is going to happen, based on all best available data and input, smoothed through best flow guesses. The order pull from the customer that is fed to the pull point at the shipping location is the trigger for all square, signaling, two-bin, or *kanban* lean visual management in the factory. The demand data, smoothed through the SOP and MPS processes and calculated by MRP, is also available for APS or line scheduling and balancing. The flow of manufacturing orders that constitutes the major maintenance burden in most manufacturing systems is basically ignored, other than to use order records to flush inventory. The same order records, as described next, can be used to generate *kanban* tickets, if desired, at BOM stocking points, although it would be preferable to call these BOM "release" points. The processes involved in implementing the model are discussed next.

LEAN CUSTOMER RELATIONSHIP MANAGEMENT

Mass production led to mass marketing, which eclipsed the importance of individual customers. This has been partially recognized in the many belated attempts at customer service and, more recently, customer relationship management. Because the primary lean production objectives include customer focus (with market-driven products and improved customer service paramount), the shift to Internet-based customer relationship processes is very appealing in the virtual lean enterprise. Lately, a lot of "buzz" and "hype" have surrounded the emerging point-and-click possibilities of Internet-based customer order management. A lot of dot.coms have learned that point-and-click is useless without pack-and-ship. Click-and-mortar is the emerging model, but even the mortar is not enough when it does not contain the inventory ordered by the customer. The latest lesson learned in e-commerce is that the emerging virtual supply chains that support new Internet-based customer relationship management must be linked to enable the production of the correct goods in time to support impatient e-customers.

The primary objective of lean customer relationship management is to maximize revenues from *a* customer over the long term, not the entire market in the short run. In the lean enterprise, the ever-changing customer requirements picture must be available to all process owners and customers who are affected by it, including suppliers. Information about customer requirements must be consistently updated throughout all planning and scheduling processes. The aggressive selling system employed by Toyota in the TPS (obtaining orders directly from the customer and pulling production with them) has led to the success of *heijunka* (production smoothing). Production smoothing keeps the total volume of production as constant as possible. In turn, the volume of business to suppliers is steady. Short-notice order changes are rare. The lean customer relationship management process forms the front end of a lean production system that is pulled by the requirements of the customer and still enables the factory to operate with less inventory, higher quality, lower costs, and quicker response to the customer.

Leading lean practitioners (such as Toyota in the North American marketplace) are now focused on a form of lean customer relationship management that uses Internet-based information technology. For Toyota, this has produced the ability to build a car to order and deliver it in 10 working days or less. Toyota announced the "10-day build" for Corolla's in 1999. The close coordination of customer relationship management, vehicle assembly, and suppliers appears to be the next major piece of the TPS, and it will be improved utilizing continuous improvement (*kaizen*) after initial implementation is complete. In some respects, it will resemble the information-technology-based, supply-chain-logistics management processes developed by American retailers such as Wal-Mart and emulated by emerging click-and-brick enterprises such as Amazon.com, but it will be leaner. And it will keep getting leaner.

The Toyota lean customer relationship management process includes mass customization that allows customers a wide assortment of order-level product options. This information-technology-enabled process allows greater standard model penetration of the market and will broaden the cost and performance gaps between the lean producers and their competition (the remaining mass producers) as a result of continuous planning demand fluctuations and short-order-cycle delivery requirements of some customers. Toyota is perfecting a direct selling system that does not depend on dealer inventory and allows the assembly factory to operate on a build-to-order basis; however, this system still relies on frequent contact with former and future customers to generate a great deal of forecast information for longer range production smoothing. The key process result is linkage of the information gathered by customer planners (manual orders and forecasts) as well as the information provided directly from customers (EDI orders and forecasts) to the entire supply chain as quickly and efficiently as possible, eliminating any and all bottlenecks.

A lean customer relationship management process interface with production must include the ability to manage contact with the customer before, during, and after the product is booked and shipped. This continued contact allows the collection of data on customer needs and preferences on a continuous, order-driven basis; the data are then fed back into the new product development process to aid in identifying market trends. Lean customer relationship management processes require intensively trained personnel and multiskilled teams trained in all aspects of the products, order processing, and customer profiling — that is, one-stop (one-person) selling, product specialists vs. professional salespeople, team cooperation vs. individual competition, and standardized pricing vs. negotiation. A lean customer relationship management process is based on the pull of customer orders (not production to stock), minimal distribution channel inventory, and short delivery cycle (e.g., 10 days at Toyota compared to 6 to 12 weeks for U.S. automakers).

LEAN SUPPLY CHAIN MANAGEMENT

In the supply chain management model, suppliers are viewed as forming a chain of linked processes. The concept is derived from the need for each producer in the chain to have its lower-tier supplier provide process inputs at the right time, in the right quantity, and to the right quality. If this is not done throughout the chain, the supplier delivering to the last link (e.g., original customer) cannot meet the final producer requirement. Pioneering lean manufacturers have demonstrated that the key to a competitive supply chain is to be found in the way shippers work in cooperation with their suppliers. Shifting the burden (and cost) of inventory down the supply chain has often been the driver behind sourcing of components with more frequent (just-in-time) deliveries. Suppliers are expected to maintain the capability to deliver, no matter how the schedule fluctuates. Inventory is used to buffer inaccurate schedules. However, shifting the burden (and cost) of inventory down the supply chain does nothing to improve the performance of the chain, and the lean enterprise is nothing more than a lean supply chain. Lean commerce processes extend a lean supply chain into a virtual supply chain.

In the lean enterprise, relationships between a supplier and customer (producer) are viewed as a set of reciprocal obligations, based on a commitment to lean principles and practices (see Table 4.1). Lean supply chain management relies on long-term cooperative vendor relationships, not adversarial relationships among several suppliers or multiple suppliers, each with a small slice of the required order. In lean supply chain management, the purchasing department is a team member in the new

Table 4.1 Customer (Producer) and Supplier Obligations in a Lean Enterprise

Producer Obligations	Supplier Obligations
Feasible production schedule	On-time delivery
Level loading, balanced flow	Capacity to meet expected demand
Assistance with supplier's lean transformation	Assistance with customer's lean requirements
Stable relationship	
Quality-certification program	Sharing continuous improvement benefits
Compliance with quality	
Pull-based production	

product introduction process and contributes to continuous improvement by coming up with new materials, services, equipment, and product ideas. Lean supply chain management utilizes multiple vendor selection criteria, not just cost. These criteria include the willingness to partner, sharing cost information, and a commitment to lean practices and continuous price reductions over the life of a part. In the lean supply chain, suppliers are expected to deliver according to lean practices, utilizing a pull-driven, continuous flow of incoming materials, with quality certified goods delivered according to just-in-time scheduling. There are no supplier-required inventories upon delivery; instead, delivery lot sizes are based on customer specifications.

LEAN PRODUCTION SMOOTHING

The lean commerce model requires *time fences* in the master production schedule. A time fence is equal to a certain period of time corresponding to a specific (selectable) demand source rule that determines the demand accumulated to drive the demand input to the calculation. The lean commerce model requires demand source rules that are selectable (hierarchical) at the system, product family, or part level and allow selection of input from a variety of sources and levels of input, with only one input source per period as defined in the production smoothing process. For mixed-model scheduling, the lean commerce model requires a calculation driver T, where T is equal to a period of time that is selectable (hierarchical) at the system, product family, production line, or part level and represents the length of time over which customer orders are to be considered as the demand driver to the calculation.

During the evolution to MRPII and ERP, the processes of forecasting, production planning, and (later) sales and operations planning (SOP) were improved to include regular meetings, usually monthly, of senior managers from all functions of the company. The SOP team makes decisions on how to allocate resources when projected demand and supply plans are out of balance, resolve any other issues (holiday or shutdown planning etc.), and agree on a single operating plan. The SOP process is utilized in many lean production environments to update a company's operating plan, project future demand, and analyze the company's resources and capacity. In lean commerce, rate-based demand and production planning leverage the existing MPS process to provide a flow of projected demand. By continuing the SOP management process performed today, an agreed-upon level of planned production can be established. Creating a seamless handoff from existing SOP processes to the lean production smoothing process, with the information being delivered just-in-time, can be accomplished through lean commerce.

In order to use a lean production smoothing process successfully, lean production processes must be in place and operating effectively. Lean production processes are designed to operate on a *pull* basis, whereas most U.S. production planning systems are *push* systems: ERP or MRP; production and inventory control systems with complex internal smoothing tools that include buffers, safety stocks, and workstation queues; and in-name-only JIT systems. ERP/MRP systems do not require lean production processes. Most lean producers have experienced difficulty mating the mass production push basis of MRP with the pull mechanisms of lean; however, ERP/MRP systems can work much more effectively in lean pull production environments than in mass production push environments because standardized production processes in lean production remove the variability from planning parameters. Setup and run time and compliance with quality specifications eliminate lot sizes and overruns that cover for scrap or rework. Production planned on process flow design complements the production input/output controls of MRP.

Lean supply chain planning systems do *not* replace ERP/MRP systems. ERP/MRP systems perform several higher level planning processes required by lean systems, including master planning, material (and other inputs) requirements planning, and capacity planning; however, several of the assumptions of ERP/MRP must be analyzed in light of how far lean has been implemented in a given firm — for example, in the areas of safety stocks, lot sizing, work-in-process inventories, large batches/long production runs, and overruns for scrap/rework. The fundamental purpose of MRPII is to establish a process that links projected demand plans to supply plans in order to anticipate demand and to plan and schedule resources in a manner that supports a company's strategic and financial goals. In an ERP architecture, the MPS is the primary tool available for production smoothing; however, linking the MPS in a lean production smoothing process to the flow of customer demand data, including both orders and forecasts, allows even greater visibility and flexibility. This approach can be utilized to drive the planning or longer lead-time buckets of the model. As newer forecasts and eventually actual orders are received, production schedules can be fluctuated up and down by product through mixed scheduling in response to daily requirements.

It is important to separate planning issues from scheduling issues. Planning involves putting in place the correct level of resources, while scheduling attempts to optimize the resources available now by relying upon timely information about the continually changing customer requirements. The planning process is essentially a push driver to the manufacturing supply chain and to the manufacturing processes. It has larger time buckets and a longer horizon and deals with products on an aggregate, usually family, basis. The scheduling process has daily time buckets and a short time horizon and deals with finite products and resources. The lean production system developed by Toyota, (TPS), is based on the principle of producing only what the customer orders when the customer orders it. In TPS, the production smoothing process begins with a forecast developed at the assembly plant that is the basis of material and capacity planning. This build plan is also given to suppliers, with revisions provided every 10 days. As customer orders come in, *heijunka* adjusts the build schedule to make the specific car the customer wants. With smoothed forecasts in place, and considering the production lead-time advantages of decades of TPS, when the customer order is received, production is pulled through the production system quickly. Used in conjunction with the time fence and demand source capabilities of most ERP-based MPS modules, the lean production smoothing process is more customer focused, which helps provide alignment between MPS planning orders and the (eventual) customer-driven production requirements. The consumption rates developed through the lean production smoothing process provide supply chain forecasts and schedules that are more in alignment with customer requirements pulled through the system. Rate-based planning also helps align upstream component schedules. Mixed-model scheduling techniques are supported to allow line and shift prioritizing of production in light of actual customer pull requirements and buffer component and finished good inventories. Product rotation and changeover based on production efficiencies are also supported, and common information about such requirements is available at both the planning and scheduling levels of the model.

In summary, the three elements of lean production smoothing are: (1) customer requirements demand pull, (2) rate-based production smoothing, and (3) mixed model production scheduling. These elements work to support (and in turn are supported by) the other lean production techniques. Lean production smoothing techniques improve the volume and pacing characteristics of demand flow manufacturing by including three rate-based elements: (1) rate-based demand and production planning, (2) rate-based order management, and (3) rate-based materials management. Rate-based order management provides a link between order promising and production scheduling through the use of an existing ERP system tool, the available-to-promise screen. Finally, mixed-model scheduling (smoothing) of the production sequence enables flexible balancing of the demand flow manufacturing processes and ensures a level demand pull across component lines and through the supply chain.

SUPPORTING A LEAN FACTORY FLOW

While these process improvements should provide an immediate benefit to customers, several other process areas can also be further improved by utilizing lean commerce. In the lean commerce model, the planning and production scheduling strength of rate-based MPS, MRP, and mixed-model scheduling processes is coupled with the pull execution of *kanban* techniques, including supplier broadcast (Internet messaging or EDI or XML fax) material pulls. Existing ERP database and master files are utilized to produce *kanban* tickets in support of mixed-model scheduling. Providing *kanban* dispatching capability produces a visual control for authorizing production, leveraging the existing work order or orderless-based records. *Kanban*, a powerful production control technique, is not a planning technique. The *kanban* can communicate to the workshop what to make, when to make it, and how much to make, but only in the current time period. *Kanbans* cannot predict what materials or how much of them will be needed in future time periods within the cost and operational efficiencies of MPS/MRP processes. However, when used within the lean commerce approach, *kanbans* provide significant benefit to production balancing efforts and corresponding quality improvements. *Kanbans* can be triggered by MRP-based buffers and "fudge factors" or on a straight zero-inventory basis at all bill of materials (BOM) levels of production in a lean environment. These system *kanbans* can then be utilized to pull the supply of components, subassemblies, and assemblies to buffers or stocking or feeder lanes.

5

LEAN PRINCIPLES, TOOLS, AND PRACTICES

LEAN CULTURAL PRINCIPLES

Process-Oriented Thinking Means What before How

When we say process-oriented thinking means what before how, we mean that understanding *what* work needs to be done comes first and is the key to determining customer value. Understanding *how* to best do the work with a new machine or tool comes next. Exploring how to use new enablers is one way to improve processes. When process performance is improved, the process result is improved. Ignoring the process reduces the chance for improved results, and ignoring the results runs the risk of missing new ideas and innovations.

Product Quality Results from Process Quality

When we say product quality results from process quality, we mean that improved process quality must be the focus of all innovation, including information technology innovation. Information system quality means meeting or exceeding process customer requirements. All improvement projects are a management activity and must use process standards. All projects must be focused on and collect data about specific processes, not just technologies.

Every Process Requires a Process Standard

Every process requires a process standard because process standards facilitate communication. Without a process standard, how can everyone agree on what the process is? Process standards connect process owners and customers with technologists. Process standards provide a basis of understanding that allows insights for improvement. Process standards make it possible to recognize downstream process requirements for timely and full availability of information, decisions, and material. Without a process standard, how would anyone know when cost, quality, and delivery parameters have improved or what to measure against? Process standards are used to stabilize a process by establishing process control and checkpoints for measurement and improvement. Process standards ensure the long-term success of an organization by protecting the company's knowledge base, by recording and preserving the company's expertise, and by facilitating cross-training. Where process standards do not exist, processes are unstable, maintenance costs are high, and improvements are not attempted or are unsuccessful.

The Process Owner Is the Process Expert

Process owners being process experts implies that today's processes are as value-added as the use of current tools and enablers allows and that process owners are doing the best job they can. When processes are identified, process owners and customers are all able to help in improvement if they are empowered. The process experts know what work must be accomplished in the process. The process customers know what they want from the process output, product, or service. Process experts design and implement process Lean Performance improvements. The process *doer* is the process *owner*, and the process *owner* is the process *expert*; therefore, the process *expert* is the process *doer*.

The Next Process Is Your Customer

By believing that the next process is the customer, every team member has the obligation to never pass on inaccurate data, information, decisions, or material. It is not okay to fix one's own process by breaking another's (or to meet the standard by sending scrap to the next process).

Loyalty to People Enables Continuous Improvement

Loyalty to people enables continuous improvement, because in a lean enterprise we do not blame; we improve. We do not judge; we fix. Mistakes are opportunities, and we challenge the obvious. In a lean enterprise, it is okay to fail in the pursuit of goals. We try because failing is okay and not trying is not okay. Using Lean Performance in a culture of cement heads does not work very well. Cement heads are people who will not consider or learn anything beyond what they already have in their heads: the set-in-concrete ideas of their own past experience and learning. Lean Performance is new learning and ideas based on experience outside of the mass production paradigm. In Lean Performance, no one gets fired for improving a process, even if that improvement eliminates the task that person performed. If we fire everyone who is good at improvement, who do we have left? Lean Performance requires commitment to lean cultural principles; the true test is when things get tough.

Process Data and Measurements Drive Process Continuous Improvement

For process data and measurements to drive process continuous improvement, we must always begin with a process standard. As stated above, without a standard, the process cannot be understood by anybody. The vast chasms that exist between the various styles and abilities of people involved in the deployment of enabling process technologies, the process owners who will employ those enabling technologies in their processes, and the process customers who must approve of the outputs of those processes are obvious to all who give the matter even a moment's thought. To deploy management policy using measurable objectives, management must have a task-based measurement of the baseline results of the process as it is currently performed. Process continuous improvement is based on measurable and identifiable process inputs, tasks, and outputs, not in opinions about them. In Lean Performance we ask questions until all the questions are asked, then we try to answer them; a new question is always the most important item. Only after asking our questions do we measure the current process results at a task level to determine existing cost measurements, quality measurements, and speed and/or delivery measurements.

LEAN TRANSFORMATIONAL PRINCIPLES*
Precisely Specify Value by Product or Family

Precisely specifying value by product or family means focusing any analysis or improvement on only the product or service that the process customer would specify as being what he or she needs as the output from a given process. It is measured by what he or she is willing to pay.

---

* This section is adapted from Womack, J., and Jones, D., *Lean Thinking: Banish Waste and Create Wealth in Your Corporation,* Simon & Schuster, New York, 1996.

Identify the Value Stream for Each Product

To identify the value stream for each product, it is necessary to identify the sequence of tasks that produce the output that the customer is willing to pay for. Note that we have not referred to the sequence of *data*. The customer is generally not interested in paying for data that support a process and are only a necessary presence (but necessary only when reducing cost, improving quality, or speeding delivery). Value-added tasks can be identified within the value stream by taking the role of the customer and asking, "If I am the customer of this process, would I be willing to pay for it?" Value-added changes are changes to a process or task that customers perceive as being changes that make the process or process output more valuable to them. The change may be at the customer's request, or it could be a legally mandated requirement or proposed by the process owner, staff, or management.

Make Value Flow without Interruption

To make value flow without interruption is simply to develop uninterrupted movement of a product through the steps in a process and between processes. Now, think about the paper and data processes; do they flow in your enterprise?

Let the Customer Pull Value from the Process Owner

To let the customer pull value from the process owner, the signal to initiate a process must come from a downstream process and ultimately the customer. In a Lean Performance project, team members develop improvements by working backward (pull) through all processes to identify customer requirements in the value stream.

Pursue Perfection

To pursue perfection, maintain and continuously improve the elements of the four preceding principles at process task level.

LEAN DIAGNOSTIC TOOLS*

3MUs

Up to this point we have discussed the use of the lean diagnostic tools almost exclusively in the physical processes, and we will consider the use

---

* This section is adapted from Imai, M., *Kaizen: The Key to Japan's Competitive Success* (McGraw-Hill, New York, 1986) and *Gemba Kaizen: A Commonsense, Low-Cost Approach to Management* (McGraw-Hill, New York, 1997).

of these tools in the management decision and information/support processes later in this book. For now, though, it should suffice to let your imagination play over the cultural impact of using these tools in the office environment, especially in the information systems "workshop."

Any discussion of the lean diagnostic tools must include the 3MUs:

- *Muda:* waste in all its forms; at a deeper level, any activity that does not add value
- *Mura:* an irregularity, discrepancy, or interruption in the flow of work, the operator's job, or the production schedule
- *Muri:* any condition that causes strain or stress for workers, machines, and work process

5S

Another lean diagnostic tool is the use of the 5Ss:

- *Sort* by classifying all items in the workplace as necessary or unnecessary. When this is done, teams can then remove all unnecessary items.
- *Straighten* by classifying necessary items according to their use and then arrange these items in such a way as to minimize search time ("a place for everything and everything in its place").
- *Scrub* by cleaning the work environment and everything in it, including machines, tools, floors, walls, storage areas — everything. Eliminate the cause or source of recurring stains, spots, and/or debris.
- *Systematize and sustain* the sort, straighten, and scrub components by developing and using checklists in a systematic way as part of the daily work routine and worker discipline.

5Ws–1H

The 5Ws–1H lean diagnostic tool focuses the effort of lean improvement on answering the who, what, where, when, why, and how questions at the process level. These tools are utilized during value-added process analysis activities.

4Ms

The 4M checklist focuses team efforts on the man, machine, material, and method issues of value-added process analysis. While these points obviously apply to physical processes, we will explore how they can also be useful in value-added analysis and improvement of management decision and information/support processes.

LEAN PERFORMANCE PRACTICES
Management Policy Deployment

In Lean Performance methodology, lean business policy and strategy drive management policy deployment. Management defines lean business policies, and lean project strategies are defined by management, key users, and project team members. Project objectives are then defined by the Lean Performance project team members, including process owners, process customers, and information systems personnel. A Lean Performance analysis determines those processes for which policies can be deployed and benefits measured, in addition to identifying software or other process enablers in need of improvement in order to meet project objectives. Modification to current systems, machines, or other process enablers are only approved when payback can be demonstrated and for processes for which the process owners are able to define performance measurements by concentrating on the three lean measurements of quality, delivery, and cost. Processes are then implemented and performance is measured by the process team, with results monitored by management. The Lean Performance analysis is then utilized to continuously deploy the lean business strategy.

Some examples of lean business policies that can be deployed include:

- Process focus and process thinking
- Putting quality first
- Total system thinking
- Support of world-class manufacturing
- Support of lean manufacturing
- Support of global standardization of processes and systems

Lean business policies are achieved in the project result by deploying lean project strategies to the team and process level. Lean project strategies communicate the business and systems strategies expressed in the business and strategic plans and are identified by the second echelon of management, the level below the policy formulators. The process of deployment continues to the manager or middle-manager level, where project objectives are developed by applying the knowledge of managers and team members to determine processes where lean project strategies can be achieved. Finally, information technology deployment is performed by information systems engineers applying their software capability and knowledge.

The process of deploying the lean business policy in support of lean manufacturing unfolds in this fashion (Figure 5.1):

- Lean project strategies:
    - Support improvement of agility and reduction of lead time.
    - Reduce storage of work-in-process and staged materials.

Lean Principles, Tools, and Practices ■ 61

Lean Business Policy:	Support Lean Manufacturing		Control Number 001
Lean Project Strategy:			
Project Objective:			
Technology Deployment:			
Process Identification:			
Lean Performance Team:			

Gap	Solution	Benefit	Performance Measurement

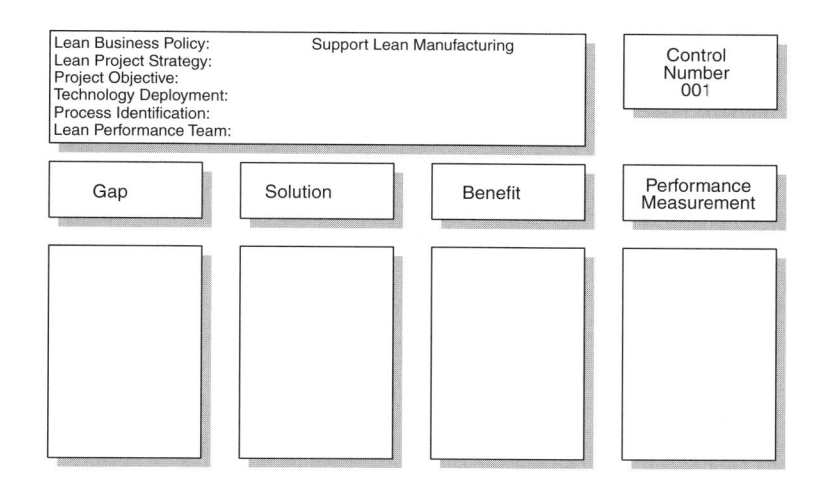

Figure 5.1   Lean Performance Analysis: Lean Business Policy Deployed

- Lean project strategy selected:
  - Reduce storage of work-in-process and staged materials.
- Project objective:
  - Reduce or eliminate the returned-goods storage room.
- Technology deployment:
  - Implement on-line credit capability of ERP software.

Lean Performance Teams

In the Lean Performance analysis, the Lean Performance teams complete a process workflow standard for each process, identifying in their process if a gap exists in meeting the deployed policy. Process or system gaps are defined as a functionality sought or needed by process owners and customers to achieve the project objectives. The Lean Performance teams document process solution or gaps and the benefits to be obtained by implementing the new process or another solution, including a software modification. A process workflow and work instructions are completed for every identified process, and the teams define Lean Performance measurements for each deployed policy/process combination. Lean Performance teams include and empower process owners and customers to take responsibility for Lean Performance. The team-based activities enable process owners, customers, and information technology engineers to improve communication and "speak with data." This synergy eventually enables shopfloor improvement initiatives to have an impact upstream. If we begin with the assumption that 85% of cost is upstream from the shopfloor, why would we concentrate our improvements only on the shopfloor?

Cross-functional Lean Performance teams are then formed to identify common processes across multiple sites and to facilitate the eventual completion of tasks necessary for implementation of enabling software. Multiple-site teams working on common or similar processes communicate and share process workflows and work instructions. With an effective prioritization and handoff of process documentation (process workflow standards and work instructions), teams at each site can more readily determine what works best in that particular process at that site and revise process standards accordingly. The cross-functional Lean Performance Teams (to be discussed below) are:

- Finance Team
- Engineering Team
- Materials Team
- Operations Team
- Information Team

To plan the project, management completes a number of tasks (discussed further below):

- Confirm lean vision
- Identify and deploy lean business policies
- Identify and deploy lean project strategies
- Develop the project mission statement
- Develop the project scope statement
- Identify and deploy project objectives

To prepare for the project, the Lean Performance project team thinks cross-functionally about how processes affect internal and external customers. Team members determine what their processes are, who their process customers are, and what their customers value as the process output and then deliver it.

Visual Management

Visual management facilitates communication between the project team, process owners and customers, company engineers, including information technology engineers, and the steering committee. Extensive use of visual management tools in the project includes:

- Project summary bar chart
- Project organization chart
- Process areas overview diagrams

Lean Principles, Tools, and Practices ■ 63

```
                    ┌───────────────────┐
            ┌───────│ Business Planning │───────┐
            │       └───────────────────┘       │
   ┌────────────┐   ┌─────────────┐   ┌─────────────┐
   │  Customer  │   │ Production and │   │   Product   │
   │Relationship│   │  Operations   │   │ Engineering │
   │ Management │   │               │   │             │
   └────────────┘   └─────────────┘   └─────────────┘
   ┌────────────┐   ┌─────────────┐   ┌─────────────┐
   │Supply Chain│   │  Inventory  │   │ Management  │
   │ Management │   │Management and│   │  Financial  │
   │            │   │  Logistics  │   │             │
   └────────────┘   └─────────────┘   └─────────────┘
            │       ┌───────────────┐       │
            └───────│  Performance  │───────┘
                    │  Measurement  │
                    └───────────────┘
```

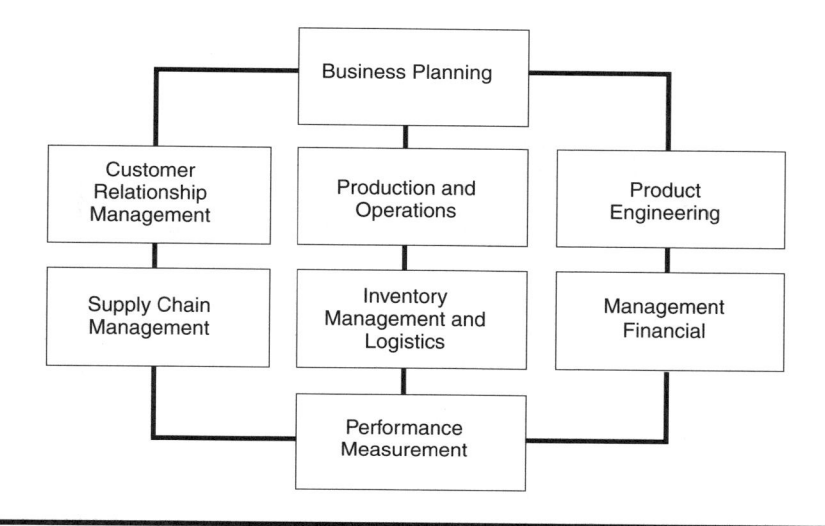

Figure 5.2 Business Process Areas

- Site configuration diagrams
- Material flow diagrams
- Workflow and work instruction diagrams

The use of visual management is as much about pushing tasks to completion as it is about using visual tools to communicate. Among other uses of visual management is the discovery and documentation of the process architecture of the firm, beginning with the assumption that processes are generally found in the areas of a manufacturing firm illustrated in Figure 5.2.

A process overview diagram is developed for each implementation site that identifies process areas according to the Lean Performance team. Figure 5.3 illustrates the process overview developed by a team at an international site.

Site-level Lean Performance teams are then defined and illustrated by the site-level Lean Performance team diagram. All processes have a process owner and customer(s) identified. The team is developed according to the process structure. Figure 5.4 depicts the team developed at the international site illustrated in Figure 5.3.

Lean Performance Analysis

After site leaders and Lean Performance teams identify the processes in each of the process areas for their sites, business process listings are

64 ■ Lean Performance ERP Project Management

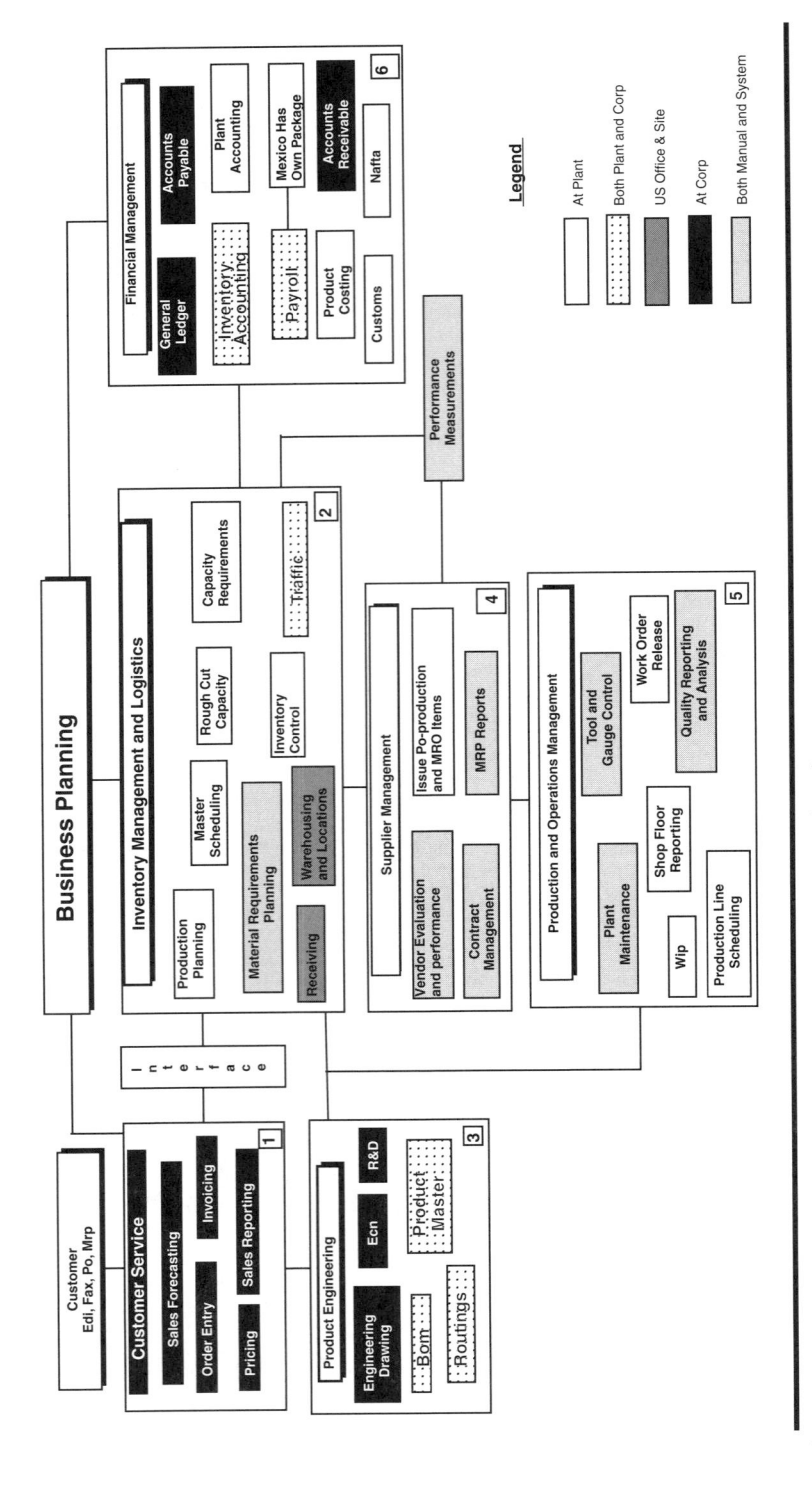

Figure 5.3 Current Process Activity Overview (International)

Lean Principles, Tools, and Practices ■ 65

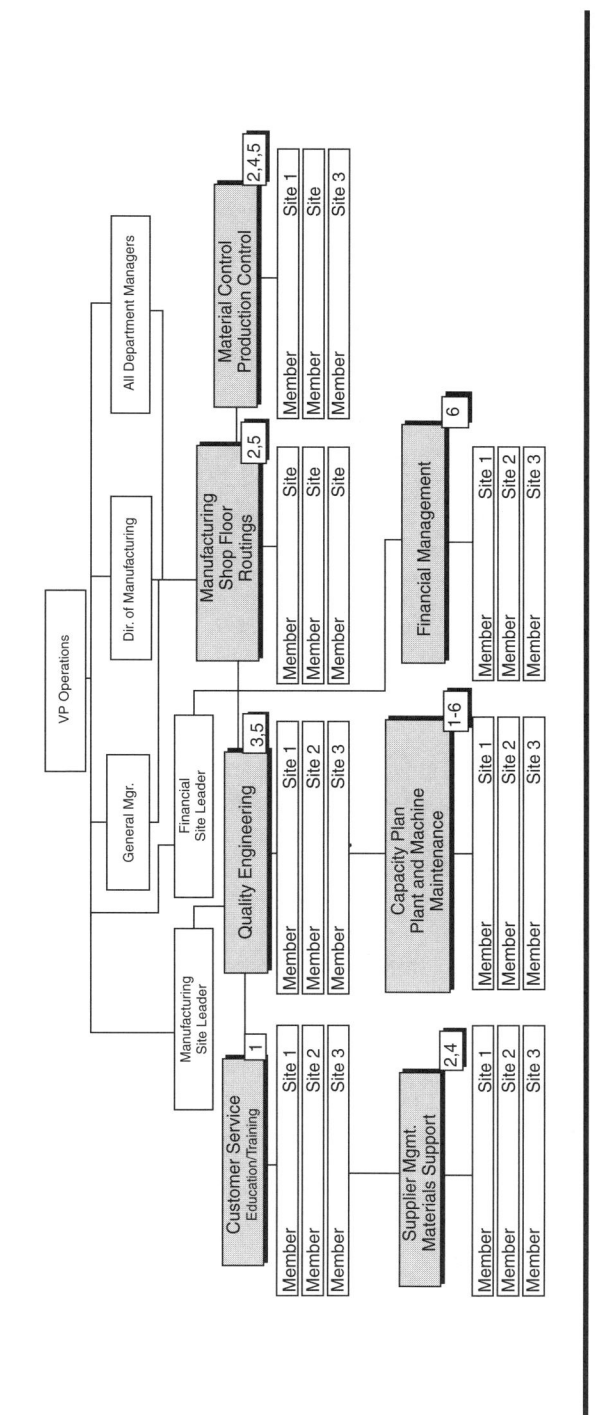

Figure 5.4 Lean Performance Team (International)

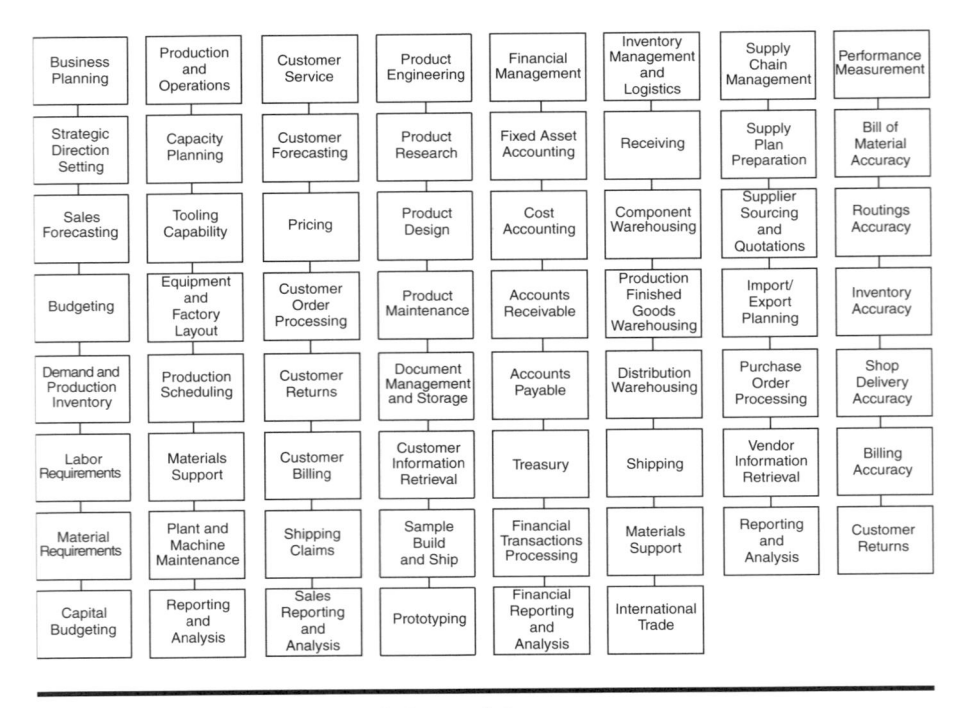

Figure 5.5 Business Process Listing and Sequence

Business Planning	Production and Operations	Customer Service	Product Engineering	Financial Management	Inventory Management and Logistics	Supply Chain Management	Performance Measurement
Strategic Direction Setting	Capacity Planning	Customer Forecasting	Product Research	Fixed Asset Accounting	Receiving	Supply Plan Preparation	Bill of Material Accuracy
Sales Forecasting	Tooling Capability	Pricing	Product Design	Cost Accounting	Component Warehousing	Supplier Sourcing and Quotations	Routings Accuracy
Budgeting	Equipment and Factory Layout	Customer Order Processing	Product Maintenance	Accounts Receivable	Production Finished Goods Warehousing	Import/Export Planning	Inventory Accuracy
Demand and Production Inventory	Production Scheduling	Customer Returns	Document Management and Storage	Accounts Payable	Distribution Warehousing	Purchase Order Processing	Shop Delivery Accuracy
Labor Requirements	Materials Support	Customer Billing	Customer Information Retrieval	Treasury	Shipping	Vendor Information Retrieval	Billing Accuracy
Material Requirements	Plant and Machine Maintenance	Shipping Claims	Sample Build and Ship	Financial Transactions Processing	Materials Support	Reporting and Analysis	Customer Returns
Capital Budgeting	Reporting and Analysis	Sales Reporting and Analysis	Prototyping	Financial Reporting and Analysis	International Trade		

developed for each site. Common primary processes and site-specific primary and subordinate processes are identified, if the project is multi-site. In a single site or multi-site project, the processes are listed in a sequence that defines the priorities best for the project. This is illustrated in Figure 5.5.

The policy deployment activity includes the opportunity for the information team to identify opportunities to utilize new technologies with which they are familiar in order to implement the policies deployed. Next, the Lean Performance teams identify the process that best addresses the policy and technology that the Lean Performance analysis technology deployment identifies. An example is shown in Figure 5.6.

Process standards are completed for each process identified, if that process survives the improvement activities. Process standards include workflows and work instructions. Figures 5.7 and 5.8 illustrate the type of documentation that should be developed to support the team efforts.

Teams will identify GAPs, solutions, benefits, and performance measurements during the project and then continuously as the central instrument of continuous improvement. This is accomplished by using a lean practice called the Lean Performance analysis. To complete Lean Performance analysis throughout the enterprise, the Lean Performance project and project teams will:

Lean Principles, Tools, and Practices ■ 67

Lean Business Policy:	Support Lean Manufacturing	Control Number
Lean Project Strategy:	Reduce Storage of WIP/stage Mat'l	001-001-001-001
Project Objective:	Eliminate Returned Goods Room	
Technology Deployment:	Implement Online Credit Capability	
Process Identification:	Fuel Pump Returns	
Lean Performance Team:	Aftermarket Operations Team	

Gap	Solution	Benefit	Performance Measurement

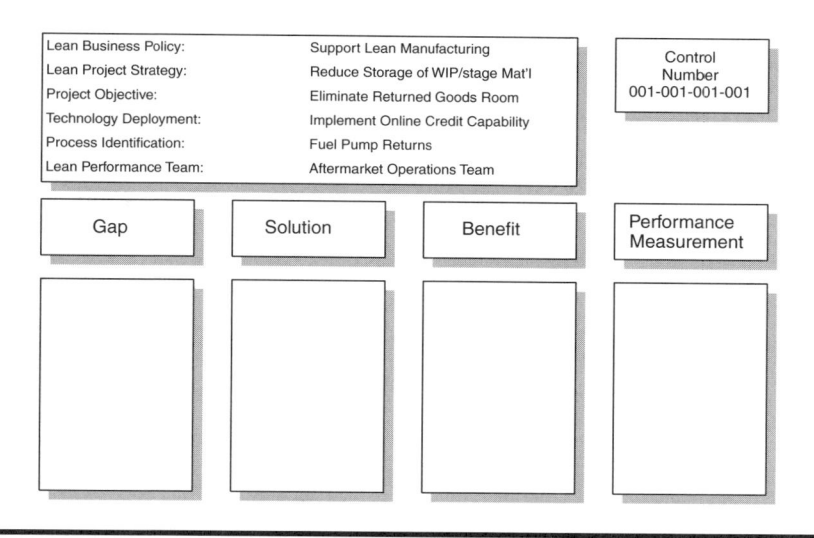

Figure 5.6 Lean Performance Analysis: Process and Team Identified

PROCESS NAME:		SITE CODE:	INDEX NUMBER:
PROCESS DESCRIPTION:	OWNER:	CUSTOMER:	
PAGE NUMBER: 1 OF	REVISION LEVEL:	DATE ISSUED:	DATE REVISED:	DATE PRINTED:
INPUT	PROCESS	OUTPUT

Figure 5.7 Workflow Diagram Template

SCREEN NAME:			SITE CODE:	INDEX NUMBER:
PAGE NUMBER: 1 OF	REVISION LEVEL:	DATE ISSUED:	DATE REVISED:	DATE PRINTED:

Figure 5.8　Work Instruction Template

- Identify all processes
- Develop process architecture
- Prioritize process standards (process workflow) definition sequence
- Perform Lean Performance analysis
- Produce process workflow standards
- Produce process work instructions

This brief introduction does not cover all of the visual management techniques nor the entire policy deployment or project process. The body of the text that follows contains a full explanation.

6

STEERING A LEAN PERFORMANCE PROJECT

MANAGEMENT IN THE LEAN PERFORMANCE PROJECT

Management in any company, in any stage of development, carries out its responsibilities through a role-set, whether it is consciously selected or is thrust upon them by the prevailing situation and organization culture. A role-set is a set of expected behaviors performed by the role player and formed over time by the interaction between the role player and the group, organization, or institution of which the role player is a member in response to the tasks pursued by the role player. Thus, managers can be viewed as role players. In fact, they may play several roles, as required (or as they perceive them to be required). A few examples of managerial roles in a Lean Performance project include:

- Advocate
- Champion
- Sponsor
- Communicator
- Motivator
- Team builder/team player
- Educator/developer
- Change agent
- Facilitator/coach/catalyst
- Mediator/negotiator

These are some of the many roles that managers (individually and as a group) can and are expected to play in a Lean Performance project. The common denominator in all these roles is the function of articulating expectations. Most people respond to concrete examples and explanations rather than plans, policies, and procedures. Let's take a closer look at the expectations for each role:

- *Advocate:* The advocate makes clear that becoming lean is the direction the company should take; assumes the role of supporter when the company is deciding whether or not to accept the challenge of becoming lean.
- *Champion:* The magnitude of the challenge of becoming lean leads to the emergence of a champion, a person that might be characterized as "leading the charge." The champion motivates, leads by example, and persuades with optimistic action.
- *Sponsor:* Management provides legitimacy to the process of becoming lean and makes it possible by providing resources and authorizing or approving changes in methods, equipment, personnel, and processes.
- *Communicator:* The role of the communicator is to eliminate the tangle of barriers to communication caused by organization structure and specialization. This person will establish new communication links and use them continuously to direct, inform, and motivate and will be the key communicator in the Lean Performance project.
- *Motivator:* Becoming lean ultimately requires an individual commitment to lean principles and practices (i.e., thinking lean); however, this is not a self-initiated process for most individuals. Management must initiate and sustain the motivation necessary to become lean through its leadership and its own commitment. Management must persuade all employees of the advantages of becoming lean and their part in the Lean Performance project.
- *Team builder/team player:* Working through committees and projects has become commonplace, but forming and sustaining Lean Performance teams is not so common. Lean Performance teams function at the task level and at the change level in the company. It is not easy for most managers and employees to operate in this mode. Management must become the team builders and themselves be team players.
- *Educator/developer:* The concepts of education and professional development in the workplace usually refer to individual education and development or career enhancement, not a united effort to change the company. Education in a Lean Performance project means acquiring the principles, tools, and practices that the Lean Performance project requires and learning the responsibilities and roles

that each must play. Management has the twofold task of educating themselves and the rest of the organization in lean thinking.

- *Change agent:* Active change agent intervention influences whether, when, where, and how a change occurs. It would be a stretch to say change agents control the change process, or even to say they manage it, although they may certainly try. The change process often results in unexpected consequences, such as too many or too few resignations to offer early retirement options. Even more important, changes are, in large measure, in the hands of the Lean Performance teams. In spite of all of these limitations, management must make it happen. They have the role of orchestrating the change process, even to the point of changing players on the Lean Performance teams if necessary.
- *Facilitator/coach/catalyst:* Lean Performance teams require assistance and guidance to make changes. It is not enough to educate, empower, and encourage. Knowledge of and interest in the action on the field, as well as providing advice and solid direction when appropriate, are necessary. Management must cause action without entering the action. As a facilitator, management helps individuals or teams pursue their objectives or solve the problems before them.
- *Mediator/negotiator:* Conflicts, turf problems, and misunderstandings are inevitable when undergoing major, rapid, or sustained change. Stress and tension gradually build before exploding into polarized viewpoints. Ideally, management should be able to anticipate and diffuse these situations, but when they are not able to do so, then they must be prepared to mediate or negotiate the conflict.

A successful Lean Performance project is predicated on effective human resource management. It is basic to all of the preceding management responsibilities and roles. Among the considerations that influence application of these roles and responsibilities in a given firm are many often-held but stunningly obsolete management assumptions regarding employees. Here are some of the most prevalent (and potentially most damaging to the process of becoming lean):

- Employees are not stakeholders in the company.
- Employees are not expected to make major contributions to the improvement process.
- Employees should focus on the jobs they are given.
- It is up to management to make improvements.
- It follows, then, that employees do not need education/training to solve problems or make improvements.

- Empowering employees to participate in the Lean Performance project entitles them to commitments that the company does not want to make.
- Human resource management becomes too problematic in a lean enterprise.
- The union does not want employees to participate in a Lean Performance project.
- We can carry out the key points of a Lean Performance project without employee involvement.

Before a management team undertakes a Lean Performance project, it must assess the extent to which they believe in these obsolete concepts. Unless members of the team are willing to discard them, little hope exists for a successful Lean Performance project. In short, lean human resource management begins with management's self-assessment and continues by adopting a set of positive assumptions. A good way to begin is to recast these obsolete assumptions in a positive light:

- Empowering employees to participate in the Lean Performance project empowers them to propose commitments the company may want to make and provides a forum for improvement.
- Employees are stakeholders in the company.
- Employees are expected to make major contributions to making improvements.
- Employees should focus on their processes and make improvements in their processes.
- Employees need education/training to solve problems or make improvements.
- Human resource management is essential in a lean enterprise.
- The union will support employee participation in a Lean Performance project.
- We will be successful in the Lean Performance project only with employee involvement.
- Employees can and should participate by identifying, developing, and implementing process improvements based on lean principles, tools, and practices.
- Employees can and should participate by making continuous improvements in their processes.
- Employees can and should participate by upgrading current and acquiring new work-related skills.
- Employees can and should participate by contributing to their Lean Performance team.

Becoming lean is no small accomplishment. It is the result of a major effort on the part of the entire organization, during which both teams and individuals make significant contributions that should not go unrecognized. All individuals involved should celebrate milestones. These need not be big events, and large monetary rewards are not necessary. In fact, some companies do not give money at all.

COMPLETING THE LEAN PERFORMANCE ASSESSMENT

The objective of the Lean Performance assessment is to consider the factors necessary to complete a successful Lean Performance project. The following is an assessment tool that includes questions about these factors. Administer this assessment with the management team that is or will be implementing a Lean Performance project in your firm. At the conclusion of the assessment, we will discuss how to use the information collected to plan the Lean Performance project. A Lean Performance project is a project cycle designed to manage implementation of the lean principles, tools, and practices at the process, management, and organization levels of a company. The Lean Performance Assessment Checklist gives participants a comprehensive understanding of their company's need for, opportunity to benefit from, and ability to undertake a Lean Performance project. It will also provide participants a means of obtaining prerequisite information in their company to develop a Lean Performance project plan tailored to their company.

To achieve the objectives, those responsible for the Lean Performance project in their firm should fill out assessment instruments, discuss points of disagreement, and reach a consensus when differences are significant. An assessment is an evaluation, a weighing of the evidence necessary to make a decision or determine a course of action (in this case, a project plan). An assessment can also be the evaluation of an activity in progress — for example, using objective measures to evaluate a lean transformation process already underway by using clearly stated assessment criteria and quantitative performance reporting. The Lean Performance assessment provides a basis for determining the scope and feasibility of undertaking a Lean Performance project by determining the extent of a company's readiness to begin. The assessment, thoroughly administered and completed, helps the management of a company decide whether or not to even begin the lean journey. The assessment also helps a company avoid formula approaches that assume all companies are alike.

As much as these assessment factors may seem like nothing more than common sense, they are all too often ignored. The results are lean transformations that are limited in scope, unnecessarily disruptive, and short-lived. Avoiding, or at least minimizing, these and other negative consequences is well worth the time involved in an initial assessment.

LEAN PERFORMANCE ASSESSMENT

The Lean Performance Assessment Checklist has been designed to assist the management team in evaluating the company's readiness to complete a successful Lean Performance project in four critical areas:

- Company readiness
- Opportunity to make lean applications
- Company capability to become lean
- Lean Performance project constraints

Company Readiness

1. **Assess the company's need to become lean** (check as many as applicable):

Priority

High	Low	Reasons
☐ ☐	☐ ☐	To meet or beat the competition
☐ ☐	☐ ☐	To be able to reduce prices
☐ ☐	☐ ☐	To keep delivery promise dates
☐ ☐	☐ ☐	To reduce new product development cycle time
☐ ☐	☐ ☐	To improve quality
☐ ☐	☐ ☐	To implement a continuous improvement program
☐ ☐	☐ ☐	To respond faster to customer orders
☐ ☐	☐ ☐	To respond flexibly to customer orders
☐ ☐	☐ ☐	To reduce costs, improve operating efficiencies
☐ ☐	☐ ☐	To improve process design
☐ ☐	☐ ☐	To redesign processes
☐ ☐	☐ ☐	To improve process operations
☐ ☐	☐ ☐	To reduce the workforce
☐ ☐	☐ ☐	To improve production planning
☐ ☐	☐ ☐	To develop a continuous flow process
☐ ☐	☐ ☐	To develop a production pull process
☐ ☐	☐ ☐	To improve production support processes
☐ ☐	☐ ☐	To improve administrative processes
☐ ☐	☐ ☐	To match/beat the competition

2. **Identify your company's current position with respect to lean** (check position or positions closest to that of your firm):

☐ Company has general but limited knowledge of lean principles, tools, and practices; thinks it may be useful in this location and wants to learn more before trying it.

☐ Company has minimal knowledge of lean principles, tools, and practices but is ready to get started; will commit resources as required.

- ☐ Company has begun to get lean in selected areas but does not know how to move from a process to an organizational level.
- ☐ Top management views lean as a shopfloor tool that does not require their involvement.
- ☐ We are midway through a lean transformation in the plant.
- ☐ We have experienced some problems of implementation.
- ☐ We have experienced some differences of opinion with the union.
- ☐ We expect to move into administrative and support processes.
- ☐ We have completed a lean transformation in the plant.
- ☐ We are now going through a lean transformation in administrative and support processes.
- ☐ Management supports the use of lean principles and practices throughout the organization.

Other/comments _____

_____

3. What other programs/approaches are you using or considering that impact the goals of lean thinking (consider their impact on the Lean Performance project):

- ☐ TQM
- ☐ SPC
- ☐ JIT
- ☐ MRP/ERP
- ☐ Computer-integrated manufacturing
- ☐ Supply chain management

Other/comments _____

_____

4. Assess the potential to apply these lean principles or level of application of these lean principles in the firm (check as many as applicable):*

Potential/Level

High			Low	Principle
☐	☐	☐	☐	Precisely specify value by product or family.
☐	☐	☐	☐	Identify the value stream for each product or family.
☐	☐	☐	☐	Make value flow without interruption.
☐	☐	☐	☐	Let customer pull value from process owner.
☐	☐	☐	☐	Continuously pursue perfection.

Other/comments _____

_____

---

* Adapted from Womack, J., and Jones, D., *Lean Thinking: Banish Waste and Create Wealth in Your Corporation,* Simon & Schuster, New York, 1996.

For a more detailed analysis, visit the management, information/support, and physical processes in the workplace. Analyze a process or processes in each area in terms of these lean transformational principles:

Precisely specify value by product or family:

1. Can you clearly identify the process?

2. Has an up-to-date process standard (bills of materials, routing, procedure, work flow, work instruction) been identified for all process tasks/steps?

3. Could anyone in the company perform the process, after some training, based on the process standards?

Identify the value stream for each product:

1. Are there any tasks performed in the process that are not included on the standard?

2. Do these tasks provide customer value and would customers pay for them if they knew we were doing them?

Make value flow without interruption:

1. Does the process have any built-in interruptions or delays?

2. Any there any side journeys for work in process (which includes paper)?

Let customer pull value from process owner:

1. Is the process directly connected to the customer?
   _____
   _____

2. Does the process owner deal directly with the end customer? If so, does the process owner review the process with the customer regularly to ensure customer satisfaction?
   _____
   _____

3. Is the process customer internal? If so, does the process owner review the process with the customer regularly to ensure customer satisfaction?
   _____
   _____

Continuously pursue perfection:

1. Is there a regular review of the performance metrics (cost, quality, delivery) of the process?
   _____
   _____

2. Is it okay for the customer to suggest improvements to the process?
   _____
   _____

List the tasks for which the lean transformational principles could be applied to improve your process (i.e., more value-added):
_____
_____
_____
_____

Identify any recent improvements and indicate whether they met the goals of the lean transformational principles:
_____
_____
_____
_____

Other observations:
_____
_____
_____
_____

5. Assess the potential to apply or the current level of application of lean diagnostic tools in your firm (check as many as applicable):

Potential/Level
High   Low   Lean Diagnostic Tool
☐ ☐ ☐ ☐   3MUs
☐ ☐ ☐ ☐   5Ss
☐ ☐ ☐ ☐   5Ws–1H
☐ ☐ ☐ ☐   4Ms

Other/comments _____
_____

For a more detailed analysis on the presence of *muda* in the workplace, send teams out to visit the process areas and then fill in this part of the assessment:

Waste (muda) in the Workplace	Where Observed
Overproduction	_____
Inventory	_____
Repairs/rejects	_____
Motion	_____
Processing	_____
Waiting	_____
Transport	_____
Manpower	_____
Technique	_____
Method	_____
Time	_____
Facilities	_____
Jigs and fixtures	_____
Materials	_____
Production volume	_____
Inventory	_____
Place	_____

Way of thinking _____
Layout _____
Distance traveled per part _____
Down time _____
Cycle time _____
Lead time _____
Queue time _____
Setup _____
Equipment utilization _____
Maintenance _____
Safety _____
Material flow _____
Standards _____
Work measurement _____
Storage areas _____
Quality assurance _____
Control points _____
Housekeeping _____

Other observations _____
_____

For a more detailed analysis of the opportunities that exist for the application of the 5Ss, send teams into the process areas to investigate and then complete this part of the assessment:

Guidelines for sorting (5Ss):

Select a designated portion of the work area that can be worked on immediately:_____.

Limit the area to allow visible results of an intensive, thorough sorting (do not make a superficial sort of a particular item over a large area); remove anything from the work area that will not be used within 30 days. List those items here:

_____
_____
_____
_____
_____
_____

If in doubt about the necessity of an item, red tag it and decide later; list red-tagged items here:

If an employee thinks a red-tagged item is necessary, have the employee demonstrate its necessity and document the item here:

Find out why unnecessary items have accumulated (for example, determine what kind of ordering system is in place); list reasons given here:

What kind of scheduling system is in place?

Guidelines for straightening (5Ss):

Classify items by use; list classifications here:

Arrange items to minimize search time and provide the arrangement scheme here:
_____
_____
_____
_____
_____

Designate a permanent place for each item and the volume necessary to keep on hand, if multiple units are required; list the items and their quantity, and locations here:
_____
_____
_____
_____
_____

Mark floor space for designated items and indicate those items here:
_____
_____
_____
_____
_____

Provide wall boards, bins, etc., as needed for required tools, fixtures, jigs, parts, maintenance equipment, etc.; indicate here how many were placed and where:
_____
_____
_____
_____
_____

When this part of the assessment has been completed, abnormalities in the locations of items should be readily apparent; is anything still out of place? _____

82 ■ Lean Performance ERP Project Management

Guidelines for scrubbing (5Ss):

Clean everything: machines, tools, floors, walls, containers, racks, etc.; list here what got cleaned:

_____
_____
_____
_____
_____

Be observant as you clean and look for any malfunctions or other problems (e.g., oil leakage, cracks, loose fasteners); provide your findings here:

_____
_____
_____
_____
_____

Red tag all malfunctioning items and follow up to ensure action; list those items here:

_____
_____
_____
_____
_____

Paint walls and machines and list everything here that was painted:

_____
_____
_____
_____
_____

Paint floor lines designated in the straightening step and list those locations here:

_____
_____
_____
_____
_____

Guidelines for systematizing (5Ss):

Develop a systematic approach to sorting, straightening, and scrubbing, including:

    What to check

    _____
    _____
    _____

    What action to take

    _____
    _____
    _____

    Who should undertake which tasks

    _____
    _____
    _____

    When these tasks should be done

    _____
    _____
    _____

Identify all items that are part of a specific job:

_____
_____
_____

Identify supervisory and managerial roles and responsibilities:

_____
_____
_____

Guidelines for sustaining (5Ss):

How will you make the preceding four steps a way of life?

_____
_____
_____

How will your company adopt these changes as a way of working?

_____
_____
_____

How will your company continually improve based on constant reevaluation by workers, supervisors, managers, and members of the continuous improvement group or unit?

_____
_____
_____

How will your company recognize and reward both group and individual efforts through the evaluation and compensation system?

_____
_____
_____

For a more detailed analysis of 5W–1H, send teams into the process areas to investigate and then complete this part of the assessment:

5W–1H focuses the effort of lean improvement on:[*]

Who

Who does it (usually)?
_____

Who is doing it?
_____

Who should be doing it?
_____

Who else can do it?
_____

Who else should do it?
_____

Who is doing the 5Ss and muda identification in this process or area?
_____

What

What is supposed to be done?
_____

---

[*] This section is adapted from Imai, M., *Kaizen: The Key to Japan's Competitive Success*, McGraw-Hill, New York, 1986, p. 235.

What is being done?

What should be done?

What else can be done?

What else should be done?

What 5Ss and muda identification are being done?

Where

Where are we supposed to do it?

Where is it being done?

Where should it be done?

Where else should it be done?

Where are the 5Ss and muda identification being done?

When

When are we supposed to do it?

When is it done?

When should it be done?

What other time can it be done?

What other time should it be done?

Why

Why is a particular employee supposed to do it?

Why do it?

Why do it there?

Why do it then?

Why do it that way?

How

How are we supposed to do it?

How is it done?

How should it be done?

Can this method be used in other areas?

Is there another way to do it?

For a more detailed analysis of the 4Ms (man, machine, material, method), send teams into the process areas to investigate and then complete this part of the assessment:*

Man (operator)

Does he/she follow standards?
_____

Is his/her work efficiency acceptable?
_____

Is he/she problem conscious?
_____

Is he/she responsible (is he/she accountable)?
_____

Is he/she qualified?
_____

Is he/she experienced?
_____

Is he/she assigned to the proper job?
_____

Is he/she willing to improve?
_____

Does he/she maintain good working relations with co-workers?
_____

Is he/she physically able to do the job?
_____

Machine (facilities)

Does it meet production requirements?
_____

Does it meet process capabilities?
_____

---

* This section is adapted from Imai, M., *Kaizen: The Key to Japan's Competitive Success*, McGraw-Hill, New York, 1986, p. 235.

Is the oiling, greasing, or lubrication adequate?

Does it often shut down operations because of mechanical trouble?

Does it meet precision requirements?

Does it make any unusual noises?

Is the layout adequate for the machine?

Are there enough machines for the facility?

Is everything in good working order?

Material

Can you observe any mistakes in volume?

Can you observe any mistakes in grade?

Can you observe any mistakes in brand name?

Can you observe any impurities mixed in?

Is the inventory level adequate?

Can you observe any waste in the use of material?

Is the handling of material adequate (safe, sanitary)?

Is the handling of the material wasteful?

Is the work in process visible? _____

Is the layout adequate? _____

Is the quality standard appropriate or achievable with the material provided? _____

Operating method

Are the work standards adequate? _____

Is the work standard up to current standards? _____

Is it a safe method? _____

Is it a method that ensures a good product? _____

Is it an efficient method? _____

Is the sequence of work adequate? _____

Is the setup adequate? _____

Are the temperature and humidity adequate? _____

Are the lighting and ventilation adequate? _____

Is there adequate contact with the previous and next processes? _____

Other/comments _____

6. **Assess the potential or current level of applications for the following lean tools and practices in the firm** (check as many as applicable):

Potential/Level
High   Low   *Lean Tools and Concepts*
☐ ☐ ☐ ☐ ☐   Cellular production
☐ ☐ ☐ ☐ ☐   U-shaped cells
☐ ☐ ☐ ☐ ☐   Cell design and layout for flow
☐ ☐ ☐ ☐ ☐   Preventive maintenance
☐ ☐ ☐ ☐ ☐   SMED (single-minute exchange of die)
☐ ☐ ☐ ☐ ☐   Internal vs. external setup
☐ ☐ ☐ ☐ ☐   Station and operation process control
☐ ☐ ☐ ☐ ☐   Sending only what is needed
☐ ☐ ☐ ☐ ☐   Error proofing (poke–yoke)
☐ ☐ ☐ ☐ ☐   Work group/team error proofing
☐ ☐ ☐ ☐ ☐   ZD (zero defects)
☐ ☐ ☐ ☐ ☐   Cycle time
☐ ☐ ☐ ☐ ☐   Takt time
☐ ☐ ☐ ☐ ☐   Kanbans
☐ ☐ ☐ ☐ ☐   Part conveyance between stations
☐ ☐ ☐ ☐ ☐   Mixed flow lines
☐ ☐ ☐ ☐ ☐   Level loading
☐ ☐ ☐ ☐ ☐   Small lot production
☐ ☐ ☐ ☐ ☐   Balanced flow
☐ ☐ ☐ ☐ ☐   One-piece flow
☐ ☐ ☐ ☐ ☐   Synchronous flow

Other/comments _____

_____

Opportunity to Make Lean Applications

7. **Assess the potential or current application of value-added process analysis to your processes** (check as many as applicable):

High   Low   *Value-Added Process Analysis*
☐ ☐ ☐ ☐ ☐   Analyzing sequential processes
☐ ☐ ☐ ☐ ☐   Time-based activity analysis
☐ ☐ ☐ ☐ ☐   Analyzing concurrent processes
☐ ☐ ☐ ☐ ☐   Analyzing organizational complexity
☐ ☐ ☐ ☐ ☐   Identifying value-added and non-value-added activities
☐ ☐ ☐ ☐ ☐   Identifying handoffs
☐ ☐ ☐ ☐ ☐   Analyzing work movement
☐ ☐ ☐ ☐ ☐   Assessing changeover times

☐ ☐ ☐ ☐ ☐ Assessing work in process
☐ ☐ ☐ ☐ ☐ Identifying problem imbalances
☐ ☐ ☐ ☐ ☐ Identifying process variability
☐ ☐ ☐ ☐ ☐ Analyzing defects and errors
☐ ☐ ☐ ☐ ☐ Analyzing process yields

Other/comments _____

8. **Assess your organization's potential to implement (or see actual results from implementing) the following lean cross-functional processes** (check as many as applicable):

High   Low   Cross-Functional Processes
☐ ☐ ☐ ☐ ☐ Lean quality management
☐ ☐ ☐ ☐ ☐ Lean maintenance
☐ ☐ ☐ ☐ ☐ Lean new product introduction
☐ ☐ ☐ ☐ ☐ Lean design and engineering

Other/comments _____

9. **Assess your organization's potential to implement (or see actual results from implementing) the following lean cross-enterprise processes** (check as many as applicable):

High   Low   Cross-Enterprise Processes
☐ ☐ ☐ ☐ ☐ Lean customer relationship management
☐ ☐ ☐ ☐ ☐ Lean sales and operations planning
☐ ☐ ☐ ☐ ☐ Lean supply chain management

Other/comments _____

10. **Lean process improvements are possible in all company/enterprise processes; assess the potential or current level of attainment of lean processes in the following process areas of your company** (check as many as applicable):

High   Low   Lean Processes
☐ ☐ ☐ ☐ ☐ Order processing
☐ ☐ ☐ ☐ ☐ Accounting
☐ ☐ ☐ ☐ ☐ Customer service
☐ ☐ ☐ ☐ ☐ Warranty processing

☐ ☐ ☐ ☐ ☐   Mailroom activities
☐ ☐ ☐ ☐ ☐   Advertising
☐ ☐ ☐ ☐ ☐   Human resources

Other/comments _____

_____

Company Capability to Become Lean

11. Identify personnel that have leadership qualities, a willingness to make major changes in company operations and will be available to participate in a Lean Performance project in your firm (the functions that these leaders would perform in the Lean Performance project include project manager, facilitator, coordinator, trainer, and process area team leader):

Name	*Department*	*Job Title*
_____	_____	_____
_____	_____	_____
_____	_____	_____
_____	_____	_____
_____	_____	_____
_____	_____	_____

12. Our experience in implementing organization change may be characterized as:

☐ No major organization changes have been made to date.
☐ We have only made small incremental changes.
☐ We have made several changes in machinery, methods, product line, processes, and organization.
☐ Changes made are all within our current policies.
☐ Changes made are not all within our current policies.
☐ Changes made have had departmental impact.
☐ Changes made have had organizational impact.
☐ Changes made have had cross-functional impact.
☐ We have made at least one major change in our operation that has been cross-functional in scope (e.g., TQM, ISO 9000, MRP/ERP, JIT).
☐ We have been through a major merger that has impacted the entire organization.

Other/comments _____

_____

13. **Evaluate your management's characteristics that have the potential to facilitate or inhibit a Lean Performance project in your firm:**

Strong	Weak	Management Characteristic
☐ ☐	☐ ☐ ☐	Innovative
☐ ☐	☐ ☐ ☐	Long-run vision
☐ ☐	☐ ☐ ☐	Supports education and development
☐ ☐	☐ ☐ ☐	Sustains effort once a program is underway
☐ ☐	☐ ☐ ☐	Desire to benefit all stakeholders (employees, customers, suppliers, management, owners)
☐ ☐	☐ ☐ ☐	Desire to be an industry leader
☐ ☐	☐ ☐ ☐	Growth oriented
☐ ☐	☐ ☐ ☐	Attention to detail
☐ ☐	☐ ☐ ☐	Personal interest in improving operations
☐ ☐	☐ ☐ ☐	Human resource skills

Other/comments _____

14. **Assess the capacity of your management to play the roles necessary to complete a Lean Performance project** (check as many as applicable):

High	Low	Role
☐ ☐	☐ ☐ ☐	Advocate
☐ ☐	☐ ☐ ☐	Champion
☐ ☐	☐ ☐ ☐	Sponsor
☐ ☐	☐ ☐ ☐	Planning coordinator
☐ ☐	☐ ☐ ☐	Communicator
☐ ☐	☐ ☐ ☐	Motivator
☐ ☐	☐ ☐ ☐	Team builder/player
☐ ☐	☐ ☐ ☐	Educator/developer
☐ ☐	☐ ☐ ☐	Change agent/manager
☐ ☐	☐ ☐ ☐	Facilitator/coach
☐ ☐	☐ ☐ ☐	Cross-functional manager
☐ ☐	☐ ☐ ☐	Process manager
☐ ☐	☐ ☐ ☐	Mediator/negotiator

Other/comments _____

Lean Performance Project Constraints

15. Assess the extent to which your firm is characterized by the organizational consequences of a mass production system as the primary basis of structure and operation. This is a key issue because mass production systems, especially those in older, established industries, pose the greatest challenges to lean thinking. Precisely because they once were the most advanced manufacturing organizations and management systems, it is difficult to convince proponents of such systems that they are now industrial dinosaurs. Recognizing these dysfunctional systems helps identify the scope and direction of a Lean Performance project.

High	Low	Characteristic
☐ ☐	☐ ☐	Command and control management systems
☐ ☐	☐ ☐	Multilayered management hierarchy
☐ ☐	☐ ☐	Departmental/job focus, not process/task
☐ ☐	☐ ☐	Priority of departmental objectives over organization objectives
☐ ☐	☐ ☐	Emphasis on the status quo, not innovation
☐ ☐	☐ ☐	Processes not flowing across departmental boundaries
☐ ☐	☐ ☐	Innovation focused on product but not process development
☐ ☐	☐ ☐	Systematic improvement considered a staff activity, not a worker responsibility
☐ ☐	☐ ☐	Quality standards being maintained, not improved
☐ ☐	☐ ☐	No documentation of systems and operations processes
☐ ☐	☐ ☐	No established standard ways of operating
☐ ☐	☐ ☐	Performance measures are primarily financial, not operational or process
☐ ☐	☐ ☐	Controls being maintained, not continuously improved

Other/comments _____

---

16. We can anticipate apathy or resistance to a Lean Performance project in our firm from the following sources. Enthusiastic advocates of lean often ignore resistance, only to wonder later on why lean fails to take hold in their company. Whatever its form, resistance or apathy, if not dealt with from the start and whenever and wherever it occurs, will kill all chances of a Lean Performance project; we must anticipate this resistance and apathy in all its forms.

- ☐ Top management _____
- ☐ Middle management _____
- ☐ Supervision _____
- ☐ Production support processes _____
- ☐ Administrative processes _____
- ☐ Professional staff _____
- ☐ Professional personnel _____

Administrative personnel:
- ☐ Union _____
- ☐ Non-union _____

Production personnel:
- ☐ Union _____
- ☐ Non-union _____

17. The key issues/problems in our company facing the Lean Performance project are:

- ☐ What to do with excess personnel
- ☐ How to work with the union
- ☐ How to overcome resistance/apathy in the workforce
- ☐ How to gain the confidence and trust of the skeptical
- ☐ How to determine the size of the one key personnel reduction, if made
- ☐ What to do about a key manager that is openly hostile
- ☐ How to pace our transformation effort over time so as to sustain effort
- ☐ How to internalize lean thinking
- ☐ How to move past "low-hanging fruit" and motivate personnel to tackle less obvious problems
- ☐ How to develop Lean Performance teams
- ☐ How to resolve conflicts between process areas
- ☐ How to gain the support of the information technology group

Other/comments _____

ANALYZING LEAN PERFORMANCE ASSESSMENT RESULTS

In the category of company readiness, if the general management does not perceive a need to become lean, does not understand the nature and scope of a Lean Performance project, or is expending major effort on other programs, except those consistent with lean thinking (e.g., TQM, ISO 9000, etc.), then a Lean Performance project should not be undertaken at this time. Instead, more education on lean thinking is in order, and any major tasks (say, a merger or acquisition) should be completed. In the meantime, the Lean Performance Assessment Checklist can be utilized to assess opportunities to apply lean principles, tools, and practices in the company. Doing so is important in order to focus the Lean Performance project on the most productive combinations of technique applications and receptive areas and to determine what types of additional education and/or training would be most beneficial. Finally, we need to gauge the scope and depth of whatever Lean Performance project can be undertaken.

Where is your firm successful in applying lean foundation tools and practices? Where are the opportunities to apply lean principles, tools, and practices? Readiness and opportunity are not enough to ensure an effective Lean Performance project. There must be a management capability in place to direct and implement the project, with the collective skills, abilities, and, above all, willingness to accept the challenges and responsibilities that becoming lean entails. Management must be scrupulously honest in assessing its collective capabilities to implement lean thinking. If management cannot ensure at least a critical minimum effort, the project is better reconsidered for a later date. This, of course, is with the understanding that what seems optional today is all too often mandatory tomorrow, and later should only be a matter of months.

Now consider the major factors that can constrain any Lean Performance project, even to the point of torpedoing it entirely:

- Rigid organizational structures
- Inflexible thinking
- Autocratic management

Do any of these three legacies of your mass production system remain? Legacy issues may necessitate shutting down, breaking up, or spinning or selling off assets when lean thinking is not likely to take root. It is hoped that in most situations this is not the case and that a small entry point can be found to initiate lean thinking.

Two other factors that, in their most virulent form, may preclude a Lean Performance project (but not necessarily permanently) are resistance and apathy. These two factors may produce an unmanageable number of cement heads and/or an intransigent union. The assessment must be completed by considering honestly whether or not the company contains an unmanageable number of cement heads or uncooperative union. Such situations must be addressed prior to beginning a project. In conclusion, thoughtful consideration of the assessment factors will have well served its purpose if it causes the management team to assess the possibilities for a successful Lean Performance project. It also will help the company plan and manage a Lean Performance project that is truly based on the company's unique configuration of objectives and resources available to achieve those objectives.

PREPARING FOR THE LEAN PERFORMANCE PROJECT

To determine if your company can, should, and is willing to begin a lean transformation or to extend already existing lean practices across the enterprise by initiating a Lean Performance project, appoint a leader/champion and develop a support group to initially coordinate the wider effort. Allow an initial trial period of 6 to 12 weeks. Focus on one process area (usually production) throughout this trial phase, and select a process that is not controversial. The emphasis of the trial is on gaining lean experience at both the team and management levels in order to determine if your company is in a position to begin or extend its lean transformation.

Acquire a basic education in lean principles, tools, and practices for managers and supervisors. Develop two or three Lean Performance teams to work on unrelated products/processes in order to gain a wider experience base. Identify several potential processes to improve. Give all team members training in the use of lean principles, tools, and practices and have an experienced lean team facilitator work with these teams. Be sure to initiate weekly team meetings on company time, and at least each month hold inter-team meetings at which the teams present their results and proposed changes. Proposed changes that the teams have approved can be implemented through a developing management process that can monitor results and measure improvement.

Continue to provide assistance to the teams as required, such as training, facilitating, or providing in-house expertise. It may be desirable to expand the lean activity by using Lean Performance teams to complete tasks in data accuracy, inventory reduction, and quality. Continue for 6 to 12 weeks, and be sure to document all significant activities and improvements. Less experience that is well documented is preferred over a greater amount of hastily conceived and executed experience that is undocumented. After the 6 to 12 weeks, reassess the company to be sure all the issues relevant to the Lean Performance project are being considered. This is the time to review and evaluate the results to date. At this point, you may decide to stop, to gather more experience and information, or to expand Lean Performance to include a formal project organization.

11

LEAN PERFORMANCE PLANNING MODULES

The two objectives of Lean Performance planning are:

1. Develop a plan for the Lean Performance project based on your firm's need, opportunity, and capability to develop unique company attributes.
2. Understand how planning can be useful to integrate lean processes throughout the transition to Lean Performance management.

Planning for Lean Performance differs from traditional corporate planning. Initial project plans cannot be based on past experience with lean transformation, because there is none. Experience in lean thinking must be acquired before a valid planning process can be undertaken. Lean thinking runs counter to the basic assumptions of mass production, upon which current manufacturing planning practices are based, so most non-lean firms are not in the lean thinking mindset, and even lean firms, as we discussed above, are generally not lean in the management decision and information/support processes. A Lean Performance project plan must be designed and implemented based on the unique lean-vision-driven configuration of a firm's organization, processes, technology, and culture. The plan must be derived from the foundational premise that all of these will change before the project is completed. Planning is necessary to facilitate the impact of changes in essential processes. Previous organizational planning did not require these considerations, because no significant process changes were assumed while planning organizational structural changes and perhaps personnel requirements. Even if planning for the Lean Performance project may seem unimportant in the early stages, the benefits obtained from good project planning will be evident as the project proceeds. The Lean Performance project methodology begins with a management project planning process that includes the deployment of management policies and strategies downward into the business.

7

DEPLOYING MANAGEMENT POLICY MODULE

MANAGEMENT TASKS

Organizing the Steering Committee

The first element of the planning process is the formation of a project steering committee. The steering committee is an expansion of the existing lean support group or, if a support group is not in place, the key individuals in the business as well as a Lean Performance project manager and a business "owner" from all process areas in a single-site project or each project site in a multiple-site project. Management personnel identified during the Lean Performance assessment as being capable of playing the various roles required within the lean transformation project are appropriate individuals for the steering committee responsibilities:

- Advocate
- Champion
- Sponsor
- Communicator
- Motivator
- Team builder/team player
- Educator/developer
- Change agent
- Mediator/negotiator
- Facilitator/coach/catalyst

Management personnel identified for these roles during the Lean Performance assessment should be called upon now to assist in the development of lean project strategies. Prior to formal deployment of the lean business policies and strategies at the project inception, roles should be formalized and a steering committee introduced.

Confirming the Lean Vision

A company's vision is its desired future state, i.e., what it hopes to become. The company lean vision must incorporate the breadth and depth of the Lean Performance project. The current company vision statement can usually be expanded and focused to incorporate lean elements. A visioning session or sessions can also be conducted.

Identifying and Deploying Lean Business Policies

Lean business policies express the views of the lean sponsor or champion of the Lean Performance project. Typically, this person is the chairman or CEO/president of the business. Lean business policies define the lean business mission and are the drivers for development of lean project strategies. Executive management often expresses lean business policies in business plans delivered to the organizational level or in existing company policy communication vehicles such as business plans and strategic planning documents (including the previously mentioned lean vision statement). The project sponsor/champion should also incorporate the lean business policies developed during the Lean Performance Assessment. Figure 7.1 illustrates a sampling of lean business policies. The deployment and eventual project/process team implementation of these lean business policies will be tracked throughout the project text that follows.

Lean business policies are formalized and communicated to the organization and eventual project team through the use of a deployment practice known as the Lean Performance analysis (Figure 7.2). The lean sponsor or champion completes the lean business policy portion of the Lean Performance analysis form, listing only one policy per form. These Lean Performance analysis masters are numbered and distributed for review and development of lean business strategies by members of the project steering committee.

Identifying and Deploying Lean Project Strategies

The lean business policies that have been identified and articulated are now disseminated, understood, and followed throughout the project; in other words, they will be deployed to the process level. A company's

—Support lean manufacturing

—Support lean thinking in the global standardization of engineering processes

—Support lean thinking in the global standardization of financial processes

—Support lean thinking in the global standardization of information systems management

Figure 7.1 Lean Business Policies

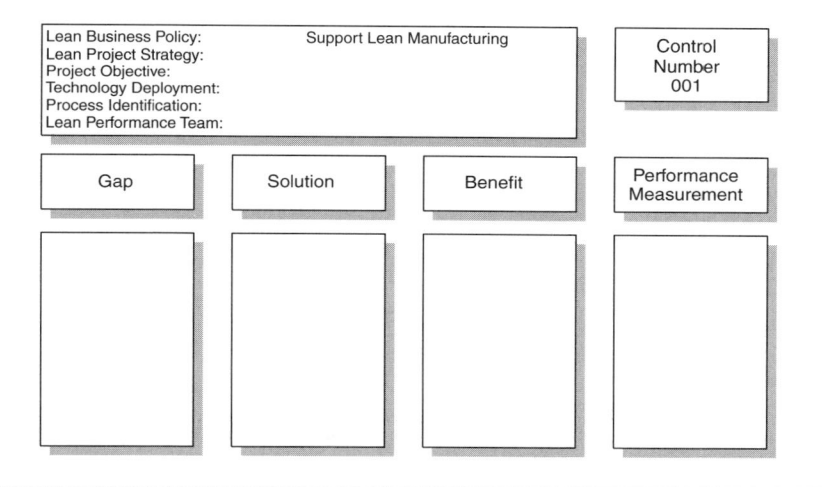

```
┌─────────────────────────────────────────────────────┐  ┌──────────┐
│ Lean Business Policy:     Support Lean Manufacturing│  │ Control  │
│ Lean Project Strategy:                              │  │ Number   │
│ Project Objective:                                  │  │   001    │
│ Technology Deployment:                              │  │          │
│ Process Identification:                             │  │          │
│ Lean Performance Team:                              │  │          │
└─────────────────────────────────────────────────────┘  └──────────┘

┌──────────┐   ┌──────────┐   ┌──────────┐   ┌─────────────┐
│   Gap    │   │ Solution │   │ Benefit  │   │ Performance │
│          │   │          │   │          │   │ Measurement │
└──────────┘   └──────────┘   └──────────┘   └─────────────┘
```

Figure 7.2 Lean Performance Analysis: Lean Business Policy Deployed

policy-driven strategies are the guidelines within which it operates while pursuing and fulfilling its lean mission. Following the lead of the lean champion or project sponsor who has deployed the lean business policies, members of the emerging project steering committee communicate the lean strategies that they would like to see pursued in their business organization or process areas. To identify lean project strategies, steering committee members and key business unit, divisional, and/or section managers interpret lean business policies that are likely to impact or be impacted by process requirements. The Lean Performance project, which now incorporates these managers' knowledge of the business and technology trends and developments and the lean policy requirements in their respective areas, is directed toward specific attainable benefits. Discussions should also be held at this time with actual and potential

- Lean project strategies for the lean business policy support lean manufacturing include:
  - Reduce manufacturing lead time
  - Reduce manufacturing inventory
  - Implement flexibility for low volume products
  - Implement supplier partnerships and certification
  - Implement activity-based costing
  - Implement process integrated document tools
  - Implement process integrated bar coding
- Lean project strategies for the lean business policy support lean thinking in the global standardization of engineering processes include:
  - Design and utilize concurrent engineering processes
  - Provide a standard software format for engineering product data management
- Lean project strategies for the lean business policy support lean thinking in the global standardization of financial processes include:
  - Implement central cost management
  - Implement centralized integrated processing of period financial closings with local "soft closes"
  - Implement centralized integrated data support, processing and monitoring of the business plan
- Lean project strategies for the lean business policy support lean thinkin standardization of information systems management include:
  - Implement global standard hardware and software
  - Implement global information technology processes and organization

Figure 7.3 Lean Project Strategies

steering committee members to identify additional lean strategies for project deployment.

Lean strategies are also derived from the results of the Lean Performance assessment (Figure 7.3). Examples of lean project strategies that support lean manufacturing used throughout the project text that follows include:

- Reduce manufacturing lead time.
- Reduce manufacturing inventory.
- Implement flexibility for low-volume products.
- Implement supplier partnerships and certification.
- Implement activity-based costing.
- Implement process-integrated document tools.
- Implement process-integrated bar coding.

Examples of lean project strategies that support lean thinking in the global standardization of engineering processes used throughout the project text that follows include:

- Design and utilize concurrent engineering processes.
- Provide a standard software format for engineering product data management.

Lean Business Policy: Lean Project Strategy: Project Objective: Technology Deployment: Process Identification: Lean Performance Team:	Support Lean Manufacturing Reduce Storage of WIP/Stage Mat'l		Control Number 001-001
Gap	Solution	Benefit	Performance Measurement

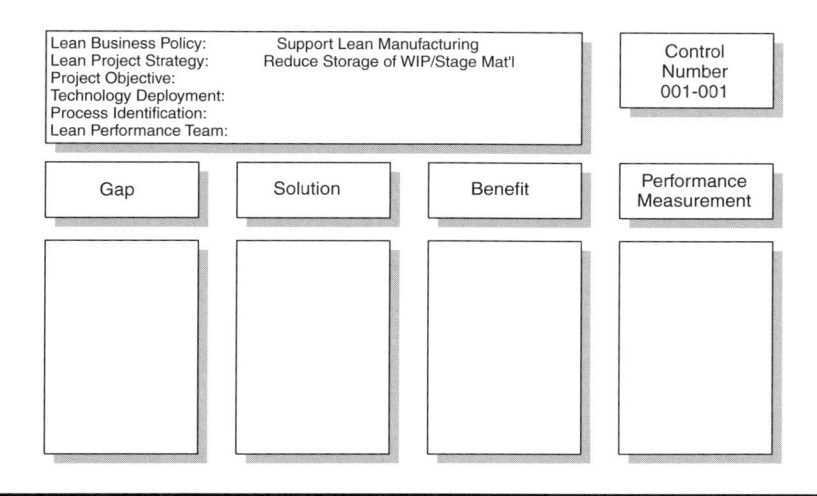

Figure 7.4 Lean Performance Analysis: Lean Project Strategy Deployed

Examples of lean project strategies that support lean thinking in the global standardization of financial processes used throughout the project text that follows include:

- Implement central cash management.
- Implement centralized, integrated processing of period financial closings with local "soft closes."
- Implement centralized integrated data support, processing, and monitoring of the business plan.

Examples of lean project strategies that support lean thinking in the global standardization of information systems management used throughout the project text that follows include:

- Implement global standard hardware and software.
- Implement global information technology processes and organization.

The lean project strategies are deployed to the organization for review and development of project objectives through the further use of the Lean Performance analysis masters. To deploy lean policies and strategies for use in the development of project objectives (Figure 7.4), the Lean Performance analysis and masters are distributed, with one numbered master for each lean business policy/lean project strategy combination.

Defining the Project Mission

Lean project strategies also define the project mission, which is the purpose and reason for existence of the project. When completed, the project should fulfill the mission. Management is responsible for seeing that the Lean Performance project mission statement articulates the lean dimensions of its mission as incorporated in the lean project strategies. It is important for the project mission to recognize and state the project boundaries. Looking at the process redesign and system design methodologies discussed earlier, we can see the fundamental differences. For example, a reengineering mission statement would define the future state of the business structure and key business structures as far as:

- Corporate mission
- Corporate structure or ownership
- Markets
- Products or services
- Core business processes
- People
- Buildings
- Machinery

A process innovation project has a different mission statement, one that would define:

- Process goals or measurements driving the requirement for innovated processes
- The process selected for innovation
- Key business elements of the process selected for innovation, including people, buildings, and machinery

A systems approach mission statement would define:

- System hardware and software future state
- Key business elements of the process areas selected for improvement, including business goals or measurements driving the requirement for redesigned processes as well as the process areas installing new system enablers

A Lean Performance project mission statement both combines and simplifies (Figure 7.5). It must define:

- Business policies and strategies driving the requirement for improved processes
- Process areas of concentration
- Future state of the system enablers

"The mission of the Lean Performance project team is to implement standard management decision and information processes utilizing unmodified package software. These improved processes must deploy management policy and facilitate process performance measurement and continuous improvement in the manufacturing information/ support processes."

Figure 7.5 Project Mission Statement

Defining the Project Scope

The project scope (Figure 7.6) defines the project boundaries within which the Lean Performance project team is empowered to (reasonably) conduct process improvement activities free from interference. The project scope includes a feedback loop and review process for the steering committee.

"The scope of the Lean Performance project is:
- To design and implement improved processes that deploy defined lean policies, strategies and objectives utilizing the project software
- To operate within the budgets, schedules, and methodology approved by the steering committee
- To report project progress, status and issues to the steering committee."

Figure 7.6 Project Scope Statement

Setting Up the Project Organization

During the year or more that it may take to complete a Lean Performance project, there must be an organization charged with the responsibility and appropriate authority to manage and execute the project tasks. The following positions and teams will be needed:

- Project manager
- Facilitator
- Training coordinator
- Lean Performance process area team leaders

- Lean Performance process area teams
- Site leaders for all sites (multisite projects)
- Lean Performance cross-functional teams
- Lean Performance cross-enterprise teams

The steering committee should establish the Lean Performance project organization as soon as the initial Lean Performance teams begin to generate a "critical mass" of activities that requires a project structure to coordinate activities in all the business process areas, as well as develop, train, and monitor teams and their activities and provide communication among company management, project management, and the various Lean Performance teams.

Why have a project organization structure? Perhaps the most important reason is that management responsibilities will increase as the Lean Performance project expands across all processes in the enterprise. Each subsequent lean improvement cycle will involve increasingly complex business processes. The pace of change will increase as the Lean Performance project expands, and more and more personnel will be involved. Team personnel and responsibilities will change occasionally, and decisions about new assignments and priorities will be required. Finally, the Lean Performance project time horizon will lengthen if the activity is not well planned and managed; the longer the Lean Performance project takes, the less likely it is that it will succeed.

The Lean Performance project manager could be the leader/advocate designated during the assessment or another capable and qualified person but should never be an external person. The most important duty of the project manager is to report to the steering committee on the progress of process improvements, including specific measures of cost, quality, and delivery or cycle improvements. The project manager must have the authority to request further action by teams through process area team leaders, as well as to send and review issues with the steering committee, where project results are presented at periodic steering committee meetings. The project manager also conducts regular (at least weekly) project team meetings.

The Lean Performance project facilitator at first could be an external person, but as soon as possible should be a trained employee. The primary responsibility of the project facilitator is to lead project meetings, including visioning sessions and process lean improvement sessions.

The Lean Performance project training coordinator is a person with training and experience in the use of lean principles, tools, and practices. The project may have to use an external person for this position at first, but in the early stages of the project the steering committee should select an employee dedicated to pursuing this role.

A Lean Performance project process area team leader will be needed for each process area identified in the enterprise. The primary responsibilities of the process area team leaders are to ensure that a team is appointed in their area, to verify that all processes in their area are identified, and to ensure that all other process teams working in other process areas are linked to their area. They will also be required to monitor team attitude and performance, including monitoring bargaining unit reaction where applicable and the level of project acceptance or resistance. Process area team leaders will continuously update the network or web-based project management tools, such as the process listing, for their area.

A Lean Performance project process area team is a group of four to seven persons in a given process area including managers and/or supervisors, area specialists, and technicians involved in process design and operation. Process owners, i.e., workers, must be included on the team. Process areas are defined early by the emerging project team. Each process area requires a process team.

Site leaders for all sites (multi-site projects) are in essence a project manager for each site who is responsible for coordinating the activities at that site. This person ensures that project communications are properly handled and project reporting is up to date. Nominally, this person reports to the project manager, but this is not a full-time position. This person may also be needed for site-level facilitation and training, depending on the organization.

Lean Performance project cross-functional teams are groups of six to ten persons from two or more process areas responsible for boundary spanning processes and interaction. Again, in addition to managers and/or supervisors, specialists, and technicians, workers must be included from all process areas participating. Cross-functional teams emerge after processes are improved at the primary process level. We will discuss the activities of several example teams below.

Lean Performance project cross-enterprise teams are groups of six to ten persons from two or more enterprise areas responsible for a company boundary spanning process. Again, in addition to managers, specialists, and technicians, workers must be included from all process areas participating. Cross-enterprise teams emerge after processes are improved at the cross-functional process level. We will discuss an example of this type of team, the lean commerce team.

Most Lean Performance projects can be handled with this basic structure. Depending on the size of the company, the specialization of the current company organization, and the tasks encountered during improvement and implementation of the processes, additional implementation teams may need to be established prior to process implementation in order to assign tasks to an existing departments (e.g., training and quality control) and developing *ad hoc* teams for tasks as they arise. The steering committee identifies candidates for all of these positions by conducting the assessment. Management policy and strategy deployment Lean Performance analysis masters should be deployed to the organization and project objectives established prior to formalizing and publishing a Lean Performance team organization chart, although it is desirable to assign a project manager to manage the formalization of project objectives. The project organization chart should be published by the team during the team development and project management activities performed early in the project. An example is included in the project management module provided below.

Identifying and Deploying the Project Objectives

Lean project strategies must be communicated in project terms in order to be effective drivers for lean change. To be communicated in project terms and to be useful, lean policies and strategies must be translated into meaningful terms at progressively lower levels of the organization. Project objectives are the actual identifiable, measurable, and quantifiable deliverables that the Lean Performance project is going to accomplish in support of deployed lean policies and strategies of the organization. Project objectives must be achievable by process owners by utilizing available project information technologies (no "missions impossible" allowed). The objectives must be tangible (recognizable) extensions at the process execution level of the lean business policies and lean project strategies deployed by the steering committee. Project objectives must be measurable. The requirement to be measurable dictates that the objectives must be attained at a process level and that those processes must have standards to be used for measurement. The objectives must also be realistic. For instance, it is unrealistic to deploy a project objective that requests a 10% cycle-time reduction in a process where further reductions are not possible due to machine speed limitations. The inclusion of project team members from the ranks of process owners and customers will mitigate against any "mission impossible."

To determine project objectives, distribute the Lean Performance analysis masters with the lean business policies/lean project strategies portions completed. Provide a copy of each master for each person involved in this task. While the core membership of this group is the steering committee and other management role players identified in the assessment, the group should also include identified process owners in the organization (e.g., the emerging project team). The emerging project teams at each project site should take a plant tour to observe current material flow, inventory support, existing machine centers, work cells, NC equipment, etc. The teams should then determine manufacturing system opportunities and plans, process simplification, and work cell integration. By interviewing key management personnel at each location, the prospective team members will gain a clear understanding of current manufacturing system capabilities, key information/support processes, and personnel assignments.

The next step is to determine the level of support necessary for manufacturing systems in each area of the company. Department managers in all critical areas should be included, such as:

- Finance
- Customer relationship management
- Maintenance
- Information systems support operations
- Engineering
- Materials
- Marketing and sales

Discussions with these managers should lead to determining the current elements and existing capabilities of the manufacturing support systems, after which the following areas can be investigated:

- CAD/CAM
- FMS and work cell
- Group technology
- AGV/ASRS
- Factory data collection and communications
- Bar coding

Finally, the existing manufacturing planning and control systems should be reviewed to determine the extent to which information integration can be achieved. Project objectives are then linked to the lean business policies and strategies by relating or deploying each suggested objective to the appropriate Lean Performance analysis master containing the relevant lean business policy/project strategy supporting attainment of that particular project objective. Obviously, if an objective cannot be linked to a lean business policy or lean project objective, it will be difficult or impossible to gain support for including that objective in the project. Some examples follow:

- For the lean project strategy of reducing manufacturing lead time, the project objectives might include implementing 24-hour turnaround of customer orders.
- For the lean project strategy of reducing manufacturing inventory, the project objectives might include implementing "pull" supplier management practices (such as standard container quantity recognition

with use of standard container quantities) and elimination of a returned-goods storeroom.
- For the lean project strategy of implementing flexibility for low-volume products, the project objectives might include implementing manufacturing line sequencing with the ability to sequence models and variations on both nondedicated and dedicated lines, implementing multiplant sourcing of finished goods, and implementing EDI/XML or other e-commerce solutions for interplant order management.
- For the lean project strategy of implementing supplier partnerships and certification, the project objectives might include implementing a pay-on-receipt process for vendors.
- For the lean project strategy of implement activity-based costing, the project objectives might include establishing product target costing/*muda*-free product target costs.
- For the lean project strategy of implementing process-integrated document tools, the project objectives might include implementing bar coding and scanning of plant documents to allow confirmation of shipments, the printing of part numbers on manufacturing orders, and the printing of manufacturing order pick lists.
- For the lean project strategy of implementing process-integrated bar coding, the project objectives might include implementing bar coding of customer requirements to improve the shipment process by allowing scanning of shipping charges and producing customer labels for filled-order items.
- For the lean project strategy of designing and utilizing concurrent engineering processes, the project objectives might include providing access to engineering product data at the manufacturing sites.
- For the lean project strategy of providing a standard software format for engineering product data management, the project objectives might include implementing a standard software package for engineering product data management
- For the lean project strategy of implementing central cash management, the project objectives might include determining and accommodating the financial requirements of Canada, Europe (EU, VAT), and Asia, in addition to such considerations as setting up a currency database, establishing a strategy to realize currency conversion rate gains and avert losses, and establishing default account structures.
- For the lean project strategy of implementing centralized integrated processing of period financial closings with local "soft closes," the project objectives might include reorganizing regional financial statements according to business segment, product group, product line,

product, customer, plant sales, gross profits, or shipments; breaking down global financial statements according to region, product group, and product line; establishing a yearly, quarterly, monthly, and month-to-date reporting structure; and highlighting global sales, global margins, and global trends.
- For the lean project strategy of implementing centralized integrated data support, processing, and monitoring of the business plan, the project objectives might include developing global standard reporting formats; monitoring, evaluating, and reporting product line and manufacturing site profitability; and developing period-to-date reporting that reflects regional sales, margins, and trends.
- For the lean project strategy of implementing standard global hardware and software, the project objectives might include implementing unmodified software packages and leveraging vendor-supplied software upgrades.
- For the lean project strategy of implementing global information technology processes and organization, the project objectives might include implementing secure data and operations processes in a system that is seamless to the users; implementing standards for information systems uptime and reliability; and providing for the measurement and reporting of performance to those standards.

For each completed lean project strategies Lean Performance analysis master, the project manager completes a project objective Lean Performance analysis master, one for each project objective deployed below that lean project strategy. The deployment links the lean business policies, lean project strategies, and project objectives to direct the teams and provides the basis for decisions about any necessary software modifications. Deploying the Lean Performance analysis also links management to the eventual performance measurements implemented to monitor the performance of the new lean processes that result from the project. These Lean Performance analysis masters are then distributed to the full project team at the first full training meeting of the team. The teams complete the information necessary to deploy the policies at the process level. Technology deployment is completed by the information team, and process identification is performed by the process area teams to link the processes used to realize the objective (Figure 7.7).

These project objectives will be achieved by employing the Lean Performance methodology to complete project tasks:

- Identify the business processes.
- Develop process standards (process workflows and work instructions).

114 ■ Lean Performance ERP Project Management

Lean Business Policy:	Support Lean Manufacturing	Control Number
Lean Project Strategy:	Reduce Storage of WIP/Stage Mat'l	001-001-001
Project Objective:	Eliminate Returned Goods Room	
Technology Deployment:		
Process Identification:		
Lean Performance Team:		

| Gap | Solution | Benefit | Performance Measurement |

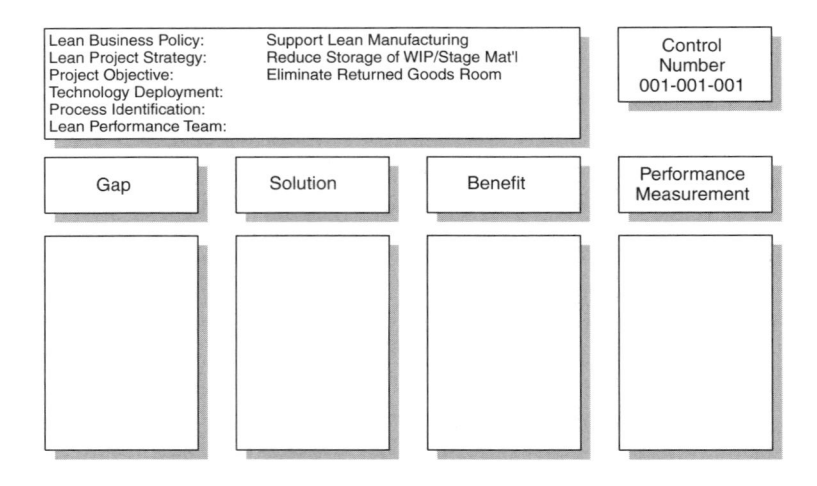

Figure 7.7 Lean Performance Analysis: Project Objective Deployed

- Complete the Lean Performance analysis.
- Develop lean improvements.
- Implement improved processes.
- Measure and manage continuous Lean Performance.

Conducting Steering Committee Meetings

The following project management tools are reviewed at the first steering committee meeting:

- Lean business policies (Figure 7.1)
- Lean Performance analysis lean business policy deployed (Figure 7.2)
- Lean project strategies (Figure 7.3)
- Lean Performance analysis lean project strategy deployed (Figure 7.4)
- Project mission statement (Figure 7.5)
- Project scope statement (Figure 7.6)
- Lean Performance analysis project objective deployed (Figure 7.7)

The steering committee communicates the lean business policies, lean project strategies, and project objectives to the Lean Performance team members at the initial team meeting and later reviews a summary of the deployed lean business policies, lean project strategies, and project objectives (Figure 7.8). A summary of the policy deployment is presented to

MANAGEMENT POLICY DEPLOYMENT AND MEASUREMENTS SUMMARY

GAP CONTROL#	LEAN BUSINESS POLICY	LEAN PROJECT STRATEGY	DEPLOYED PROJECT OBJECTIVE	TECHNOLOGY DEPLOYMENT	PROCESS IDENTIFICATION	LEAN PERFORMANCE TEAM	PERFORMANCE MEASUREMENT
001	Support Lean Manufacturing	Reduce Manufacturing Lead Time	Implement 24 hour turnaround of customer orders				
002	Support Lean Manufacturing	Reduce Manufacturing Inventory	Implement "Pull" supplier management practices				
003	Support Lean Manufacturing	Reduce Manufacturing Inventory	Eliminate returned goods storeroom				
004	Support Lean Manufacturing	Implement Flexibility for Low Volume Products	Implement manufacturing line sequencing				
005	Support Lean Manufacturing	Implement Flexibility for Low Volume Products	Implement multi-plant sourcing of finished goods				
006	Support Lean Manufacturing	Implement Flexibility for Low Volume Products	Implement EDI/XML or other E-Commerce solution for interplant orders				
007	Support Lean Manufacturing	Implement Supplier Partnerships and Certification	Implement a pay-on-receipt process for vendors				
008	Support Lean Manufacturing	Implement Activity Based Costing	Establish Product Target Costing/ MUDA Free Product Target Costs				

PAGE 1

Figure 7.8 Policy Deployment and Measurements Summary

the Lean Performance team members at their initial meeting by the project sponsor. The emerging project team will return the deployed lean business policies, lean project strategies, and project objectives to the steering committee two times during the project:

MANAGEMENT POLICY DEPLOYMENT AND MEASUREMENTS SUMMARY

GAP CONTROL#	LEAN BUSINESS POLICY	LEAN PROJECT STRATEGY	DEPLOYED PROJECT OBJECTIVE	TECHNOLOGY DEPLOYMENT	PROCESS IDENTIFICATION	LEAN PERFORMANCE TEAM	PERFORMANCE MEASUREMENT
009	Support Lean Manufacturing	Implement Process integrated Document Tools	Implement Bar Coding for Plant Documents				
010	Support Lean Manufacturing	Implement Process integrated Bar Coding	Implement Bar Coding for Customer Requirements				
011	Support Lean Thinking in the Global Standardization of Engineering Processes	Design and Utilize Concurrent Engineering Processes	Provide access to engineering product data at the manufacturing sites				
012	Support Lean Thinking in the Global Standardization of Engineering Processes	Provide a Standard Software Format for Engineering Product Data Management	Implement a standard software package for engineering product data management				
013	Support Lean Thinking in the Global Standardization of Financial Processes	Implement Central Cash Management	Determine and accommodate financial requirements of Canada, Europe (EU, VAT), Asia				
014	Support Lean Thinking in the Global Standardization of Financial Processes	Implement Central Cash Management	include currency considerations				
015	Support Lean Thinking in the Global Standardization of Financial Processes	Implement Centralized integrated Processing of Period Financial Closings	Consolidate Regional Financial Statements				
016	Support Lean Thinking in the Global Standardization of Financial Processes	Implement Centralized integrated Processing of Period Financial Closings	Consolidate global financial statements				

PAGE 2

Figure 7.8 Policy Deployment and Measurements Summary (cont.)

1. After completion of technology deployment, process identification, and team assignments
2. After identification of the proposed process performance measurements

MANAGEMENT POLICY DEPLOYMENT AND MEASUREMENTS SUMMARY

GAP CONTROL#	LEAN BUSINESS POLICY	LEAN PROJECT STRATEGY	DEPLOYED PROJECT OBJECTIVE	TECHNOLOGY DEPLOYMENT	PROCESS IDENTIFICATION	LEAN PERFORMANCE TEAM	PERFORMANCE MEASUREMENT
017	Support Lean Thinking in the Global Standardization of Financial Processes	Implement Centralized integrated Data Support, Processing and Monitoring of the Business Plan	Develop global standard reporting formats				
018	Support Lean Thinking in the Global Standardization of Financial Processes	Implement Centralized integrated Data Support, Processing and Monitoring of the Business Plan	Monitor, evaluate and report product line and manufacturing site profitability				
019	Support Lean Thinking in the Global Standardization of Financial Processes	Implement Centralized integrated Data Support, Processing and Monitoring of the Business Plan	Develop Period-To-Date reporting, including Regional Sales, Margins and Trends				
020	Support Lean Thinking in the Global Standardization of information Systems Management	Implement Global Standard Hardware and Software	Implement unmodified software packages				
021	Support Lean Thinking in the Global Standardization of information Systems Management	Implement Global Standard Hardware and Software	Leverage vendor supplied software upgrades				
022	Support Lean Thinking in the Global Standardization of information Systems Management	Implement Global information Technology Processes and Organization	Implement secure data & operations processes in a system that is seamless to the users				
023	Support Lean Thinking in the Global Standardization of information Systems Management	Implement Global information Technology Processes and Organization	Implement standards for systems uptime and reliability and measure and report performance				
024							

PAGE 3

Figure 7.8 Policy Deployment and Measurements Summary (cont.)

Preliminary Lean Performance team rosters should be established from the currently identified process areas, and these people should be invited to the initial meeting. People attending the first meeting would likely include process owners and customers in cross-functional areas of the company, such as:

- Finance
- Engineering
- Materials
- Operations
- Information

The steering committee should use this occasion to deliver their general expectations about the Lean Performance project to the team. Typically, in a project of this type management expects to identify and eliminate redundant activities; identify and eliminate "disconnected" business processes; implement uniform, documented lean business processes; and produce process standards, including process workflows and work instructions, that support training and QS/ISO documentation requirements. The project should implement a consistent information basis for manufacturing and financial business decisions, in addition to establishing process-based performance measurements. Following the Lean Performance methodology, the project process should evolve into Lean Performance management, which continuously deploys management policy to teams who implement that policy and measure performance results at a process level.

The Lean Performance project organization has legitimate expectations of the steering committee, as well. The team expects the steering committee to ensure that the project is properly focused; that is, the steering committee understands what the job is, uses the proper methodology for that job, understands the implications of using that methodology, and supports the project team in managing the consequences of those implications. The Lean Performance project team expects the steering committee to ensure that the project stays properly focused; that is, the steering committee ensures that the project sticks to the job assigned, with no "scope creep." The teams can also reasonably expect the steering committee to ensure that the methodology is followed and to support the project team while it measures and manages the improved processes that result from the project effort.

8

MANAGING THE PROJECT MODULE

PROJECT TEAM TASKS

Maintaining the Project Summary Bar Chart

A preliminary project summary bar chart should be prepared in advance of the initial team meeting in order to illustrate overall project timing. The example shown in Figure 8.1 shows the project divided into modules that correspond with the methodology being presented.

Maintaining Project Communications

To maintain effective project communications, a project web page should be established that includes a project newsletter and discussion chat room. Various project management spreadsheets will be posted by the project manager and maintained online by the project team.

Maintaining the Project Plan

A project workplan should be developed to initiate and monitor progress. The workplan must include the process implementation sequence as well as the key tasks in each process implementation (Figure 8.2). Using the project workplan as a reference, the project manager should monitor all tasks of the implementation process (including overall planning and review), in addition to coordinating the work of the Lean Performance teams toward completion of their assigned tasks. One of the primary

120 ■ Lean Performance ERP Project Management

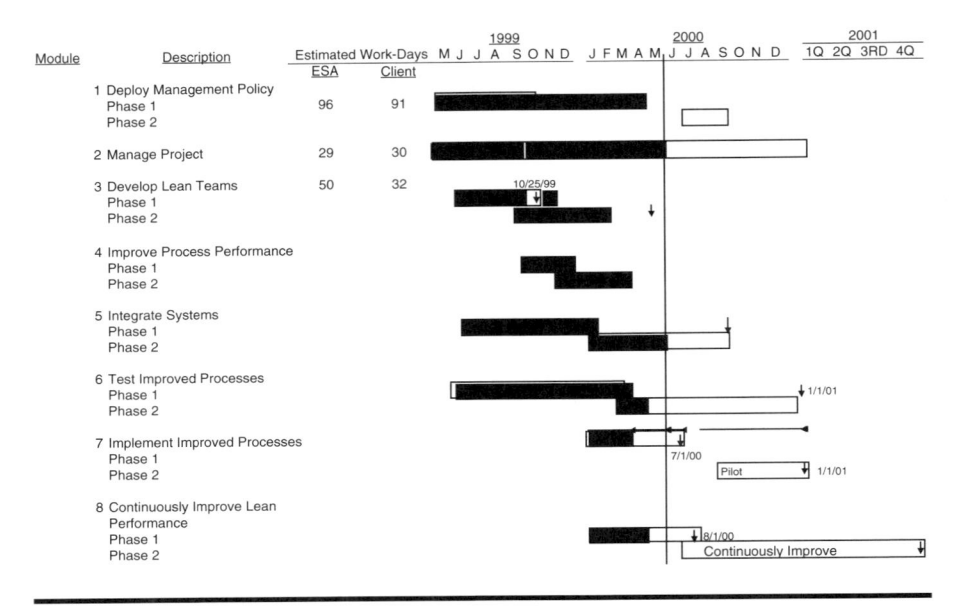

Module	Description	Estimated Work-Days ESA / Client	1999 M J J A S O N D	2000 J F M A M J J A S O N D	2001 1Q 2Q 3RD 4Q
1	Deploy Management Policy Phase 1 Phase 2	96 / 91			
2	Manage Project	29 / 30			
3	Develop Lean Teams Phase 1 Phase 2	50 / 32	10/25/99		
4	Improve Process Performance Phase 1 Phase 2				
5	Integrate Systems Phase 1 Phase 2				
6	Test Improved Processes Phase 1 Phase 2				1/1/01
7	Implement Improved Processes Phase 1 Phase 2			7/1/00 / Pilot	1/1/01
8	Continuously Improve Lean Performance Phase 1 Phase 2			8/1/00 Continuously Improve	

Figure 8.1 Lean Performance Methodology Project Summary Bar Chart

MODULE -TASK STEP	DESCRIPTION	RESPONSIBILITY	ESTIMATED WORK-DAYS ESA CLIENT	----------TARGET--------- START COMPLETE DATE DATE

1. Prepare a preliminary project summary bar chart to illustrate project timing.

   • Deliverable: project summary bar chart

2. Maintain project communications

   • Establish Web page for project communications

   • Establish the project e-newsletter

3. Develop project work plan and monitor progress

   • Define implementation responsibility by product and product line

4. Monitor all tasks of the implementation process. Provide overall planning and review.

   • Provide coordination and review among Lean Performance teams in completion of assigned tasks for each process implementation.

Figure 8.2 Project Work Plan

responsibilities of the Lean Performance project manager during the project is to review project work plan status and assignments as necessary, update the project work plan as appropriate, and use the project summary bar chart to provide project status reports to the steering committee.

Maintaining an Open Issue Resolution Process

The project manager has the responsibility to establish an open-issue-resolution process as soon as the project begins, not after issues begin to stack up. Open issues are issues encountered during the project that a team member or system user feels must be resolved before new process standards can be implemented. An Internet- or intranet-based open-issues control log (in spreadsheet form, if possible) will provide online access for all project team members. Resolved issues are documented for review by appropriate online users. The structure and operation of the open-issue process is communicated to the team through a written procedure emphasizing that the purpose of the open-issue reporting and resolution procedure is to manage the process of reporting, organizing, and resolving open issues during the project. The procedure should guarantee that all written issues will be investigated and responded to. The Lean Performance project manager assigns open-issue-resolution priority. In some cases, resolution of an open issue may be categorized as not critical or not possible to allow for initial implementation to proceed. Originators of issues that cannot be immediately addressed should be assured that these issues will be evaluated during the continuously improve Lean Performance module for inclusion in the eventual system.

Issues must be written up and submitted to the project manager by the team that encounters the issue in order for the open issue to be considered for resolution (Figure 8.3). The project manager will respond to and manage the issue as outlined in the procedure. Issues can be written in any of the following categories:

- System operations
- System security
- System bug
- Modification needed
- Business decision/policy needed
- Modification not working
- Work-around requires additional headcount
- Process work flow/work instruction updating
- Training required

Issues that do not seem to fit into a particular category should be written up and submitted anyway. The open-issue process to be followed is illustrated in Figure 8.4, which is an open-issue template with labeled entry blocks or fields; this type of open-issue template can also be created and posted on the web page for use by team members. Refer to the figure for the steps to be followed:

122 ■ Lean Performance ERP Project Management

```
                    LEAN PERFORMANCE PROJECT
                 ISSUES REPORTING AND RESOLUTION FORM

ORIGINATOR _____ ISSUE NUMBER _____ PRIORITY ___

ORIGINATING PLANT _____   ISSUE TYPE: (CHECK BELOW)

ORIGINATION DATE _____   SYSTEM OPERATIONS   ___

SYSTEM AREA _____    SYSTEM SECURITY     ___

REFERENCE:                        SYSTEM BUG          ___

PROGRAM # _____    MODIFICATION NEEDED ___

SCREEN # _____    BUSINESS/POLICY     ___

REPORT # _____    MOD NOT WORKING     ___

RESOLUTION ASSIGNED TO:           HEADCOUNT REQUIRED  ___

_____     PROCEDURE UPDATE    ___

DATE REQUIRED _____     TRAINING REQUIRED   ___

DESCRIPTION: _____
_____
_____
_____


ALTERNATE RESOLUTIONS: _____
_____
_____
_____


ACCEPTED RESOLUTION: _____
_____


RESOLUTION ACCEPTED BY: _____ DATE CLOSED: ___

DATE SUBMITTED TO SITE LEADER _____

DATE SUBMITTED TO PROJECT MANAGER_____
```

Figure 8.3 Open-Issue Form

1. *Step one:* Originator completes blocks 1, 4, 5, 6a–i, 7, 8, 9, 10, 13, and 14. The originator is the person who first encounters the issue and is responsible for defining and documenting the issue on an issue form. An originator can rely on another team member or user to write the issue; however, the originator must submit the issue and answer any questions that may be asked in order to clarify the issue and define solutions.
2. *Step two:* The originator must submit the issue to the project site leader as soon as possible. The originator also provides copies of the process standards (workflows and work instructions), screens, and reports, where applicable. Project site leaders verify completion

```
                    LEAN PERFORMANCE PROJECT
                ISSUES REPORTING AND RESOLUTION FORM

    ORIGINATOR _____1_____ ISSUE NUMBER ___2___ PRIORITY __3_

    ORIGINATING PLANT _____4_____      ISSUE TYPE: (CHECK BELOW)

    ORIGINATION DATE _____5_____      SYSTEM OPERATIONS   _6a_

    SYSTEM AREA _____7_____       SYSTEM SECURITY     _6b_

    REFERENCE:                             SYSTEM BUG          _6c_

    PROGRAM # _____8_____       MODIFICATION NEEDED _6d_

    SCREEN # _____9_____       BUSINESS/POLICY _6e_

    REPORT # _____10____        MOD NOT WORKING   _6f_

    RESOLUTION ASSIGNED TO:                HEADCOUNT REQUIRED
       _6g_

    _____11____        PROCEDURE UPDATE  _6h_

    DATE REQUIRED _____12____        TRAINING REQUIRED _6i_

    DESCRIPTION: _____13_____

    _____

    _____

    _____


    ALTERNATE RESOLUTIONS: _____14_____

    _____

    _____

    _____


    ACCEPTED RESOLUTION:
    _____15_____

    _____

    RESOLUTION ACCEPTED BY_____16_____DATE CLOSED____17___

    DATE SUBMITTED TO SITE LEADER_____18_____

    DATE SUBMITTED TO PROJECT MANAGER_____19_____
```

Figure 8.4 Open-Issue Template

of the necessary information and check the issue log spreadsheet for similar or redundant issues. Project site leaders complete block 18 and submit the issue to the project manager as soon as possible, by web posting, or fax, or in person.

3. *Step three:* The project manager completes blocks 2, 3, 11, 12, and 19; reviews alternative resolutions with users; and, where necessary, determines the need for any additional resources, such as consultants or a software help line. The project manager also:
   - Accepts the issue for resolution.
   - Assigns a number to the issue.
   - Determines issue priority, and initials decision.

- Accepts the date by which action is required or determines an alternative schedule for resolution, which is indicated on the form.
- Assigns responsibility for resolution of the issue.
- Enters the issue on the open-issue log/spreadsheet.

4. *Step four:* If the issue is a system bug, the project manager will report it to the software vendor and return the issue with a software vendor "fix" number assigned. The project manager will verify receipt of the bug fix to the originator and coordinate testing of the fix prior to closing the issue.
5. *Step five:* If the issue is a modification that is not working, or is an issue that has been approved by the steering committee for modification, the process for managing modifications begins. The modification number will be the same as the issue log number.
6. *Step six:* The person assigned to provide resolution of the issue will develop a resolution and present it to the originator and project manager. When the resolution is accepted, the issue form will be completed and the open issue log updated. The person assigned to provide resolution completes block 15, and the originator completes block 16 to verify acceptance of the resolution or returns the issue.
7. *Step seven:* The project manager reviews and closes the issue, completes block 17, and updates the issue log spreadsheet.

Maintaining the Project Organization

The key to building a project team for a successful project is to identify all process owners in the organization and include them on the organization chart (and in the project). So, to start with, all of the processes must be identified (but be warned that it is difficult to get them correct the first time through). The preliminary project organization necessary for the project is determined by identifying process areas on a preliminary basis. Processes are generally found in process areas as shown in Figure 8.5, which illustrates the corporate site of a manufacturing company. A manufacturing site engaged in assembling products for the aftermarket will probably more closely resemble the process areas shown in Figure 8.6. Finally, international (as well as many domestic) manufacturing sites will probably closely resemble the process areas illustrated in Figure 8.7.

By considering the process area structure of each site in the organization, a preliminary project organization chart of the Lean Performance team can be defined (Figure 8.8). The initial project organization chart is prepared after determining the process area owners and a site leader for each site and should include:

Figure 8.5 Business Process Areas Overview Diagram for Corporate Site of a Manufacturer

Figure 8.6 Business Process Areas Overview Diagram for Manufacturer of Products for the Aftermarket

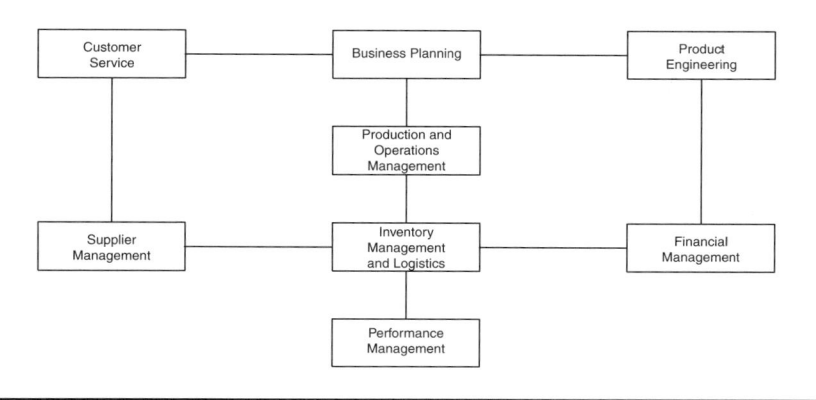

Figure 8.7 Business Process Areas Overview Diagram for International Manufacturer

- Steering committee
- Project manager
- Site leaders
- Process area owners

Maintaining the project organization chart is the ongoing responsibility of the project manager. At various points in the project, the chart will need

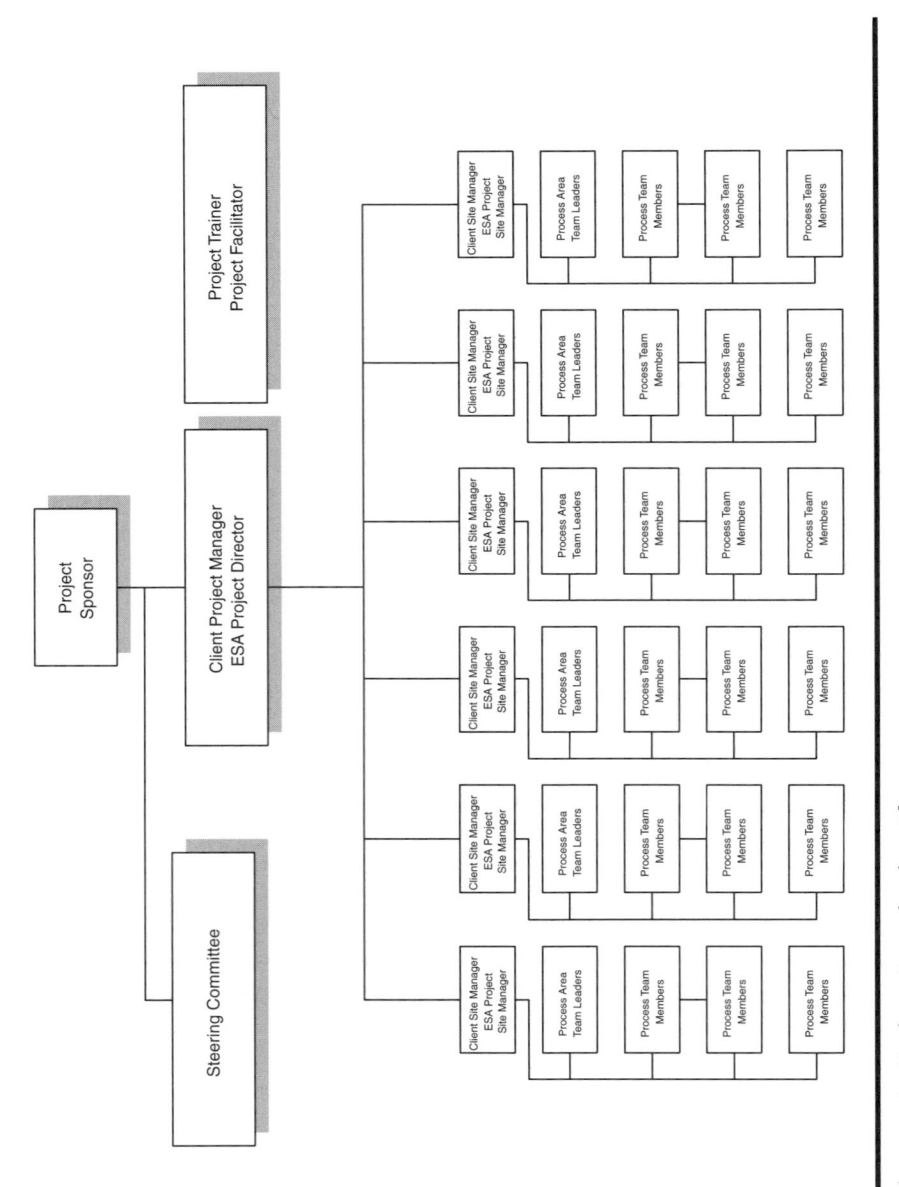

Figure 8.8 Project Organization Chart

to be updated to reflect additions to the team, especially when all processes are identified and all process owners and customers are included on the overall project team.

Maintaining the Quality Assurance Process

Maintaining the quality assurance process is another ongoing responsibility of the project manager, who is administering the project and assuring the overall quality of effort. Maintaining the quality assurance process includes monitoring project status, identifying roadblocks affecting progress, and developing project progress reporting for steering committee meetings. As we have already seen, the project manager also assists with problem identification and resolution through the open-issues process. To this point, the involvement of the project champion/sponsor has been enough to carry the effort forward and ensure the quality of the project planning result. Now that there is a formal project, with a project manager and project team, an additional resource is needed. Any quality assurance review should include a perspective from someone outside of the project who, along with the project manager, should examine the project work plan and corresponding results. The reviewers should concentrate on ensuring that the project is proceeding on schedule and on budget within the project mission and scope.

Quality assurance reviews should be conducted at project checkpoints prior to the steering committee meetings held at the completion of every project module:

1. Lean Performance planning
    First milestone: Manage project
    Second milestone: Develop Lean Performance teams
2. Lean Performance improvement
    First milestone: Improve process performance
    Second milestone: Integrate systems
    Third milestone: Test improved processes
3. Continuously improve Lean Performance
    First milestone: Implement improved processes
    Second milestone: Continuously improve Lean Performance

The project management tools should be utilized to support the quality assurance process and prepare for the steering committee meetings. All of the following topics should be addressed at the project management quality assurance review:

- Lean business policies (Figure 7.1)
- Lean Performance analysis lean business policy deployed (Figure 7.2)
- Lean project strategies (Figure 7.3)
- Lean Performance analysis lean project strategy deployed (Figure 7.4)
- Project mission statement (Figure 7.5)
- Project scope statement (Figure 7.6)
- Lean Performance analysis project objective deployed (Figure 7.7)
- Policy deployment and measurements summary, all pages (Figure 7.8)
- Lean Performance methodology project summary bar chart (Figure 8.1)
- Project work plan (Figure 8.2)
- Open-issue form (Figure 8.3)
- Open-issue template (Figure 8.4)
- Business process areas overview diagrams, as necessary (Figures 8.5 to 8.7)
- Project organization chart (Figure 8.8)

Reporting Progress to the Steering Committee

Progress is reported to the steering committee as part of the initial project team meeting by utilizing the project management diagram tools completed and reviewed at the project management quality assurance review.

9

DEVELOPING LEAN PERFORMANCE TEAMS MODULE

PROJECT TEAM TASKS

Finalizing Projects and Strategies

To assess the current projects that might adversely affect or overlap with the Lean Performance project, the project manager should develop a projects and strategies definition, beginning by organizing the information discussed at the initial project team meeting by the project steering committee and by the project team for each site. The project manager should then:

- Identify all current application or manufacturing technologies projects underway or under management review.
- Define current projects approved and/or underway in manufacturing support/systems.
- Identify other business and/or manufacturing strategies likely to affect the timing of the project.
- Confirm their inclusion and/or applicability to the lean business policies, lean project strategies, and project objectives already deployed.
- Verify that major lean business policies and strategies likely to affect the timing of lean process implementation are contained in the identified project objectives, including manufacturing system implementation or modification (especially any so-called "interim" or "phased" development).

Site: Corporate

1. Purchasing and travel card utilization will change processes in accounts payable

2. Payrolls (salary, union) will continue to be done outside of primary software. Labor interfaces may be required

3. HR systems are connected to the payroll system and will be continued outside of primary system

4. Engineering pdm database will not be addressed initially within project, however, needs review prior to engineering doing independent development

5. Project will proceed without "key" players in finance, sales, and marketing, but progress will be limited in these areas

6. Communication links for North America will be completed prior to October 2001

7. Engineering planning will not include automated information flow from cad in the initial phase

8. Pitney Bowes installation and interface will be completed in project

---

Figure 9.1   Current Projects and Strategies Definition

- Meet with site leaders to finalize the current projects and strategy definition.
- Identify projects currently underway that must be considered for system integration.
- Identify manufacturing issues that must be supported by the Lean Performance project.
- Identify and analyze scheduling and resource conflicts.

The current projects and strategies definition (Figure 9.1) provides a vehicle for reporting to the steering committee, which selects or deselects projects. The final project plans make up the final project. All project elements accepted as the responsibility of the project team should be carefully incorporated into the project plan.

Developing the Site Configuration

Site configuration diagrams are developed to document and visually communicate the system configuration decisions as budgeted. Equipment and communication lines are illustrated as they will be implemented, as are networks and intranets. Software vendor sizing profiles are updated or verified. A preliminary technical analysis of hardware requirements necessary to support the implementation is conducted to determine a site configuration. In addition, the project team should:

- Identify manufacturing considerations, including the development of project priorities, resource and budget requirements, and adequacy of software for unmodified implementation.
- Determine the degree of systems integration and identify systems interfaces required to support site needs.
- Evaluate existing projects and plans.
- Identify alternatives and priorities, where possible.
- Determine information systems resource requirements for the project and include an estimate of the long-term information systems personnel needed.
- Outline alternative short-term improvement strategies, where possible.
- Confirm hardware delivery for each site to support process workflow activities.
- Evaluate system's configuration architecture to determine adequacy.
- Complete or review the software vendor sizing profiles by analyzing:
  - Item/part masters
  - Bills of material
  - Routings
  - Throughput
  - Storage requirements
  - Communication requirements
  - Printer, terminal and personal computer requirements
- Perform initial load analysis on hardware.
- Update the hardware strategy as necessary, then review budgets with information systems management and verify completion of site preparation requirements.
- Complete and publish the site configuration diagram for the project (Figure 9.2).

Identifying All Processes

Processes are the operating structure by which an organization does what is necessary to produce value for its customers. A process is an activity that involves people, is designed to produce an output, contains a specific ordering of work activities across time and place, and is a structure for doing work. Processes utilize enablers to perform tasks that produce the business outputs of the organization. In our estimation, an enterprise resource planning (ERP), manufacturing execution system (MES), or supply

132 ■ Lean Performance ERP Project Management

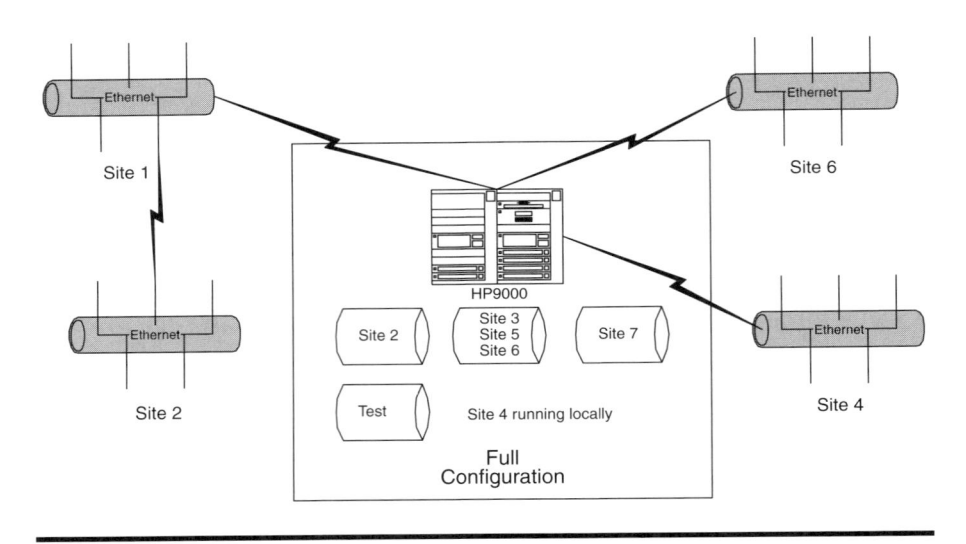

Figure 9.2 Site Configuration

chain management (SCM) system is every bit as much of a process enabler as a computer numeric controller (CNC) drill.

Lean processes are processes where we have applied lean principles, tools, and practices to the utilization of enablers in order to improve process Lean Performance. All processes are candidates for Lean Performance because processes are usually designed (if at all) at the outset of operations; thereafter, they evolve in response to new demands but not necessarily systematically, and they begin to acquire dysfunctional attributes. With the occasional exception of physical processes, most processes are not reflected in organizational structures. They do not follow existing boundaries of organizational power and authority. They are not defined or described in the same way by those who participate directly in them. Processes have boundaries, but they generally operate across organizational and/or enterprise boundaries. A process boundary can be functional, covering one department or unit, or cross-functional, covering more than one department or unit. Processes can also be cross-enterprise, covering more than one company or enterprise. Lean Performance means making work flow across functions and enterprises wherever possible. An organization that does not identify their suppliers and customers as owners and customers of processes cannot be said to be working in a cross-enterprise manner (supply chain processes, product introduction processes).

Process identification and Lean Performance analysis are integrative steps in a Lean Performance project because while a business can be thought of as one long continuous process, it cannot be improved that way. Processes are the organizational building blocks. Lean improvements

Inputs	Throughputs	Outputs
Data	Logic, Distribution and Other Applications to Tasks	Information, Reports Instructions, Documents

Figure 9.3 Information/Support Process Characteristics

cannot be made between cross-functional and cross-enterprise processes until they have been made within these processes. Lean processes are necessary for a lean management team, staff, organization, and work force and a virtual lean enterprise. Process identification enables process integration, which uncovers those processes that are not organized or performed in the appropriate department, that are "flat" (i.e., the customer order process could be improved to more readily perform shipping or other customer relationship tasks), and that are not completely defined or standardized. Process identification also reveals duplication or lack of integration between areas where a process (or part of a process) might be performed more than once (Figure 9.3).

Processes have owners, who are responsible for the design and execution of their processes and for ensuring that their customers' needs are met by the processes. Process owners have the primary responsibility to maintain and utilize the process to produce their output. Information/support process owners have the primary responsibility to maintain and utilize their processes, not to maintain the data (machine) process that enables the information/support process.

Processes have identifiable recipients or customers, who use the process output, whether internal or external. Customers are generally found downstream from the process owner. Information/support processes are designed to produce and consume information at interim and final outputs, and an information/support process customer uses the process output — the information. In Lean Performance, process customers must agree that the process delivers the output that they require (and sign off on such a statement).

All processes in all process areas should be identified at each site by site leaders through interviewing and exploration with managers, key users, process owners, and customers. The project manager and site leaders have already defined process areas (not necessarily departments), and the business process areas diagrams that resulted have been presented to the steering committee. These diagrams are a good place to start the discussion necessary for the Lean Performance team to identify all of the process areas at each site; it should be noted that the areas in which processes are found by the emerging project site teams probably will be different than those originally documented on the business process areas diagrams, as identifying process areas and processes is a little like peeling an onion.

The full set of process areas should be verified by the Lean Performance team at each project site. The project site teams should collect summary documentation of existing systems to ensure that all of the identified process areas have been verified for each location. An overview of the areas in which processes are found should then be completed by the site-level Lean Performance team and illustrated in diagrams such as those shown in Figures 9.4 to 9.6. A number of discrete processes (where the work is being performed) will generally be found within each of the process areas. Identifying these discrete processes is usually a simple task: You just have to ask somebody what they do (and asking anybody but the process owners is a big mistake). In process identification, however, the focus is not so much on what people do but rather on what happens to the data, material, or work they produce. The discrete process begins at the raw material or data inputs (beginning boundary) and ends at the finished product or information output (ending boundary).

Tasks being performed in any process must be discrete enough to improve and are generally performed to produce outputs for internal customers. Individual process steps and tasks usually are separated by queues and waiting times that involve the movement of interim outputs from place to place and provide for the involvement of more than one individual in the overall process sequence. Identifying a process as being individual tasks and operations or a group of duties performed by one individual or department is usually wrong. If no output has been produced by a group of tasks, a process has not been completed. Remember, the focus is not on what people do but rather on what happens to the material or work. In summary, a discrete process:

- Has an identifiable owner
- Has an identifiable input or set of inputs, such as labor, information, materials, and/or instructions
- Consists of sets of tasks, steps, operations, or functions performed in sequence
- Produces an identifiable output such as a physical product, service, or information
- Has an identifiable customer for the output
- Has boundaries (i.e., a definite beginning and a definite ending)

As mentioned previously, the starting point (boundary) of any process is the point of input of the data or material for the first task that processes or changes that input. The ending point (boundary) of any process is the point of output of the product of that process.

Developing Lean Performance Teams Module ■ 135

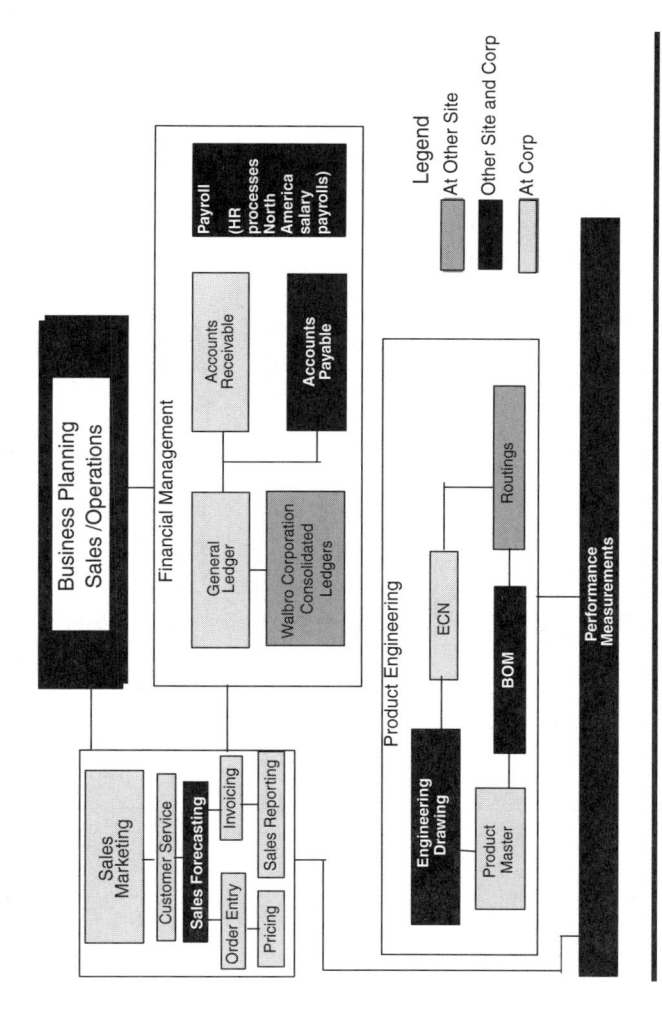

Figure 9.4 Current Process Activity Overview Diagram (Corporate)

136 ■ Lean Performance ERP Project Management

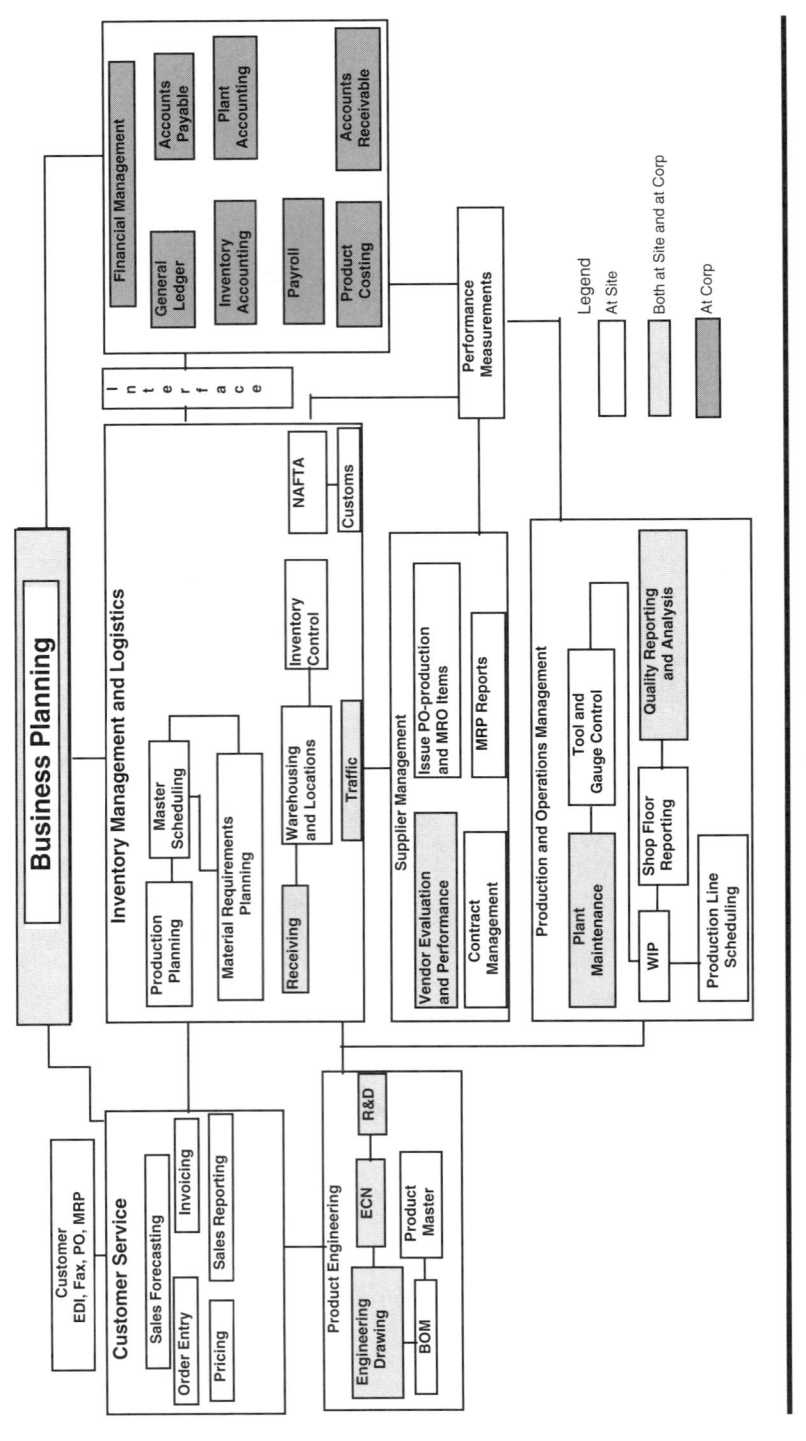

Figure 9.5   Current Process Activity Overview Diagram (Aftermarket)

Developing Lean Performance Teams Module ■ 137

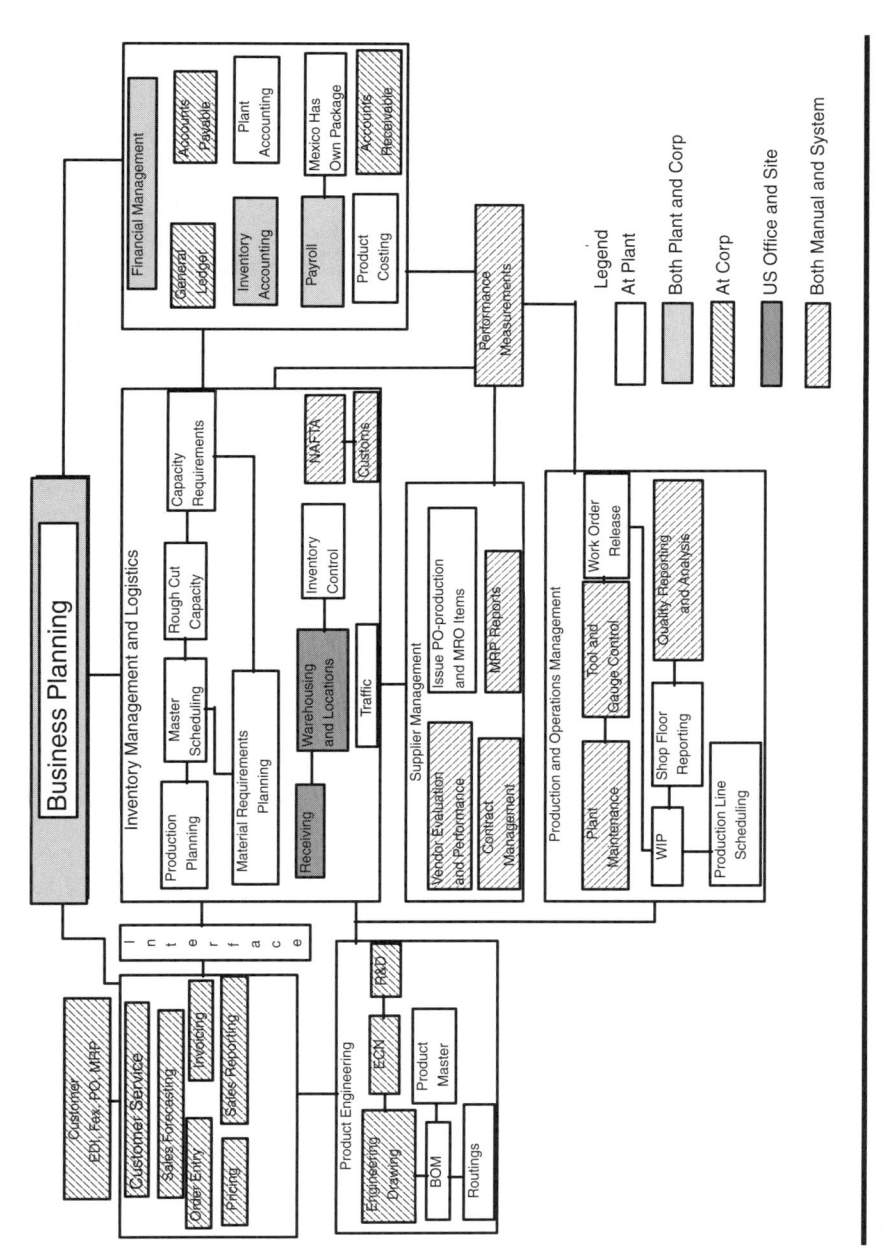

Figure 9.6 Current Process Activity Overview Diagram (International)

After all of these processes are identified, lists of processes for each site are submitted to the project manager. These process lists are consolidated, and common primary processes and site-specific processes are identified. Doing so allows multiple-site teams to work without redundant effort, resolves differences in identification and terminology of the various sites processes, and determines the sequence of assigning workflow standards and process areas by location (Figure 9.7). Taken together, the process areas overview diagrams and the process listing and sequence provide a process view of the organization. A process view is a dynamic view of what value is delivered by the organization, and how it is delivered. Viewing the virtual lean enterprise in a process view inevitably highlights cross-functional and cross-enterprise processes for lean improvement.

Developing Site Teams

Site teams are defined and illustrated by the site-level project team diagram. When a process owner has been identified for each process, it is a simple matter to determine the site teams and their assignments. All process owners are on the team, and their assignment is to complete implementation of their lean improved processes. When Lean Performance site teams are identified (Figures 9.8 to 9.10), the project manager will:

- Verify project team members and determine assignments for the project.
- Identify resource personnel for team members.
- Identify key system users.
- Arrange for participation of project team, resource personnel, and key users.
- Estimate and publish time commitments for all.
- Arrange for project team facilities at each location (including any requirements for terminals, tables, chairs, etc.)

Developing Lean Performance Team Training

The education and training necessary for team members to properly configure and operate the supporting software are defined in conjunction with appropriate resources from the software vendor; the actual classes and rosters for software education will be developed later in the project. To be successful at Lean Performance, the training provided by the software vendor must be completed only after the project team members complete the process requirements definitions for their processes. To accomplish this, team members must receive specific team-development

Developing Lean Performance Teams Module ■ 139

Primary Process	Activity Area	Supporting Process	Subordinate Process	Master Index No.	Translation	Workflow	System Map	Schedule Completion
Customer service	Service	Quality reporting	Customer returns	CS-01	Complete	Open	Open	
Customer service	Invoicing	Invoicing		CS-02.01	Open	Open	Open	
Customer service	Invoicing	Cumulative shipped reconciled		CS-02.02	Open	Open	Open	
Customer service	Pricing	Pricing		CS-03	Open	Open	Open	
Customer service	Sales forecasting	Sales forecasting		CS-04.01	Open	Open	Open	
Customer service	Sales forecasting	Quoting		CS-04.02	Open	Open	Open	
Customer service	Order entry	Order processing		CS-05.01	Open	Open	Open	
Customer service	Order entry	Purchase order maintenance		CS-05.02	Open	Open	Open	
Customer service	Order entry	Aftermarket order procedure		CS-05.03	Open	Open	Open	
Inventory management and logistics	Master scheduling	Master scheduling	Demand determination	IL-01.01	Open	Open	Open	
Inventory management and logistics	Master scheduling	Master scheduling	Production mix/quantity	IL-01.02	Open	Open	Open	
Inventory management and logistics	Receiving	AZ warehouse		IL-02.01	Complete	Open	Open	
Inventory management and logistics	Receiving	Incoming at plant		IL-02.02	Complete	Open	Open	
Inventory management and logistics	Receiving	Stockroom		IL-02.03	Complete	Open	Open	
Inventory management and logistics	Receiving	Incoming inspection		IL-02.04	Complete	Open	Open	
Inventory management and logistics	Receiving	MRO supplies		IL-02.05	Complete	Open	Open	
Inventory management and logistics	Receiving	Sample parts		IL-02.06	Open	Open	Open	
Inventory management and logistics	Traffic	Finished goods exportation		IL-03.01	Complete	Open	Open	
Inventory management and logistics	Traffic	Exportation of HAZMAT		IL-03.02	Complete	Open	Open	
Inventory management and logistics	Traffic	Finished goods warehousing		IL-03.03	Complete	Open	Open	
Inventory management and logistics	Traffic	AZ warehouse		IL-03.04	Complete	Open	Open	
Inventory management and logistics	Traffic	Returnable containers		IL-03.05	Open	Open	Open	
Inventory management and logistics	Traffic	Bar-code labeling		IL-03.06	Open	Open	Open	
Inventory management and logistics	Inventory control	Cycle count		IL-04.01	Complete	Open	Open	
Inventory management and logistics	Inventory control	Production report		IL-04.02	Complete	Open	Open	
Inventory management and logistics	Inventory control	Lot control		IL-04.03	Complete	Open	Open	
Inventory management and logistics	Inventory control	Parts recovery		IL-04.04	Open	Open	Open	
Inventory management and logistics	Inventory control	Piece count verification		IL-04.05	Open	Open	Open	
Inventory management and logistics	Inventory control	Bulk issues		IL-04.06	Open	Open	Open	
Inventory management and logistics	Inventory control	Physical inventory		IL-04.07	Open	Open	Open	
Inventory management and logistics	Work order release	Designation		IL-05.01	Complete	Open	Open	
Inventory management and logistics	Warehousing	Warehouse configuration		IL-06	Open	Open	Open	
Supplier management	MRP reports	MRP plans	Review	SM-01	Complete	Open	Open	Open

Figure 9.7   Lean Performance Project Process Listing and Sequence

140 ■ Lean Performance ERP Project Management

Primary Process	Activity Area	Supporting Process	Subordinate Process	Master Index No.	Translation	Workflow	System Map	Schedule Completion
Supplier management	Contract mgmt.	Purchase order process	Requisitions	SM-02.01	Complete	Complete	Complete	Open
Supplier management	Contract mgmt.	Purchase order process	Purchase order generation	SM-02.02	Complete	Complete	Complete	Open
Supplier management	Contract mgmt.	Purchase order process	Spot buys	SM-02.03	Complete	Complete	Open	Open
Supplier management	Contract mgmt.	Purchase order process	Expedite (domestic)	SM-02.04	Complete	Complete	Open	Open
Supplier management	Contract mgmt.	Purchase order process	Expedite (For.)	SM-02.05	Complete	Open	Open	Open
Supplier management	Contract mgmt.	Purchase order process	Reschedules	SM-02.06	Complete	Open	Open	Open
Supplier management	Contract mgmt.	Purchase order process	Tooling orders	SM-02.07	Complete	Open	Open	Open
Supplier management	Contract mgmt.	Purchase order process	Mailing purchase order	SM-02.08	Complete	Open	Open	Open
Supplier management	Contract mgmt.	Purchase order process	MRO purchase order	SM-02.09	Complete	Open	Open	Open
Supplier management	Supplier evaluations	Sourcing/quotations	Selection	SM-03.01	Complete	Complete	Open	Open
Supplier management	Supplier evaluations	Sourcing/quotations	AVL	SM-03.02	Complete	Open	Open	Open
Supplier management	Supplier evaluations	Sourcing/quotations	Supplier setup	SM-03.03	Complete	Complete	Complete	Open
Supplier management	Supplier evaluations	Sourcing/quotations	RFQ	SM-03.04	Complete	Complete	Complete	Open
Supplier management	Supplier evaluations	Reporting	Performance rating	SM-03.05	Complete	Open	Open	Open
Supplier management	Prod. line scheduling	PO-01	Complete	Open	Open			
Production and operations	Prod. line scheduling	Pilot runs		PO-01.01	Open	Open	Open	Open
Production and operations	Work in process	Machining/castings		PO-02.01	Complete	Open	Open	Open
Production and operations	Work in process	Machining/covers		PO-02.02	Complete	Complete	Complete	
Production and operations	Work in process	Material flow		PO-02.02.01	Complete	Complete	Complete	
Production and operations	Work in process	Preassembly		PO-03.01	Open	Open	Open	
Production and operations	Work in process	Final 1 assembly		PO-03.02	Open	Open	Open	
Production and operations	Work in process	Final 2 assembly		PO-03.03	Complete	Open	Open	
Production and operations	Work in process	Material flow for preassembly, final 1, final 2		PO-03.03.01	Complete	Complete	Complete	
Production and operations	Work in process	WED production		PO-04.01	Complete	Open	Open	
Production and operations	Work in process	Material flow for MA series		PO-04.01.01	Complete	Complete	Complete	
Production and operations	Work in process	Material flow for MB series		PO-04.01.02	Complete	Complete	Complete	
Production and operations	Work in process	Diecasting — TPP		PO-05.01	Complete	Open	Open	
Production and operations	Work in process	Diecasting material flow		PO-05.01.01	Complete	Open	Open	
Production and operations	Shopfloor reporting	Production reporting		PO-06.01	Open	Open	Open	
Production and operations	Shopfloor reporting	Labor reporting		PO-06.02	Open	Complete	Open	
Production and operations	Work order	Releases		PO-07.01	Complete	Open	Open	
Production and operations	Work order release	Component requisitioning		PO-07.02	Complete	Open	Open	

Figure 9.7 Lean Performance Project Process Listing and Sequence (cont.)

Developing Lean Performance Teams Module ■ 141

Primary Process	Activity Area	Supporting Process	Subordinate Process	Master Index No.	Translation	Workflow	System Map	Schedule Completion
Production and operations	Plant maintenance	Preventive maintenance		PO-08.01	Open	Open	Open	
Production and operations	Quality reporting	Deficiency reporting		PO-09.01	Complete	Open	Open	
Production and operations	Quality reporting	Sort/rework/scrap/RTV		PO-09.02	Complete	Open	Open	
Production and operations	Quality reporting	Component sampling		PO-09.03	Open	Open	Open	
Production and operations	Quality reporting	Small parts inspection		PO-09.04	Complete	Open	Open	
Production and operations	Quality reporting	Machine line inspection		PO-09.05	Complete	Open	Open	
Production and operations	Quality reporting	Preassembly inspection		PO-09.06	Complete	Open	Open	
Production and operations	Quality reporting	Final 1 inspection		PO-09.07	Complete	Open	Open	
Production and operations	Quality reporting	Final 2 inspection		PO-09.08	Complete	Open	Open	
Production and operations	Quality reporting	Final teardown		PO-09.09	Complete	Open	Open	
Production and operations	Quality reporting	Final visual		PO-09.10	Complete	Open	Open	
Production and operations	Quality reporting	Scrap accounting		PO-09.11	Complete	Open	Open	
Production and operations	Tool/gauge control			PO-10	Open	Open	Open	
Financial management	Customs	Importation of production material		FM-01.01	Complete	Open	Open	
Financial management	Customs	MRO importation		FM-01.02	Complete	Open	Open	
Financial management	Customs	Exportation invoicing		FM-01.03	Complete	Open	Open	
Financial management	NAFTA	Certificates of origin		FM-02.01	Complete	Open	Open	
Financial management	NAFTA	Assembly description		FM-02.02	Complete	Open	Open	
Financial management	Product costing	Product costing		FM-03.01	Complete	Open	Open	
Financial management	Product costing	Standard costs		FM-03.02	Complete	Complete	Complete	
Financial management	Product costing	CRNs		FM-03.03	Complete	Open	Open	
Financial management	Product costing	Quality cost reporting		FM-03.04	Open	Open	Open	
Financial management	Cash management	Petty cash disbursement		FM-04	Complete	Open	Open	
Financial management	Payroll	Distribution		FM-05	Complete	Open	Open	
Financial management	Accounts payable	Accounts payable		FM-06	Complete	Open	Open	
Financial management	General ledger	Finance statements		FM-07.01	Complete	Open	Open	
Financial management	General ledger	WALBRO policy		FM-07.02	Complete	Open	Open	
Financial management	General ledger	Government reporting		FM-07.03	Complete	Open	Open	
Financial management	General ledger	Taxes		FM-07.04	Complete	Open	Open	
Financial management	General ledger	Month-end closing		FM-07.05	Open	Open	Open	
Financial management	Inventory accounting	Valuation		FM-08	Complete	Complete	Complete	
Business planning	Business planning	Business planning		BP-01	Complete	Complete	Open	
Business planning	Business planning	Labor requirements		BP-01.01	Complete	Complete	Open	

Figure 9.7 Lean Performance Project Process Listing and Sequence (cont.)

142 ■ Lean Performance ERP Project Management

Primary Process	Activity Area	Supporting Process	Subordinate Process	Master Index No.	Translation	Workflow	System Map	Schedule Completion
Business planning	Business planning	Materials requirements		BP-01.02	Complete	Complete	Complete	
Business planning	Business planning	Purchase plan		BP-01.02.01	Complete	Complete	Open	
Product engineering	ECN	ECN setup		PE-01.01	Complete	Complete	Complete	
Product engineering	ECN	Change notice		PE-01.02	Open	Open	Open	
Product engineering	ECN	Change coordination		PE-01.03	Open	Open	Open	
Product engineering	Bill of materials	Parts list maintenance		PE-02	Open	Open	Open	
Product engineering	Res. & develop.	Development		PE-03.01	Open	Open	Open	
Product engineering	Res. & develop.	New product releases		PE-03.02	Open	Open	Open	
Product engineering	Product masters	Where first used list		PE-04.01	Open	Open	Open	
Product engineering	Product masters	Data maintenance		PE-04.02	Open	Open	Open	
Product engineering	Engineering drawing	Print distribution		PE-05.01	Open	Open	Open	
Product engineering	Engineering drawing	Drawing maintenance		PE-05.02	Open	Open	Open	

Figure 9.7 Lean Performance Project Process Listing and Sequence (cont.)

Developing Lean Performance Teams Module ■ 143

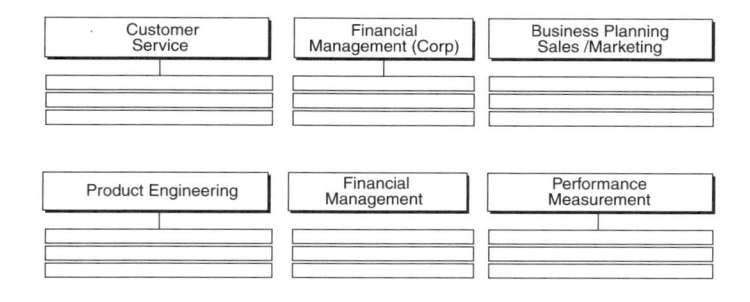

Figure 9.8 Lean Performance Team (Corporate)

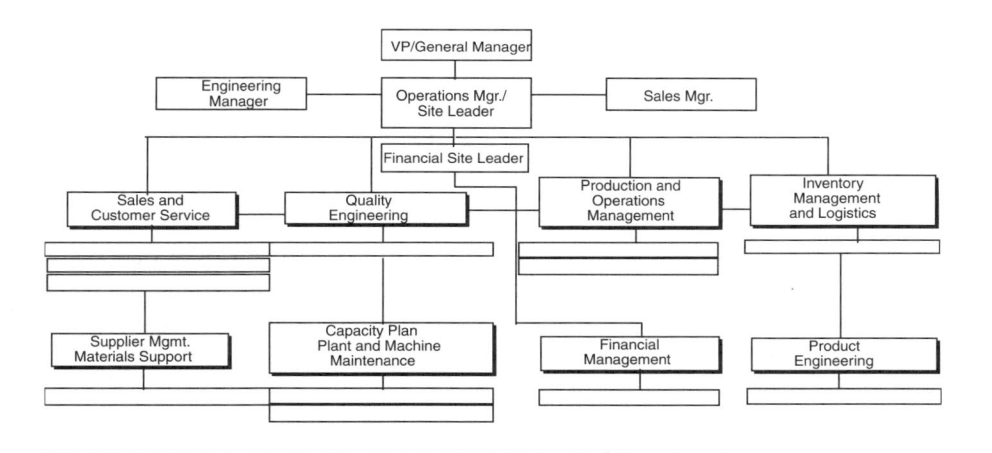

Figure 9.9 Lean Performance Team (Aftermarket)

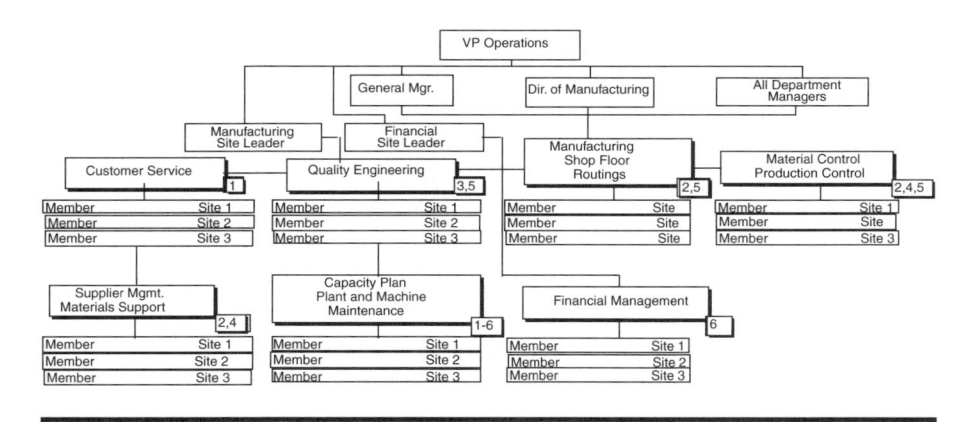

Figure 9.10 Lean Performance Team (International)

and process-improvement training. This training should be completed prior to beginning any work on improving processes. The team-development and process-improvement training should be conducted by the project trainer and project facilitator, respectively.

Initial team-development training should include all team members from all sites. Team-development training should:

- Teach and empower the process owners and customers to take responsibility for enterprise Lean Performance and the virtual lean enterprise.
- Enable process owners, customers, and information systems support to improve communication and operate from a process-oriented focus.
- Provide insight into the use of process standards and measurements to manage continuous improvement.
- Inform the process owners that the Lean Performance teams have identified common processes across multiple sites; multiple teams working on common or similar process workflow standards and work instructions will communicate and share the work and will determine what works best in their processes at their sites.

Above all, the message should be sent that teams enable shopfloor physical process lean improvements to impact upstream. In most manufacturing companies, 85% of cost is upstream from the shop. During the training, the Lean Performance teams should be reminded that their activities include establishment of site-level project plans; development of process standards, process workflows, and work instructions; software and process GAPs identification; open-issues resolution; and eventual process-level proposed performance measurements.

The project manager should record any systems problems or requirements brought to light during steering committee or team meetings, including team training sessions. The project manager should also complete an evaluation summary for each meeting or training session, as this Lean Performance team training develops the team dynamics for a successful project. Later in the project, additional training will be needed to complete the process-improvement training required by team members.

The team-development training should fully address questions about why the project is being undertaken, especially questions concerning the project methodology itself. The training orientation message should be something like the following:

> Traditionally, the experts would decide what's best for you and deliver a new system or process and tell you how to operate it. That never works very well. Another way we could go forward would be to bring in experts and let them decide how you ought

to do processes. Then we could get the process owners, customers, and users involved to see if the experts got it right. We could then make changes where necessary and deliver you a new system or process. This is known as the user-involved approach. A third way we could go forward would be to let the process owners, customers, and key users determine the best way to do the processes and then deliver a new system or process in support of your design. This is the Lean Performance team approach.

Lean Performance team members are cooperative, mutually respectful, collaborative, dedicated to the approach, and powerful, and they share a vision. The process of team development is to start as a group, using outside facilitation or assistance, and then to grow into a self-directing team with no further facilitation or assistance required. Our purpose is to last beyond the project.

It is always the decision of the team member to join the Lean Performance team. Team members join because they see the vision, like it, and want to be a part of it. Some individuals may not see the vision but would still like to participate, either now or later. It's entirely up to the individual. Of course, not participating may have adverse job consequences.

These are the Lean Performance team ground rules:

- Meetings start on time
- Meetings finish on time
- Do not bite, scratch, or kick team members (or facilitators)
- Do not throw things at each other
- Decisions are by consensus
- Participate
- Keep an open mind to change
- There is no such thing as a dumb question
- Maintain a positive attitude
- Never leave a disagreement unvoiced
- Create a blameless environment
- Practice mutual respect every day
- Treat others as you want to be treated
- One person, one vote
- There is no position or rank
- There is no magic wand

This is about training and working smarter. We will begin every team session by reviewing the results of the last session. We will evaluate the session, not the performance of individuals. We will explore how each team member felt the session went. We will determine what we as a team did well and propose what we could do better. We will end every team session by summarizing the results of that session. Again, we will evaluate the session, not the performance of individuals. We will explore how each team member felt the meeting went and ask what we as a team did well and not so well. We will attempt to learn what we could we do better.

After the orientation, the next important item on the team-training agenda is instruction on the development of process standards. The objectives of the process workflow and work instruction standard development are to develop documentation to help manage processes with new software and to document those processes consistent with ISO and QS compliance requirements. We also complete process documentation for handoff to other project sites so our best processes can be implemented throughout the organization without duplication of effort. To develop process workflow standards, process owners first determine what their processes do. Only after that will site leaders, facilitators, or software vendors present software-specific training to demonstrate how process requirements are performed by enabling software. Process owners document the process input/output cycle by adding the who, where, and when information to the process documentation.

Process owners then review the processes and outputs with process customers for acceptance. It is likely that there will be some reluctance to complete the process standards on the part of some (if not most or all) of the team members. Completing the process standards is beginning to resemble a lot of extra work. Some skeptical team member is bound to ask why we are developing process standards for management decision and information/support processes? Here are some answers:

- Standards establish communication and connect information systems support and system users.
- We would not even consider introducing a new machine or process to a physical product process without developing a standard (bill of materials, routing) for performing the process or a standard cost.
- Lean Performance utilizes process standards for information/support processes in order to maximize the use of unmodified, vendor-supported software because:
  - Vendor-supported software lowers complexity, and less complexity means less downtime for the computers, networks, and customer; cost, quality, and delivery performance improves.
  - As we have learned in the lean factory, process standards must be established before a process can be stabilized, and a process must be stabilized before a technological innovation can be implemented.

- Standards are needed to develop process control and checkpoints for measurement and improvement; again, the lean factory has demonstrated that improving process performance improves the process result.
- Standards ensure the success of the organization.
- Standards are needed to protect the company's knowledge base by recording and preserving expertise.
- Standards are needed in order to facilitate cross-training.

Lean Performance methodology uses process standards as a driver in any information technology implementation or improvement project. Development and acceptance of a process standard precede developing any modifications. Development of process standards focuses the requirements definition on the information technology customer, the process owner. In the project, the requirements of the improved processes are defined using the process workflow standard technique, at first without references to the software and later with the addition of screen references from the software. Process improvements are undertaken in sections by small groups, then reviewed and approved in the weekly team meetings. Figures 9.11 and 9.12 illustrate the results of process standards development.

A copy of the project control spreadsheet is distributed to all process owners, and the team is instructed on how to locate and update the project control spreadsheet on the project web page. Steering committee reporting will be based on the presentation of graphs developed from reports on the status of process workflow and work instruction. Figure 9.13 is an example of a project control spreadsheet that supports graphic (visual) progress reporting.

When the Lean Performance team meeting mechanics are introduced, it should be emphasized that weekly meetings are held for updates, reviews, and decisions; they are not process improvement working sessions. Working sessions are small group meetings (involving process owners and customers) that are held as needed to get work done. A team leader is selected for each team to assume the responsibilities of developing the agenda for weekly meetings, reserving a meeting room, and notifying team members of the meeting. The team leader also conducts weekly meetings, makes sure the meetings stay on track (with the assistance of the facilitator), and meets with the facilitator afterward to determine ways to improve the next meeting. During the week, team leaders monitor the progress of the small groups toward completing their assigned tasks. In some cases, the team leader assignment may be rotated among team members. No decisions should be made at weekly meetings if more than one team member will be absent. Team leaders hold updates with project management to report team status and progress. Finally, the teams

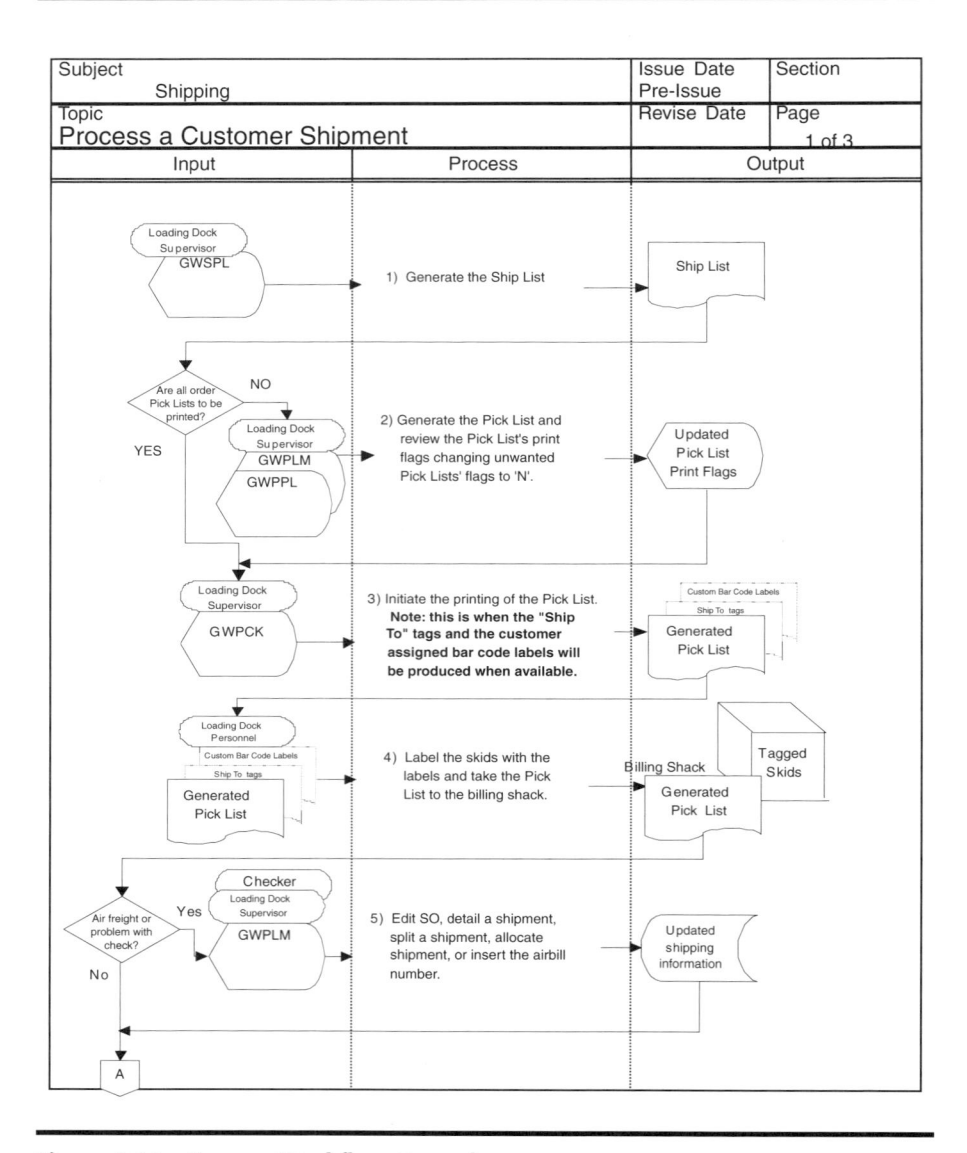

Subject Shipping		Issue Date Pre-Issue	Section
Topic Process a Customer Shipment		Revise Date	Page 1 of 3
Input	Process	Output	

[Flowchart content:]

1) Generate the Ship List
- Input: Loading Dock Supervisor GWSPL
- Output: Ship List

Decision: Are all order Pick Lists to be printed?
- YES → (continues)
- NO → 2) Generate the Pick List and review the Pick List's print flags changing unwanted Pick Lists' flags to 'N'.
  - Input: Loading Dock Supervisor GWPLM, GWPPL
  - Output: Updated Pick List Print Flags

3) Initiate the printing of the Pick List.
Note: this is when the "Ship To" tags and the customer assigned bar code labels will be produced when available.
- Input: Loading Dock Supervisor GWPCK
- Output: Custom Bar Code Labels, Ship To tags, Generated Pick List

4) Label the skids with the labels and take the Pick List to the billing shack.
- Input: Loading Dock Personnel, Custom Bar Code Labels, Ship To tags, Generated Pick List
- Output: Billing Shack, Generated Pick List, Tagged Skids

5) Edit SO, detail a shipment, split a shipment, allocate shipment, or insert the airbill number.
- Input: Checker, Loading Dock Supervisor GWPLM
- Decision: Air freight or problem with check? Yes/No
- Output: Updated shipping information

A

Figure 9.11 Process Workflow Example

are empowered to act within the project mission and scope and also within the parameters of the lean principles.

Teams will employ the lean transformation principles in the Lean Performance analysis. In the project, teams will be creating or enhancing an already existing lean culture, and all team members are empowered to invoke the lean cultural principles during team activities. As a reminder, the lean cultural principles are:

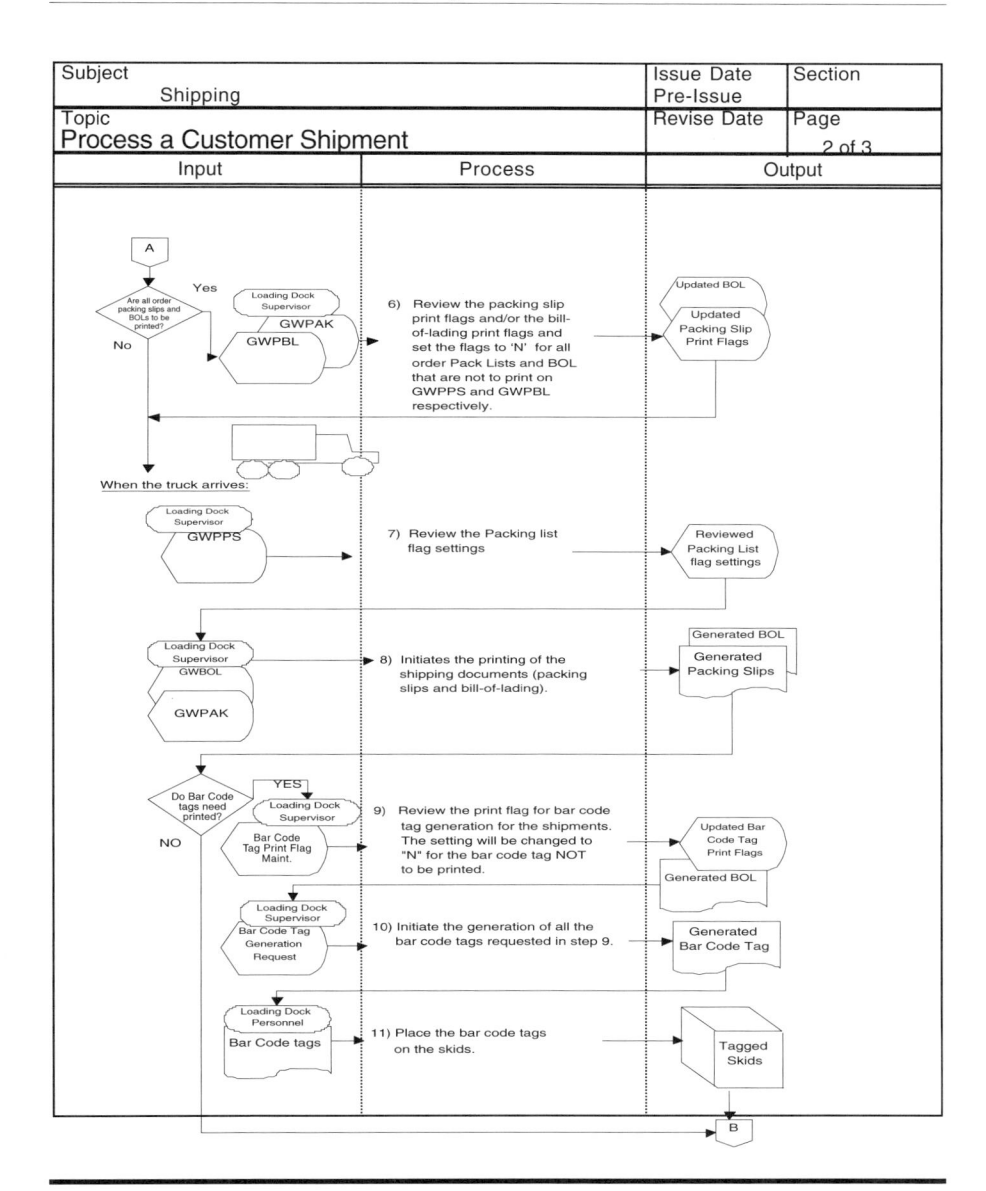

Subject Shipping	Issue Date Pre-Issue	Section
Topic Process a Customer Shipment	Revise Date	Page 2 of 3
Input	Process	Output

[Flowchart continues from connector A:]

- Decision: Are all order packing slips and BOLs to be printed?
  - Yes → Loading Dock Supervisor: GWPAK, GWPBL
  - 6) Review the packing slip print flags and/or the bill-of-lading print flags and set the flags to 'N' for all order Pack Lists and BOL that are not to print on GWPPS and GWPBL respectively.
  - Output: Updated BOL, Updated Packing Slip Print Flags

When the truck arrives:
- Loading Dock Supervisor: GWPPS
- 7) Review the Packing list flag settings
- Output: Reviewed Packing List flag settings

- Loading Dock Supervisor: GWBOL, GWPAK
- 8) Initiates the printing of the shipping documents (packing slips and bill-of-lading).
- Output: Generated BOL, Generated Packing Slips

- Decision: Do Bar Code tags need printed?
  - YES → Loading Dock Supervisor: Bar Code Tag Print Flag Maint.
  - 9) Review the print flag for bar code tag generation for the shipments. The setting will be changed to "N" for the bar code tag NOT to be printed.
  - Output: Updated Bar Code Tag Print Flags, Generated BOL

- Loading Dock Supervisor: Bar Code Tag Generation Request
- 10) Initiate the generation of all the bar code tags requested in step 9.
- Output: Generated Bar Code Tag

- Loading Dock Personnel: Bar Code tags
- 11) Place the bar code tags on the skids.
- Output: Tagged Skids

[Connector B]

Figure 9.11   Process Workflow Example (cont.)

- Process-oriented thinking means putting what before how; first, understand what work needs to be done, then understand how best to do the work with a new system.
- Product quality results from process quality; improved process quality is the focus of the project.

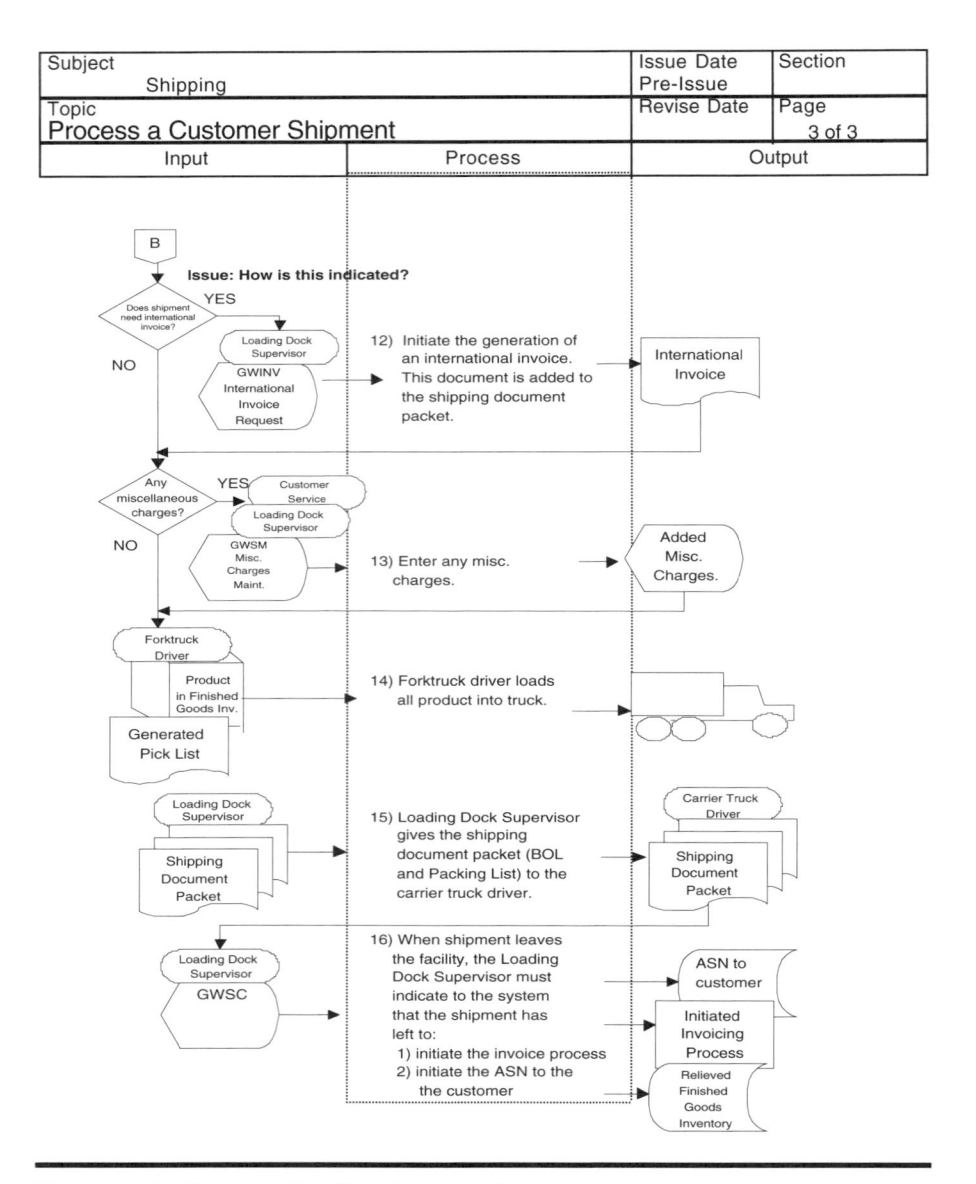

Figure 9.11 Process Workflow Example (cont.)

- Every process must have a process standard; without a process standard, no one can agree on what the process is.
- The process owner is the process expert; when in doubt, the process owner carries the discussion.
- The next process is your customer; of course, the customer can override the process owner when it comes to the output of any

SCREEN NAME:	**WORK INSTRUCTION**	SCREEN NUMBER:	INDEX NUMBER:
CYCLE COUNT WORKSHEET PRINT		3.13	IM

1. Set print range restrictions as desired.

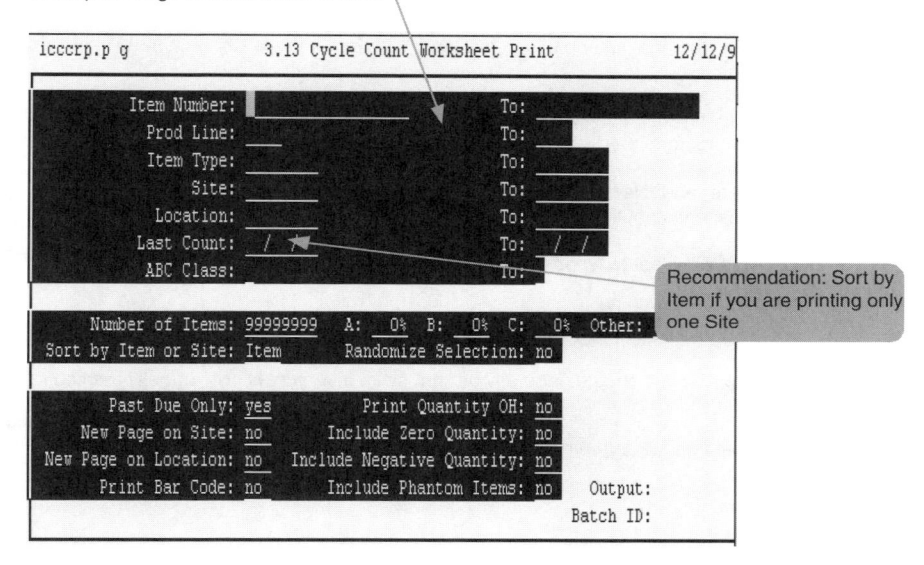

```
icccrp.p g              3.13 Cycle Count Worksheet Print              12/12/9

              Item Number:  _____          To:  _____
                Prod Line:  _____          To:  _____
                Item Type:  _____          To:  _____
                     Site:  _____          To:  _____
                 Location:  _____          To:  _____
               Last Count:  __/__/__                To:  __/__/__
                ABC Class:  _____          To:  _____

          Number of Items: 99999999    A: 0%   B: 0%   C: 0%   Other: ____
          Sort by Item or Site: Item    Randomize Selection: no

             Past Due Only: yes         Print Quantity OH: no
          New Page on Site: no       Include Zero Quantity: no
      New Page on Location: no    Include Negative Quantity: no
             Print Bar Code: no      Include Phantom Items: no    Output: _____
                                                                 Batch ID: _____
```

Recommendation: Sort by Item if you are printing only one Site

2. Set the "Number of Items" for which worksheets are desired. "99999999" will cause all items that are due for counting to print.

3. If something other than "99999999" is entered for "Number of Items," enter the per cent of each class that should be included in the print.

4. Choose "Sort by Item" if you are printing only one Site.

5. If you choose "Randomize Selection" equal "no," and you have chosen "Number of Items" to be something less than "99999999", you will get a selection of "A" Class items in item number sequence equal to the percent of "A" parts specified, beginning with the lowest item number. Otherwise, you will get a random selection from all item numbers equal to the percent of "A" parts specified. The same thing will occur with "B," "C," and "Other" parts.

Figure 9.12   Work Instruction How-To Example

process, and if the process customer is not happy with the process output then the process is not yet improved.
- Loyalty to people enables continuous improvement, and the golden rule principle applies; treat others on the team as you would have them treat you.
- Process data and measurements drive process continuous improvement; measurements level the playing field of ideas — better ideas tend to produce better processes, and better processes produce better results.

WORK INSTRUCTION		
SCREEN NAME: CYCLE COUNT WORKSHEET PRINT	**SCREEN NUMBER:** 3.13	**INDEX NUMBER:** IM

6. When "Past Due Only" is set to "yes," only those parts that have passed the specified number of days since last count will print. Setting this to "no" will cause the days since last count to be ignored. Note that setting this to "no" and "Number of Items" to "99999999" will cause all items to print.

7. Setting "Print Quantity OH" (On Hand) to "yes" will cause to worksheet to show the current inventory figure according to the System. "No" will suppress this data.

8. "New Page on Site" and "New Page on Location" can be used to control page breaks in the printing and may make distribution of the worksheets easier.

9. If "Print Quantity OH" is set to "yes," then "Include Zero Quantity" and "Include Negative Quantity" will take effect.

10. "Print Bar Code" should be "no".

11. "Include Phantom Items" should generally be "no" since inventory is not normally tracked for phantoms.

12. Press PF1 to print the worksheets.

DATE: 12/17/00 11:57:24 AM
PAGE: 2

Figure 9.12 Work Instruction How-To Example (cont.)

Reporting Progress to the Steering Committee

The project manager conducts a Lean Performance planning quality assurance review. The key report for this review is a progress report for the steering committee that utilizes graphs generated by the project control spreadsheet and based on project team process owners' updates. Figure 9.14 to 9.17 illustrate the type of visual reporting generated by a fairly rudimentary spreadsheet. The project manager also includes updates of all of the project management tools in the report.

WHAT FOLLOWS LEAN PERFORMANCE PLANNING?

Phase two of the Lean Performance methodology is called Lean Performance improvement and includes three modules of project tasks to be performed by the teams:

1. Improve process performance.
2. Integrate systems.
3. Test improved processes.

Level							
1	Business Planning					Sales	
2	Analyze Sales History	Analyze Open Orders	Analyze Seasonal Trends	Analyze Other Business Trends	Generate Forecast	Pricing	Analysis
3							
4							
MASTER INDEX NUMBER	1100	1200	1300	1400	1500	2100	2200
APPLICABLE							
WORK							
INSTRUCTIONS							
PRIORITY							
C/S	C	C	C	C	C	C	C
STATUS	O	O	O	O	O	O	O
OPEN	1	1	1	1	1	1	1
ACTIVE							
FLOWED							
MAPPED							
WORK INST							
TESTED							
TOTAL	1	1	1	1	1	1	1

Figure 9.13 Project Control Spreadsheet

154 ■ Lean Performance ERP Project Management

Level														
1	Customer Service													
2		New Customer Qualification/ Set Up	Establish Part Cross References	Maintain Credit Data	Maintain Price Codes	Order Entry						Customer Returns		Customer Invoicing	Customer Credit
3						Receive Non-EDI Order	Receive EDI Order	Enter Order (Non Blanket)	Process Order (Blanket) Enter Order (Blanket)	Schedule Orders (Blanket)	Allocate Available Inventory	Customer Order Change Management	Customer Returns - Fuel Pump	Customer Returns - Carburetor		
MASTER INDEX NUMBER	CS06	CS07	CS08	CS03	CS09	CS10	CS11	CS15	CS16	CS12	CS13	CS0102	CS0103	CS0201	CS14
APPLICABLE	020101	0116	070801	011001	NA		0701	07060113 07060301 07060302	07060305 07060306	0710 071201 071202	0701	NA	NA	0715 0716	
WORK															
INSTRUCTIONS															
PRIORITY C/S	S	S	S	S	S	C	S	S	S	S	C	C	C	S	C
STATUS	W	W	M	W	W	O	W	A	A	W	W	W	W	W	M
OPEN						1									
ACTIVE			1					1							1
FLOWED	1	1		1	1		1		1	1	1	1	1	1	
MAPPED															
WORK INST															
TESTED															
TOTAL	1	1	1	1	1	1	1	1	1	1	1	1	1	1	1

Figure 9.13 Project Control Spreadsheet (cont.)

Developing Lean Performance Teams Module ■ 155

Level											
1	Production & Operations Management										
2		Capacity Planning		Routing Maintenance		Production Scheduling			Produce Product	Material Scheduling	
3			Capacity Data Management		Maintain Packing Specs	Maintain Labor Data	Analyze Sales Forecast	Generate Rough Cut Plan	Review/ Replan	Release to Production		Review Rough Cut Plan	Review/ Replan	Release to Purchasing
4				Determine Machine Capacities	Monitor For Accuracy									
MASTER INDEX NUMBER			4111	4112	4210	4220	PO-6.4.1	PO060402	PO060403	PO0703	P0-11	4510	4520	4530
APPLICABLE											1807			
WORK											1814			
INSTRUCTIONS														
PRIORITY C/S			C O	C O	S O	C O	C A	C A	C A	S A	S W	C O	C O	S O
STATUS														
OPEN			1	1	1	1	1	1	1	1		1	1	1
ACTIVE														
FLOWED														
MAPPED											1			
WORK INST											1			
TESTED														
TOTAL			1	1	1	1	1	1	1	1	1	1	1	1

Figure 9.13 Project Control Spreadsheet (cont.)

156 ■ Lean Performance ERP Project Management

Level		Product Engineering		
1		Maintain New Release Part Data	Maintain ECN Part Data	Maintain BOM Data
2				
3				
4				
MASTER INDEX NUMBER		5100	PE0602	5300
APPLICABLE				
WORK INSTRUCTIONS				
PRIORITY		C	C	S
C/S STATUS		A	A	A
OPEN				
ACTIVE		1	1	1
FLOWED				
MAPPED				
WORK INST				
TESTED				
TOTAL		1	1	1

Figure 9.13   Project Control Spreadsheet (cont.)

Developing Lean Performance Teams Module ■ 157

Figure 9.13 Project Control Spreadsheet (cont.)

158 ■ Lean Performance ERP Project Management

Level										
1	Inventory Management & Logistics									
2	Receiving	Receiving Inspection	Warehousing		Shipping			Shop Floor Reporting	Maintain MRP Planning Data	
3			Cycle Counting		Physical Inventory	Order Picking	Prepare Shipments			
4			Set Up Cycle Count	Perform Cycle Count						
MASTER INDEX NUMBER	IL0207	IL0204	IL0401	IL0402	IL0407	IL0701	IL0702	IL08	IL10	
APPLICABLE	030401	030401	010405	0313	0401	071204	071213	030401	010407	
WORK	051301	030606	030603	0314	0402			0307		
INSTRUCTIONS		0307	0324	0315	0404			180801		
		05050505		032101	0406			180805		
		051307		032102	0407			180806		
		1913		1307	0411					
					0412					
					0421					
					0423					
PRIORITY C/S	C	C	S	S	C	S	C	S	C	
STATUS	W	W	W	W	W	W	W	W	W	
OPEN										
ACTIVE										
FLOWED										
MAPPED										
WORK INST TESTED	1	1	1	1	1	1	1	1	1	
TOTAL	1	1	1	1	1	1	1	1	1	

Figure 9.13   Project Control Spreadsheet (cont.)

Level										
1	Quality Management			Financial Management						
2	Supplier Quality Monitoring	Material Deviation Control	Product Certifications	Receivables	Payables	General Ledger	Budgeting	Fixed Assets	Costing	
3										
4										
MASTER INDEX NUMBER	8100	8200	8300	9100	9200	9300	9400	9500	9600	
APPLICABLE										
WORK										
INSTRUCTIONS										
PRIORITY C/S	C	C	C	C	C	C	C	C	C	
STATUS	O	O	O	O	O	O	O	O	O	
OPEN	1	1	1	1	1	1	1	1	1	37
ACTIVE										9
FLOWED										0
MAPPED										2
WORK INST										20
TESTED										0
TOTAL	1	1	1	1	1	1	1	1	1	68

Figure 9.13   Project Control Spreadsheet (cont.)

Developing Lean Performance Teams Module ■ 159

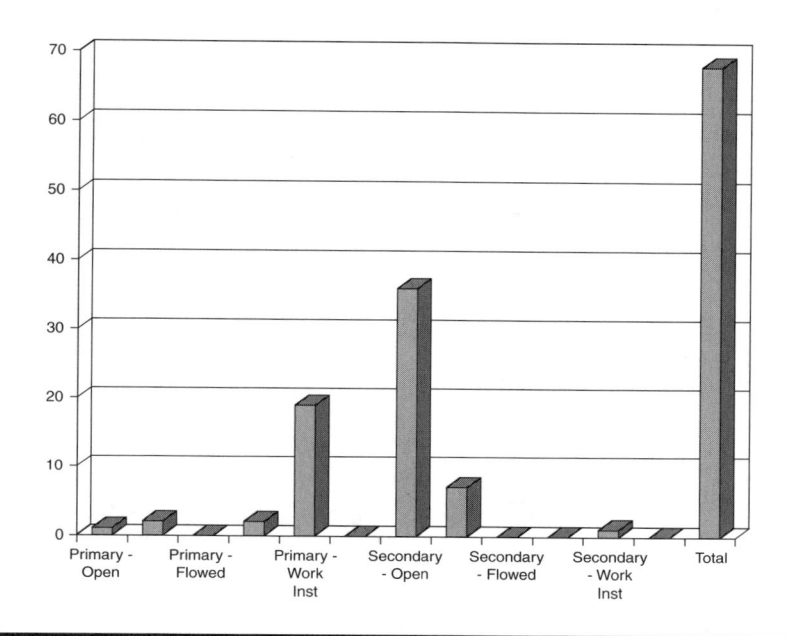

Figure 9.14 Process Workflow Diagram: Status for All Business Areas for Aftermarket Site

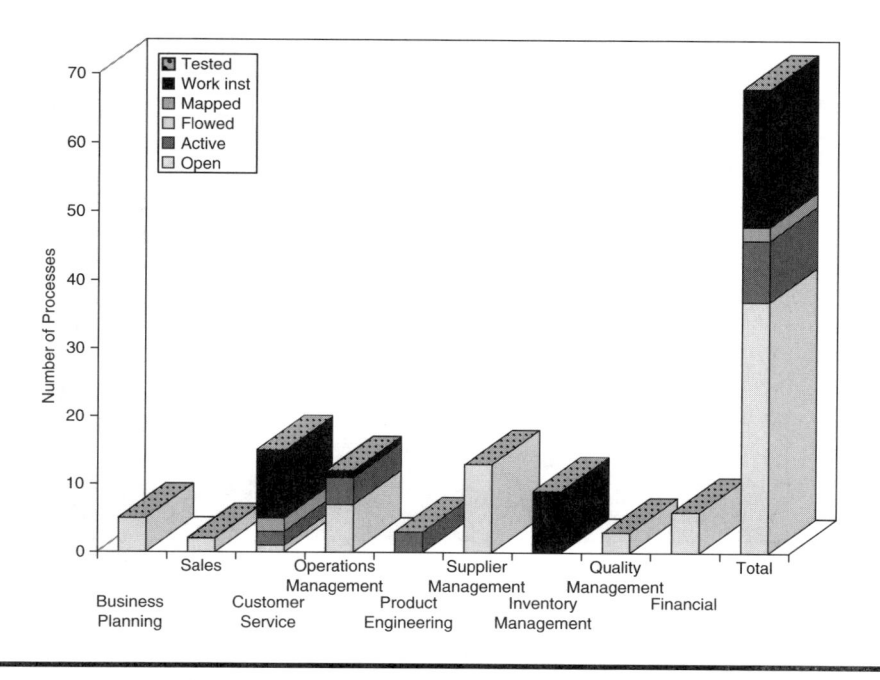

Figure 9.15 Progress by Major Business Areas for Aftermarket Site

160 ■ Lean Performance ERP Project Management

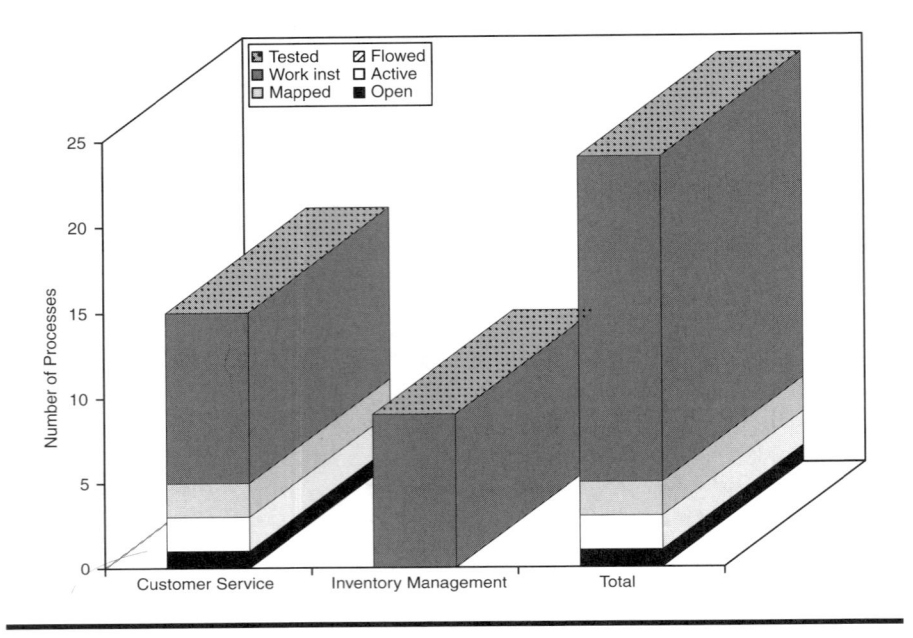

Figure 9.16 Progress by Primary Business Areas for Aftermarket Site

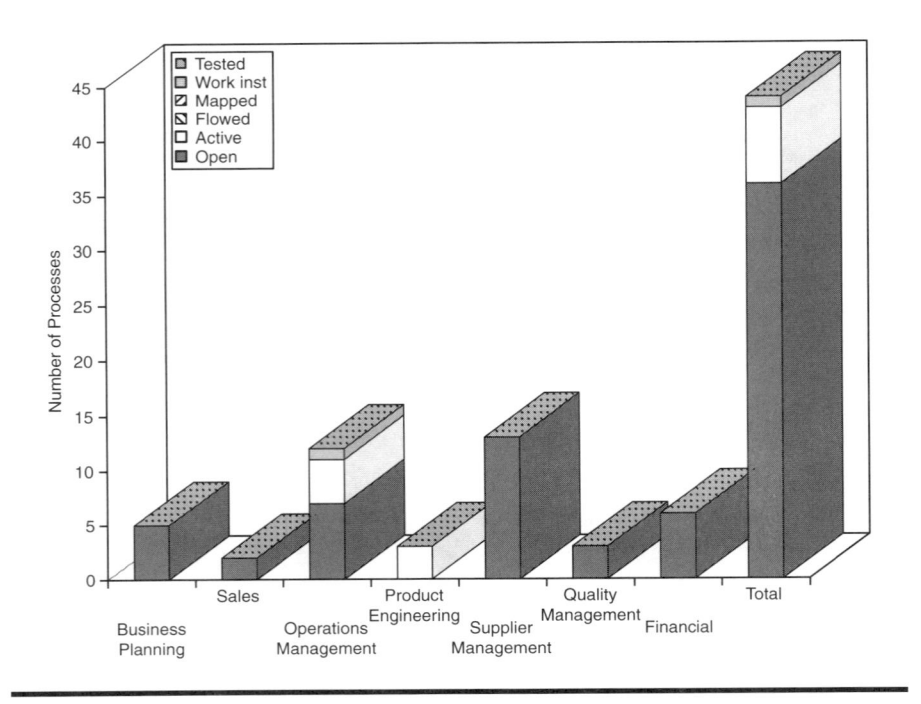

Figure 9.17 Progress by Secondary Business Areas for Aftermarket Site

Improving process performance includes these tasks:

- Development of process standards, including workflow and work instructions
- Finalization and documentation of software system controls and codes
- Lean Performance analysis
- Lean Performance team education

Integrating systems includes these tasks:

- Development of software improvements to close process and system GAPs.
- Planning, programming, and testing of data conversion and software programs.
- Installation and testing of software and communications capabilities.

Phase two concludes with testing the improved processes and includes these tasks:

- Developing test procedures
- Prototype and pilot testing
- Process testing
- Updating process workflow/work instruction
- Conducting the user training program

Phase three of the Lean Performance methodology is the continuous Lean Performance phase. This project phase includes two modules of tasks:

- Implement improved processes.
- Continuously improve Lean Performance.

Implementing the improved processes includes monitoring the successful completion of all tasks necessary for process implementation, in addition to:

- Maintaining Lean Performance teams
- Implementing Lean Performance management
- Continuously deploying lean policy and strategy

The Lean Performance methodology concludes with continuously improving Lean Performance, which includes defining and initiating Lean Performance measurements to:

- Ensure system integrity.
- Deliver key management data.
- Provide continuous improvement data.

III

LEAN PERFORMANCE IMPROVEMENT MODULES

In phase two, the shift from planning to improve processes to actually improving processes occurs. Processes that require improvement usually reside in departmental silos, although we have taken the first step toward improvement by identifying project processes in process areas rather than departments. These processes are going to be converted into cross-functional and cross-enterprise processes, and at the end of the project an entirely different process configuration may be in place. Phase two should be planned to continue for 4 to 6 months, and the sequence of processes improved should be:

- Physical processes
- Information/support processes
- Cross-functional processes
- Cross-enterprise processes

10

IMPROVING PROCESS PERFORMANCE MODULE

MANAGEMENT TASKS

Maintaining Lean Performance Teams

Lean Performance teams are the gathering point for the process owner and customer process standards definition activity. The two types of standards to complete are (1) process workflow standards, which are classic input–task–output flowcharts, historically derived from Taylor and the School of Scientific Management, and (2) process work instruction standards, which are derived from the initiators of lean production in regard to their visual management attributes but which are also very connected to the information technology system innovation school, in that many implementation consultancies use them or something like them to document procedures during implementation. Several of the better enterprise resource planning (ERP) software vendors supply a set of system screen work instructions along with their training modules. Often, these work instructions are user maintainable. Sites that have a software enabler with this attribute should use it but should be cautious about using the prepackaged "processes" that are also supplied by some vendors. While these programs are a noble attempt (and frequently handy if they can be maintained by the user), they are no substitute for conducting a business-specific, value-added process analysis to prepare for implementation.

The majority of the important tasks of the Lean Performance teams are performed in this phase of the project. The first of these tasks has already begun: identifying, analyzing, and improving processes. The teams will also develop process workflows and work instructions (process standards) with process owners and customers and perform the Lean Performance Analysis. From a steering committee perspective, it is critical to the eventual success of the project to monitor the composition of the project team. Once established, the Lean Performance teams will have to be modified from time to time for various reasons, including expanding the scope of the processes being improved, changing personnel or assignments, eventual formation of the cross-functional and cross-enterprise teams, and formalization of product- or process-based teams for ongoing Lean Performance management. The Lean Performance site and process team leaders and the project manager have the task of recommending team changes and selecting members of the cross-functional and cross-enterprise teams. The steering committee has the task of accepting those recommendations or seeking alternatives.

Members of the initial Lean Performance cross-functional teams are identified in this project phase and are drawn from the following process area teams:

- Finance
- Engineering
- Materials
- Operations
- Information

The next significant change to the Lean Performance team structure also occurs during this project phase: nominating members of the lean commerce team. Forming the lean commerce team occurs as the initial process identification and improvement activities conclude. This team is charged with the responsibility of designing and implementing lean commerce processes and the cross-enterprise virtual lean enterprise.

Conducting Steering Committee Meetings

During phase two, the first report at each steering committee meeting should be the report of the project manager on the project progress to plan. Utilizing the project tools presented previously, the project manager should be able to present the results of process and progress monitoring, including the summary bar chart and process graphs. Probably the most important function provided by the steering committee is to critically judge how well the improved processes are performing for the customer, based on performance standards and other expectations. Although a formal audit activity will be performed on the project results during the final phase of the project, steering committee members represent process areas, and their process area team leaders are responsible to report process lean improvements to them. Steering committee members should also examine records and interview process owners and customers in their process areas in order to make recommendations for changes and/or corrections. One important point to make here, though, is that any time the steering committee or its members interact with the project team on project issues, the lean cultural principles in place within the project team govern, and steering committee members are expected to abide by them. Not abiding by and endorsing these principles dooms the project and the eventual adoption of Lean Performance management. As a reminder, these lean cultural principles include:

- Process-oriented thinking means putting *what* before *how*.
- Product quality results from process quality.
- Every process requires a process standard.
- The process owner is the process expert.
- The next process is your customer.
- Loyalty to people enables continuous improvement.
- Process data and measurements drive process continuous improvement.

Regardless of the extent to which employees are empowered to design, redesign and/or improve processes, it remains management's responsibility to oversee and ultimately authorize any proposed changes. Carrying out this responsibility includes authorizing expenditures, reviewing proposed operational procedures, and providing for allocation of personnel. The Lean Performance Analysis is the mechanism deployed by the steering committee to coordinate the design and development of company-wide standards for measuring, monitoring, and improving processes. The Lean Performance Analysis is completed by the project team during phase two of the project and is the management tool for further policy and strategy deployment in phase three, in addition to being the "bottom-up" mechanism for requesting software enhancements and defining and reporting process level measurements on an ongoing basis.

PROJECT TEAM TASKS

Lean Performance Team Education

Education is critical to helping team members participate effectively. When the Lean Performance team education is being organized ensure that membership of the teams includes everyone necessary to perform the team tasks. Membership of the teams should be viewed as being inclusive rather than exclusive. These teams are not status or prestige assignments within the corporate culture. They need to be working teams, and they have quite a bit of work to do. Process owners and customers should not be excluded from team membership; they must be in on the teams from the start.

The first education activity for team members is becoming familiar with what is expected of them in the Lean Performance project itself. The training begins with a review of all the project plans, diagrams, and reports generated by the Lean Performance planning activities and covers all of the project tasks to be accomplished in this section of the workplan, as well as the Lean Performance improvement practices that will be employed to accomplish those tasks.

The Lean Performance Analysis builds from the already completed identification and deployment of lean business policies, lean project strategies, and project objectives. It also includes:

- Technology deployment
- Identifying teams and processes
- Developing process standards
- Identifying process and system GAPs
- Determining solutions for those GAPs
- Identifying benefits and process performance measurements

Early in the Lean Performance improvement phase, the project manager will issue the process standards documentation templates, which incorporate the columns and headings illustrated in Figures 10.1 and 10.2. During the Lean Performance improvement phase, the project manager should occasionally review the process listing and sequence to remove eliminated processes, identify or include new or missing processes, and resolve differences in terminology of the process identifications.

During Lean Performance team training, the teams should complete several project tasks, the first of which is to determine what vendor software classes should be conducted and who should attend, based on the process listing and sequence identification. The on-site software classes should not be held until after the process requirements are defined and each process value-added *what* is fully recognized and understood. Development of company software expertise is critical to answering the process owners' questions about software support for their processes.

The Lean Performance project manager and training coordinator should schedule appropriate software education for all Lean Performance teams based on the requirements of their respective processes. A review of the process identifications should provide some insight. Final decisions on who should attend what training can be delayed until the process requirements are understood and documented. When process owners attend software training, the process requirements portion of their process workflow standards should be completed; they can then use the classes to

PROCESS NAME:		SITE CODE:	INDEX NUMBER:
PROCESS DESCRIPTION:	OWNER:	CUSTOMER:	
PAGE NUMBER: 1 OF	REVISION LEVEL:	DATE ISSUED:	DATE REVISED: DATE PRINTED:
INPUT	PROCESS		OUTPUT

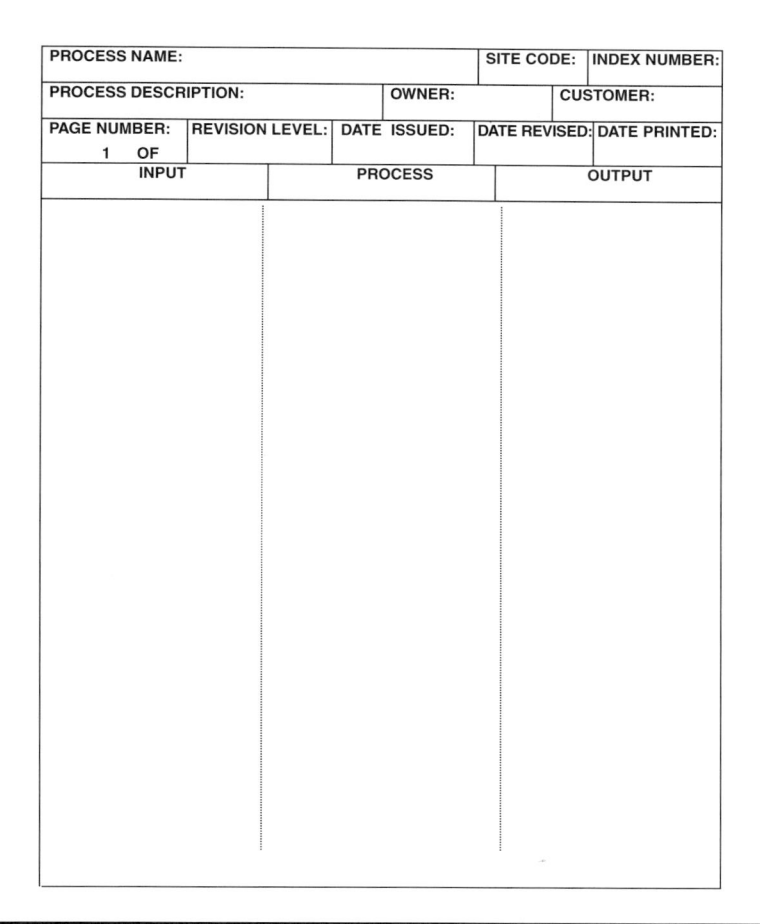

Figure 10.1   Workflow Diagram Template

begin to complete their decisions and documentation. An education and training plan should then be developed that incorporates the initial software and hardware competency training into a longer term plan. The education and training plan is developed by the training coordinator and referred to the steering committee for approval. It becomes the basis of the ongoing company practices in Lean Performance education and training. The education and training plan must address the training classes, Internet courses, video training, rosters, and sequence and timing of classes. The plan should consider the ongoing competency of personnel, especially transfers and new hires, and should include standards or other techniques to ensure the periodic measuring of competency and to provide for skills updating, especially those demanded by software upgrades and modification.

SCREEN NAME:			SITE CODE:	INDEX NUMBER:
PAGE NUMBER: 1 OF	REVISION LEVEL:	DATE ISSUED:	DATE REVISED:	DATE PRINTED:

Figure 10.2　Work Instruction Template

From a general competency perspective, classes that should be offered include:

- Orientation to material requirements planning (MRPII) and software terms (1/2 hour of classroom)
- MRPII overview: What will MRP II do for me? (1 hour of classroom)
- Getting started: What do I do to support software? (1 hour of classroom)
- Keyboard familiarity: How to navigate the system (1/2 hour of classroom)
- Train the trainer (for process owners; 1 hour of classroom)

	A	B	C	D	E	F	G	H	I	J	K	L	M
1	Last Name	First Name	Plt	D	Phone	New Phone	Dept	Area	Computer	Getting Started	MRP Overview	Job Specific	
2	Smith	Kelly	1B	7	2490	NTHQ		Admin					
3	Smith	Julie	1F	8	-	N/L		AP/AR Clerk					
4	Smith	Tania	17	7				Bus. Planner		D			
5	Smith	Betty	17	7	3543	3759	1780	Cust. Service					
6	Smith	Melinda	17	7	-			Cust. Service					
7	Smith	George	17	7	2870	3723	1780	Cust. Service					
8	Smith	Vickie	17	7	3893	3893	1780	Cust. Service					
9	Smith	Nancy	17	7	3310	3748	1780	Cust. Service					
10	Smith	Rhonda	1O	7	-	N/L		Data Entry					
11	Smith	Deborah	1O	7	-	N/L		Data Entry					
12	Smith	Cindy	1M	7	2513	6445		EDS Admin		I			
13	Smith	Shay	1E	7				Engr					
14	Smith	Mel	17	7	3284	3744	1762	Engr Indust					
15	Smith	Bill	17	7	3844	3844	1763	Engr Indust			X	X	X
16	Smith	Greg	17	7	3060	3728	9503	Engr Product					
17	Smith	Vickie	1S	7	-	N/L		Engrng					
18	Smith	Jennifer	1F	7	3346	6537	9585	Finance		D		AR/INV	
19	Smith	Debbie	1F	7	-	N/L		Finance					
20	Smith	Charlotte	1F	7	2161	6412		Finance	PC				
21	Smith	Jo	1F	7	2854	6490	9585	Finance					
22	Smith	Joan	1F	7	3941	6616	9585	Finance					
23	Smith	Ron	1F	7	2351	6430	9585	Finance		X	X	X	
24	Smith	Gene	1F	7	3034	6504	9595	Finance	PC				
25	Smith	Julie	1F	7	2286	6425		Finance		X	X	X	
26	Smith	Carol	1F	7	6996	6623	9585	Finance					
27	Smith	Mike	1F	7	3979	6618	9585	Finance					
28	Smith	Chris	42	7	2329	3709		Finance		X	X	X	
29	Smith	Kim	1F	7	3992	6619	9585	Finance					
30	Smith	Susie	1F	7	2285	6423		Finance					
31	Smith	Dave	1F	7	2271	6420	9585	Finance					
32	Smith	Angela	1F	7	-	N/L		Finance		D	X	I	
33	Smith	Pam	1F	7	3464	6550	9585	Finance		D	X	I	

Figure 10.3 Training Assignments Spreadsheet

- General system use and important inquiries (for all system users; 1 hour of classroom)
- Report generation (for interested system users; 1 hour of classroom)

User-specific training and exercises are presented just before going live with the new process and should include task or user process-specific process workflow and work instruction training. The reason for holding off on this training at this point is that specific training by facility for plant- or facility-identified processes is enhanced once the teams have uncovered the common processes of the plants. Project trainers should work with the project manager to develop and maintain a spreadsheet to manage and communicate project training schedules (Figure 10.3).

Finance Team Tasks

The finance team is responsible for the activities of process owners and customers in the following process areas:

- Financial management
- Plant accounting
- Business planning

172 ■ Lean Performance ERP Project Management

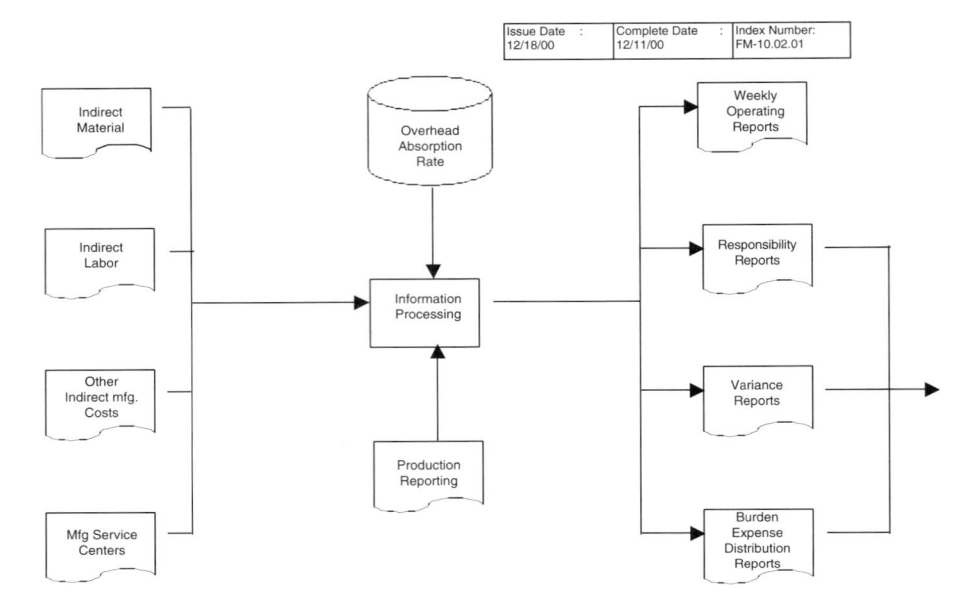

The overhead cost accumulation overview illustrates how indirect manufacturing costs are accumulated, reports are generated, and the final journal entries are produced to record the absorption or recovery of manufacturing overhead and the charge to make to work-in-process inventories. Overhead costs are accumulated in established departments or cost centers through the coding structure and the normal accounting process of sorting and summarizing transactions.

Figure 10.4 Overhead Cost Accumulation Model

Finance team activities include reviewing project objectives deployed during Lean Performance Planning. Along with the other teams, the finance team will complete appropriate Lean Performance Analysis masters to connect their processes to the lean business policies and lean project strategies. The finance team also determines how to provide all other performance measurements proposed during the Lean Performance Analysis through the use of system central data. This task usually involves determining system structural setup issues, including the financial perspective on database structures.

The finance team also conducts a review of system setup criteria to determine how data setup will include product lines and/or business segments or units in item masters and how the data setup will include standard base account structures to minimize the use of reference fields in financial consolidations and to enable faster period-end reporting with minimum account reconciliation. The finance team develops an overhead allocation method that allocates corporate and regional costs at the plant-site level to allow appropriate full-absorption costing and timely reporting of costs and determines appropriate usage of variable vs. full-absorption costing (see Figure 10.4 for an example).

The finance team also conducts a review of software package setup requirements and audits the existing system for accounting data completeness, accuracy, and effectiveness in costing manufacturing processes. The team verifies system files and all accounting data subject to data load and/or conversion, including work centers, and enters correct accounting data where needed. The finance team rolls up system standard costs and verifies that they are accurate. They determine how to provide financial management performance reporting that ensures support for level-by-level performance measurements through an appropriate general ledger accounts structure (Figure 10.5). The finance team also recommends financial entity or site configurations that allow the collection and reporting of financial data according to lean business policies and strategies and project objectives and includes a determination of how to handle entities for joint ventures (Figure 10.6). Other tasks that are accomplished by the finance team include reviewing and establishing product line designations, setting up an exchange-rate system, and taking advantage of the system capability to establish budgets.

The finance team also works with the information team to determine an accounting and financial data conversion strategy that includes the steps to map accounting and financial system data with engineering item master data. The conversion strategy should include an audit of accounting data for completeness, accuracy, and effectiveness in regard to costing manufacturing processes. The finance team will enter accounting data where appropriate and roll up system standard costs and verify them. Finally (and especially because very often the finance team will tend to be ahead of other teams in their system training), the finance team does not make any final decisions on the use of system codes that have any bearing on other processes. Full Lean Performance team input will be included in final system setup decisions at the process test.

Engineering Team Tasks

The engineering team is responsible for the activities of process owners and customers in all engineering process areas. The engineering team is also assigned responsibility for improving the new product introduction and design and engineering processes described previously. Other engineering team activities include reviewing project objectives deployed during Lean Performance Planning and completion of Lean Performance Analysis masters to connect their processes to lean business policies and lean project strategies deployment. Engineering team activities also include comparing item masters and bills of materials (BOMs) to drawings, especially finding items referenced on drawings as manufactured that may be purchased instead. The team is also responsible for verifying correlation

Default System Accounts

Issue Date:	Complete Date:	Index Number:
Draft	12/11/00	FM-10.01

The following table lists all of the accounts that are set up in the SYSTEM/ACCOUNT control file.

Account	Type	Use	Account No.
Receivables (AR[a])	Asset	Invoice post, AR	01000
Sales	Income	Invoice post	21000
Sales discount	Expense	Invoice post	21010
(Tax) exempt sales	Income	Invoice post (Canadian)	Not used
PST[b]	Liability	Invoice post (Canadian)	Not used
Sales tax 1	Liability	Invoice post	11611
Sales tax 2	Liability	Invoice post	11611
Sales tax 3	Liability	Invoice post	11611
Sales terms (credit)	Expense	AR payment	21010
Sales cash	Asset	AR payment, AP checks	00100
Sales finance	Income	AR	70600
COGS[c] material	Expense	SO[d] shipment	30000
COGS labor	Expense	SO shipment	31000
COGS burden (variable)	Expense	SO shipment	40000
COGS overhead (fixed)	Expense	SO shipment	40010
COGS subcontract	Expense	SO shipment	30010
Payables	Liability	Vouchers, checks	11000
AP[e] discount	Income	Checks	70610
Expensed item receipt	Expense	Vouchers	42600
Expensed item usage variance	Expense	Vouchers	Not used
Expensed item rate variance	Expense	Vouchers	Not used
Cost of production	Expense	Nonproductive labor, SFC[f] transfer	42000
Labor (absorbed)	Expense	SFC, repetitive, WO[g] close	31200
Burden (absorbed)	Expense	SFC, repetitive, WO close	49800
Inventory	Asset	Inventory transactions	02000
PO[h] receipts (accrued AP)	Liability	PO receipt, voucher	11000
Purchases	Expense	PO receipt (noninventory)	42600
Overhead applied	Expense	PO receipt	49810
Subcontract	Expense	PO receipt (if no work order)	46000

Figure 10.5   General Ledger Accounts

of system fields in item masters, BOMs, work centers, and routings between new and old enabling software.

The engineering team takes on the responsibility of proposing manufacturing BOMs and routings to the operations and materials Lean Performance teams. By *proposing*, we mean exactly that. The engineering team assumes ownership of product data, and many system data management functions are dependent on product data settings and structures. By proposing manufacturing BOMs and routings to the operations and materials teams, the engineering team is recognizing that, while they may have the system authority to control how system data are established and

Default System Accounts

	Issue Date:	Complete Date:	Index Number:
	Draft	12/11/00	FM-10.01

The following table lists all of the accounts that are set up in the SYSTEM/ACCOUNT control file.

Account	Type	Use	Account No.
Scrap	Expense	WO receipt	42200
Work in process	Asset	WO, backflush, repetitive	02100
Inventory discrepancy	Expense	Inventory counts	30210
Cost revalue	Expense	GL^i cost change	30220
Floor stock	Expense	WO close	30280
PO price variance	Expense	PO receipt	30230
AP usage variance	Expense	Voucher	30240
AP rate variance	Expense	Voucher	30250
Method variance	Expense	WO close	30260
Transfer variance	Expense	Multisite transaction	30270
Material usage variance	Expense	WO close	30241
Material rate variance	Expense	WO issue, WO close	30251
Labor usage variance	Expense	SFC, repetitive, WO receipt	31240
Labor rate variance	Expense	SFC, repetitive	31250
Burden usage variance	Expense	SFC, repetitive, WO receipt	49840
Burden rate variance	Expense	SFC, repetitive	49850
Subcontract usage variance	Expense	WO close	30242
Subcontract rate variance	Expense	WO close	30252

[a] AR = accounts receivable.
[b] PST = **DEFINE**.
[c] COGS = cost of goods sold.
[d] SO = **DEFINE.**
[e] AP = accounts payable.
[f] SFC = **DEFINE**.
[g] WO = work order.
[h] PO = purchase order.
[i] GL = general ledger.

Figure 10.5   General Ledger Accounts (cont.)

maintained, they recognize the value of the input of process owners who use that system data in the actual manufacture of products. The Lean Performance approach allows for the establishment of appropriate hand-offs and checks and balances in the development of product structures while recognizing that the ownership responsibility and maintenance of the BOM and routing standards properly belongs to engineering. Reciprocally, the operations and materials teams are responsible for communicating through the use of these BOMs and routing standards as they establish system operations and transactions. The materials team and operations team will also produce their own standards (material flow

176 ■ Lean Performance ERP Project Management

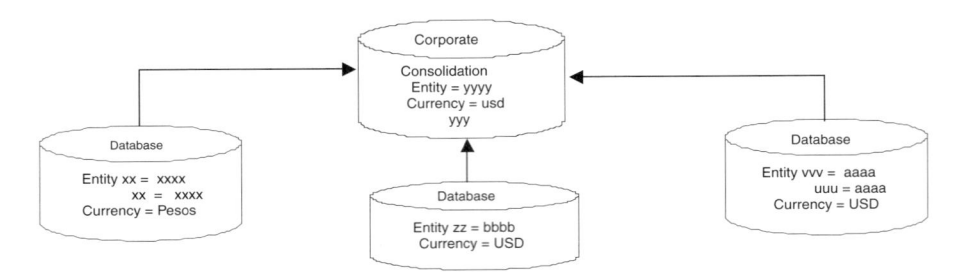

```
                          ┌─────────────────┐
                          │    Corporate    │
                          │  Consolidation  │
                          │  Entity = yyyy  │
                          │  Currency = usd │
                          │      yyy        │
                          └─────────────────┘
     ┌──────────────┐              ▲              ┌──────────────┐
     │   Database   │              │              │   Database   │
     │              │    ┌─────────────────┐      │              │
     │ Entity xx =  │    │    Database     │      │ Entity vvv = │
     │     xxxx     │    │                 │      │    aaaa      │
     │  xx = xxxx   │    │ Entity zz = bbbb│      │  uuu = aaaa  │
     │Currency=Pesos│    │ Currency = USD  │      │Currency = USD│
     └──────────────┘    └─────────────────┘      └──────────────┘
```

1. Can set up one database for each site and separate financials for each entity
2. Sites 1 and 2 are in one database, separated by entity code
3. Site 3 in a separate database
4. Financials consolidated at Corporate
5. Can use alphanumeric characters or all numeric to identify entities and sites
6. Each entity can have its own financials
   - Income Statement, Balance Sheet
7. We can share common master files
   - i.e, Customer files, Vendor files
8. The field size is 4 characters
   1st field represents the division = assigned by corporate
   2nd field represents the geographic area = assigned by corporate
   3rd and 4th fields will be assigned by the respective sites

Figure 10.6   Database Financial Entities

diagrams) to communicate and manage the flow of product and corresponding system transactions (more about this topic later).

Ownership and management of system data used by other process owners includes a recognition of responsibility to abide by the lean cultural principles, particularly the one proposing that *the next process is your customer.* The engineering team has several tasks to perform in order to ensure that all downstream customers of system data are receiving or have access to adequate and accurate data. The terms *adequate* and *accurate* in this context imply the attribute of quality. Data maintained in processes owned by the engineering team drive many other processes downstream, and quality data are as important to the satisfaction of the external customer as are quality materials or physical processing of those materials. To ensure the quality of system product data, the engineering team will audit engineering BOMs for completeness, accuracy, and manufacturing effectiveness. The team will copy the engineering BOMs to the manufacturing BOM data area in the software or enter the manufacturing BOMs (where needed). The engineering team will audit manufacturing routings for completeness, accuracy and effectiveness in supporting manufacturing processes, and copy or enter routings to the new software where needed.

It is usually appropriate to assign ownership of the item master file to the engineering team, because they generally are the first to enter part-identified data into the system, as well as any additional necessary product data for all sites. The engineering team is responsible for maintaining the accuracy and completeness of system product data and has the task of determining team ownership of engineering BOMs as well as usage of product codes in an item master. Another issue of ownership that must be settled by the engineering team is that of determining design engineering questions such as the local or central ownership of product drawings or the governance of product drawings maintained away from the engineering location. The engineering team is also responsible for communicating policy decisions regarding these and other relevant engineering team items to the greater project team. The engineering team will work with the information team to develop a plan to convert existing system fields in the item master, engineering BOMs, work centers, and routings to the new system. They will also develop a plan to input any additional necessary product data information.

A key issue for the engineering team on many projects is to determine how item masters and engineering BOMs will be downloaded or otherwise made available to the appropriate manufacturing site or sites when released for production. In addition, the team will often need to determine the engineering data conversion strategy (including a plan to map and convert engineering data along with other system data) and the policies and processes required to maintain the product data after the system is live. Often, an engineering data maintenance policy is issued to clarify and communicate these policies; for example, the item master is maintained by the engineering drawing owner, and central or perhaps corporate product engineering owns the item master file. In this case, item masters are downloaded or otherwise made available to a manufacturing site upon release of the product for manufacture. Correspondingly, in this example, central or corporate product engineering owns the BOM and communicates that policy (along with the process to make engineering BOMs available to the manufacturing sites) via download or other transmission upon the release of product.

Project result: preliminary bills of materials and routings

Materials Team Tasks

The materials team is responsible for the activities of process owners and customers in the following process areas:

- Customer relationship management
- Sales and marketing

- Inventory management and logistics
- Supplier management
- Purchasing

The first materials team activity is to review project objectives deployed during Lean Performance Planning. Along with the other teams, the materials team completes the appropriate Lean Performance Analysis masters to connect their processes to lean business policies and lean project strategies. The materials team should also review and verify relevant system files, including those containing materials planning data, vendor master data, and price and customer master data that are subject to data load and/or conversion.

The most challenging task that the materials team will complete is developing an overview diagram of each manufacturing and warehouse facility, one that includes a representation of all physical material movement and storage. This material flow diagram will be the standard for discussions and decisions on a wide range of questions and issues and is a further use of the visual management practices of lean production, modified to include the purposes of data and information/support process integration. The material flow diagram includes:

- Work centers
- Work cells
- Assembly lines
- Quality control inspection areas
- Quality control hold areas
- Quality control test areas
- Shipping
- Component staging
- Vendor returns
- Component storage
- Receiving purchased materials
- Receiving outside operations materials
- Customer returns
- Work-in-process staging, racks, lanes
- Finished goods storage, racks, lanes
- Pull locations, racks, lanes
- Scrap areas
- Rework areas
- Shipping lanes
- Docks

The materials team includes on the material flow diagrams the sequence of production activity and material moves for all products, product lines, and production lines. The materials team completes the material flow analysis by verifying one complete BOM and routing for each major product. To complete this important task, the team begins with the finish point of the product and "pulls" through the final assembly, assembly, subassemblies, and raw materials until the complete product structure is accounted for.

Using material movement labels, the team identifies all material consumption, staging, and storage points in the flow by work center or line. Team members verify locations required for material support and illustrate all material storage, staging, and consumption by warehouse, location, and work center or line. Team members use material movement indicators to highlight any material queues and label all pull locations and/or lanes. Care should be taken to highlight stocking levels, paypoints, checkpoints, and backflush points. Figure 10.7 shows an example of the type of diagram that should be produced. Recommended transaction points are labeled on the diagram, and the necessary system transactions are documented. Product flow cycle times (expressed in shifts per day) are also noted. Figure 10.8 provides an example of material flow transactions.

Operations Team Tasks

The operations team is responsible for the activities of process owners and customers in the process areas of production and operations management, maintenance, and quality. The operations team is also assigned the responsibility of improving the previously described maintenance and quality management processes. Along with the other teams, operations team activities include reviewing the project objectives and completing the appropriate Lean Performance Analysis masters to connect their processes to the lean business policies and lean project strategies. The operations team begins by reviewing the proposed BOMs, routings, and material flow generated by the engineering team and the proposed material flow documented by the materials team. Using these preliminary standards, the operations team analyzes product flow, backflush, and the use of paypoints to evaluate their accuracy and adequacy. The team illustrates any process tasks or conditions that are based on or are the result of decisions taken due to plant layout or other physical limitations. If desired, team members can provide recommendations for new layouts where they might be beneficial. Team members identify and correct any work-in-process conditions where material is issued, consumed, and/or moved for longer than one shift per day without a controlling backflush transaction. They also draw attention to any condition where material moves across more than one work center without a controlling backflush or paypoint,

180 ■ Lean Performance ERP Project Management

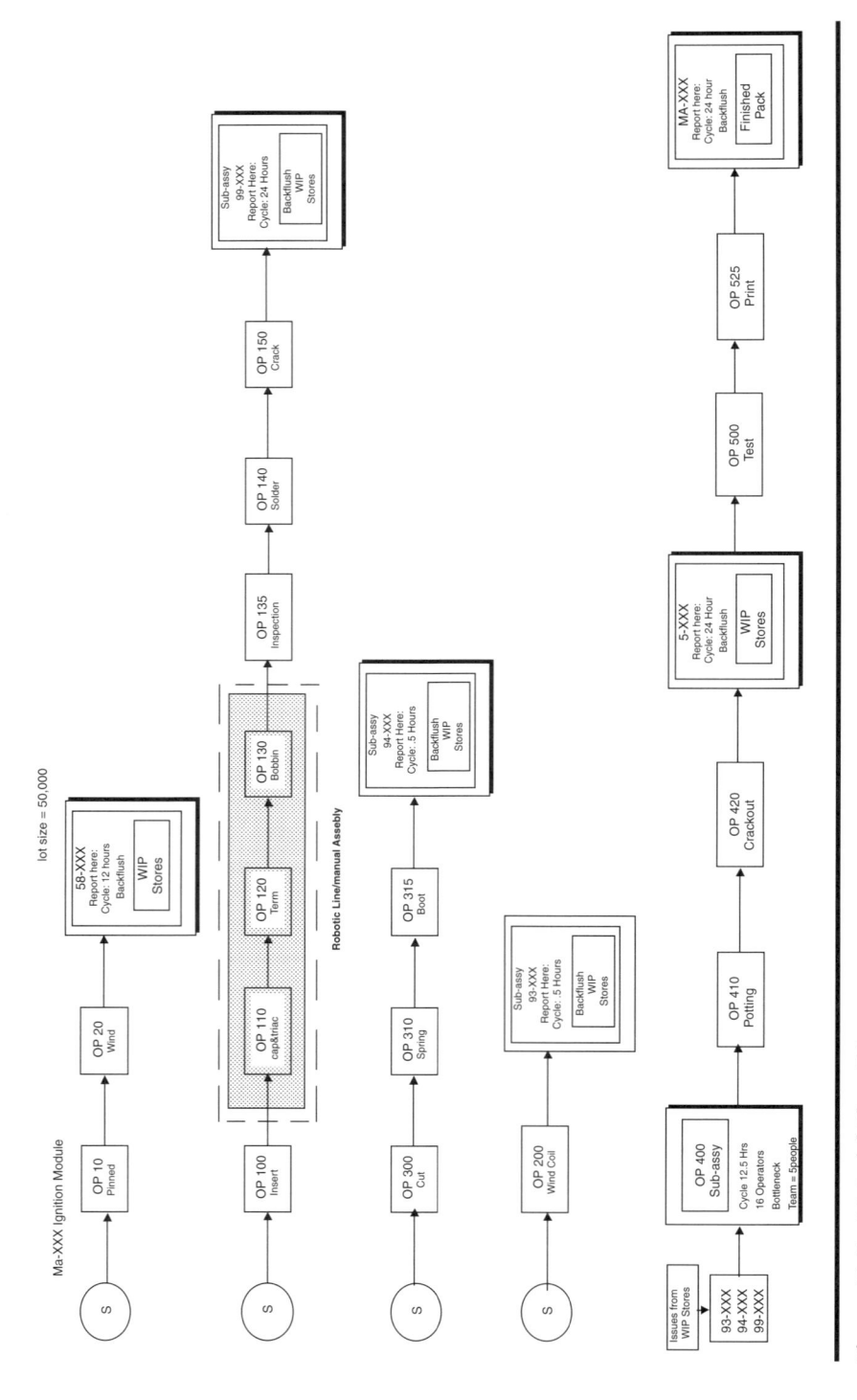

Figure 10.7 Material Flow Diagram

Improving Process Performance Module ■ 181

No.	Description	Transaction	Flow Rate (per hour)
1	Receive raw material, components, and subassemblies from suppliers, outside processes, or outside subassembly department	Receipt to stock location	80
2	Production reporting of finished field coil subassembly by pieces; link to final assembly schedule	Routing paypoint; backflush raw materials	80
3	Production reporting of finished outer frames by standard pallet load	Routing paypoint; backflush frame from storage	80
4	Production reporting of pole face, shift levers, lams, commutators, and commutator ends	Routing paypoint; backflush raw materials	80
5	Receive bar stock	Purchased receipt to stock	80
6	Issue bar stock to production	Material issue to production	80
7	Production reporting of clutch and pinion assembly	Routing paypoint; backflush components	80
8	Production reporting of frame assembly	Routing paypoint; backflush components	80
9	Production reporting of brush	Routing paypoint; backflush raw material	80
10	Production reporting of powder metal inner frame	Routing paypoint; backflush raw material	80
11	Production reporting of shell and pinion; send to outside	Routing paypoint; report scrap operation	80
12	Receive shell and pinion from outside operation	Receive to stock	80
13	Production reporting of shaft; send to outside operation	Routing paypoint; report scrap	80
14	Receive shaft from outside operation	Receive to stock	80
15	Production reporting of armature assembly	Routing paypoint; backflush components	80
16	Production reporting of completed housings	Routing paypoint; backflush components	80
17	Final assembly and paint	Routing paypoint; backflush components; finished goods to stock	80
18	Shipment to customer	Finished goods deduction from stock	80

Figure 10.8 Material Flow Transactions

unless this material flow is continuous without interruption. If the flow is not continuous, the team should develop improvement suggestions and research and test them until a resolution is achieved.

Project result: final BOMs and routings

The operations team also validates the representation of material storage, staging, and consumption by warehouse, location, and work center or line on the material flow diagrams. Team members also confirm the accuracy of the material movement indicators on the material flow diagrams to ensure that all locations required for material support are included. Team members add or delete locations as required.

Project result: final material flow diagrams

Project result: final material flow transactions

Information Team Tasks

One of the more important information team tasks is to plan the data conversion strategy. Working with the finance and engineering teams, the information team considers how to convert the financial and accounting data and map the data to the engineering item master data, wherever possible, as well as how to automate the data load wherever practical. Early on in the planning of the data conversion, the information team should verify the database configuration, which could involve considering a database for simulations and planning and ensuring that multisite product planning and sourcing can be performed if necessary. Consultation with the materials team should provide insight into those issues. The data conversion plan should also define postimplementation system data policy and processes, including real-time data updates and local ownership of processes. The data conversion plan also determines appropriate data export/import and transfer capability among databases after system implementation, especially for special cases such as product designed in one region (data entity) but manufactured in another region (data entity). The information team consults with the project trainer and facilitator to determine the use of the database for training, including periodic refreshes of data and use of data in system testing.

The information team also verifies the findings of the finance, engineering, and materials teams concerning system files subject to data load and/or conversion. This pertains to all engineering data: item masters, BOMs, routings, all finance and accounting data (including work centers), and all materials data (including planning data and vendor masters). The information team has the responsibility of mapping all system fields in the item masters, BOMs, work centers, routings, planning data, customer and vendor masters, etc., for conversion. The information team also verifies basic system capabilities and compatibility and identifies any required data elements that are not provided in the standard software.

The information team obtains agreement from other teams and establishes the structure and use of numbering conventions for implementation, including customer numbers, part numbers, drawing numbers, vendor numbers, and all other system numbering conventions. Needless to say, this can turn into a project in itself. A recommendation here is to avoid the use of significant numbering schemes, at all costs. In fact, this is a good time to revisit the use of numbering schemes in light of the data search capabilities of today's systems and to consider scrapping outdated numbering significance schemes. The information team should also review all team code definitions and recommend revisions where necessary. The team should examine any team-recommended requirements to assign values to available system fields and resolve the use of alphanumeric capabilities.

The information team finalizes ongoing training and education to support the technical aspects of the software and hardware. The information team is responsible for all system-integration tasks, such as those involving customer data, EDI, XML, or FAX. The team coordinates the establishment of systems communications capability and all hardware and software setup (more on this topic below) later in the project cycle. As for the other teams, information team activities include reviewing all lean policies and strategies deployed by the steering committee through the Lean Performance Analysis. The information team contributes to achieving the project objectives by leveraging their knowledge of new system capabilities and providing suggestions to all other teams about the use of new technologies available.

The information team adds their input to the Lean Performance Analysis by completing the information system deployment area of the Lean Performance Analysis masters. The goal here is for the information team members who are specialists in software support to share their knowledge of specific software capability to support management strategies and objectives. In this way, we hope to leverage team members' knowledge of existing business processes and their insights into how new technologies might improve those processes. Information system deployment defines information system functionality sought by team members (system users) to achieve the project objectives. The technology must link to the lean policies and strategies deployed by the steering committee. Essentially, information technology deployment provides the basis for completion of the Lean Performance Analysis. Participation in policy deployment enables any information technical expertise to benefit the project by demonstrating the practical use of new system capabilities. In this way, the information

184 ■ Lean Performance ERP Project Management

```
Lean Business Policy:          Support Lean Manufacturing           Control
Lean Project Strategy:         Reduce Storage of WIP/Stage Mat'l    Number
Project Objective:             Eliminate Returned Goods Room        001-001-001-001
Technology Deployment:         Implement Online Credit Capability
Process Identification:
Lean Performance Team:
```

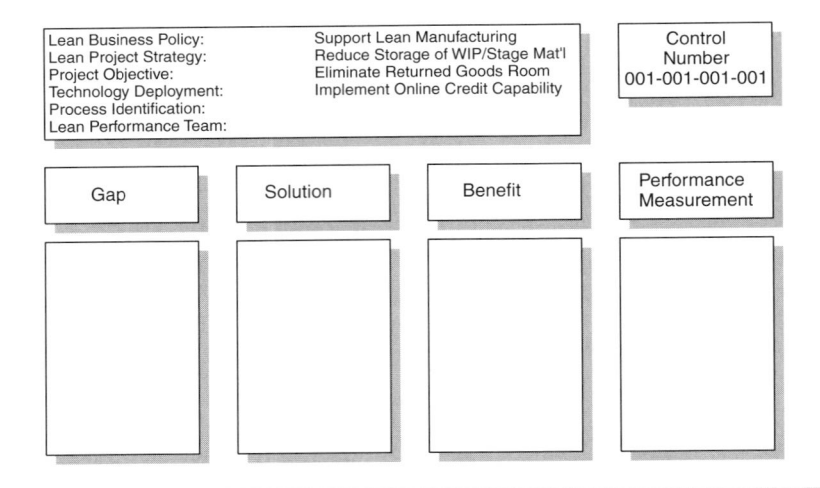

Gap	Solution	Benefit	Performance Measurement

Figure 10.9 Lean Performance Analysis: Technology Deployed

team members are pointing the way to other teams to consider the use of new technologies in their processes.

Upon completion of the Lean Performance Analysis, information system deployment occurs when the information systems support engineers review the project strategies and suggest new or improved system capabilities that they have uncovered in the enabling software already present in the business or available to the project, whether it be enterprise resource management (ERP), manufacturing execution system (MES), operations planning system (OPS), customer relationship management (CRM), or supply chain management (SCM). The information systems support engineers tend to have more familiarity with new and available systems capabilities, and they can assist process owners in taking best advantage of the new system tools at a process level. Later, during the Lean Performance Analysis GAP exercise, information team members will play a critical role in suggesting software improvements to close documented system GAPs as they arise. For example, to support a deployed lean business policy of *supporting lean manufacturing* with a deployed lean project strategy of *reducing manufacturing inventory* which generates a project objective of *eliminating the returned-goods storeroom*, technology deployment might include *utilizing the online credit capability of the software* (Figure 10.9).

The appropriate process team reviews the Lean Performance Analysis technology and investigates the potential for incorporating this new tool at the process level, for whatever process the team members feel is appropriate. The Lean Performance Analysis masters are distributed to the project team for review. Consider an aftermarket operations team determining that the fuel pump return process is a viable candidate for online credit capability. By revisiting the Lean Performance Analysis masters, the team is able to provide a summary report for the steering committee early in the Lean Performance Analysis. At this point, the masters should be distributed to all project team members for review and identification of the necessary processes and teams. Figure 10.10 summarizes the technology deployment examples that correlate to the lean business policies, lean project strategies, and project objectives examples shown in Figure 7.8. The information team activities also include managing the data conversion activities and system enhancements that are supported by the Lean Performance Analysis and approved by the steering committee. We will discuss the information team responsibility of performing and administering the stress test below.

Lean Commerce Team Tasks

Lean commerce relies upon an integrated approach to products, product structures, and data systems to supply the materials to manufacture what customers want when they want it. As the process test and eventual system implementation draw nearer, confidence in full-system integrated functionality becomes more critical. A preliminary process is necessary to determine the validity of critical EDI/XML and system programs and transactions affecting customer order recognition, order processing, and shipping, including ASNs. These lean commerce team activities are necessary to validate customer-sensitive system results and develop and perform data and logic testing on critical customer-facing processes. It may be necessary to design, develop, test, and implement additional system processes and capabilities to produce accurate EDI/XML data and enhance the customer-facing processes.

The lean commerce team reviews and expands the use of lean principles, tools, and practices across all the business processes in the company now that the team members have gained wider experience with lean applications as well as familiarity with the capabilities of new software to support the improved processes. This is especially necessary in environments where a best-of-breed solution is being leveraged and multiple vendors and packages have to be utilized in single or related cross-functional and eventually cross-enterprise processes. After testing, the lean commerce team designs new processes for utilizing the EDI/XML data for production planning and master scheduling to incorporate lean production smoothing and advanced production scheduling (APS) techniques. The lean commerce team should design new processes for customer data management, where needed, including customer masters, pricing (including retroactive pricing) contracts, and order management data. The team also

MANAGEMENT POLICY DEPLOYMENT AND MEASUREMENTS SUMMARY

GAP CONTROL#	LEAN BUSINESS POLICY	LEAN PROJECT STRATEGY	DEPLOYED PROJECT OBJECTIVE	TECHNOLOGY DEPLOYMENT	PROCESS IDENTIFICATION	LEAN PERFORMANCE TEAM	PERFORMANCE MEASUREMENT
001	Support Lean Manufacturing	Reduce Manufacturing Lead Time	Implement 24 hour turnaround of customer orders	Use system capability to generates pick/pack lists throughout the day			
002	Support Lean Manufacturing	Reduce Manufacturing Inventory	Implement iPulli supplier management practices	Set the item master to create commodity order recommendations at quantity/price break chosen			
003	Support Lean Manufacturing	Reduce Manufacturing Inventory	Eliminate returned goods storeroom	Utilize online credit capability of software			
004	Support Lean Manufacturing	Implement Flexibility for Low Volume Products	Implement manufacturing line sequencing	Utilize system capability to sequence models and variations within a model on all lines.			
005	Support Lean Manufacturing	Implement Flexibility for Low Volume Products	Implement multi-plant sourcing of finished goods	Implement multi-plant MPS capability, including capacity simulations			
006	Support Lean Manufacturing	Implement Flexibility for Low Volume Products	Implement EDI/XML or other E-Commerce solution for interplant orders	Use messaging feature to notify placement of multiplant requirements immediately			
007	Support Lean Manufacturing	Implement Supplier Partnerships And Certification	Implement a pay-on-receipt process for vendors	Allow vendors access into delivery and schedule screens to manage JIT deliveries			
008	Support Lean Manufacturing	Implement Activity Based Costing	Establish Product Target Costing/ MUDA Free Product Target Costs	Establish simulation costing database for development of additional cost data			

Figure 10.10 Policy Deployment and Measurements Summary — Technology Deployed

designs any required new processes from customer order entry through shipping, evaluates packaged software alternatives to existing EDI or XML systems, and prepares cost analyses for any additional capability sought.

An evaluation of the benefits and costs of bringing in a new software system vs. enhancing the current system should be completed prior to any

MANAGEMENT POLICY DEPLOYMENT AND MEASUREMENTS SUMMARY

GAP CONTROL#	LEAN BUSINESS POLICY	LEAN PROJECT STRATEGY	DEPLOYED PROJECT OBJECTIVE	TECHNOLOGY DEPLOYMENT	PROCESS IDENTIFICATION	LEAN PERFORMANCE TEAM	PERFORMANCE MEASUREMENT
009	Support Lean Manufacturing	Implement Process Integrated Document Tools	Implement Bar Coding for Plant Documents	System can be set up to print readable part #'s on orders and pick lists			
010	Support Lean Manufacturing	Implement Process Integrated Bar Coding	Implement Bar Coding for Customer Requirements	Use system capability to scan confirm shipment, scan shipping charges, and produce labels			
011	Support Lean Thinking in the Global Standardization of Engineering Processes	Design and Utilize Concurrent Engineering Processes	Provide access to engineering product data at the manufacturing sites	Use system capability to support online real-time access at all sites, at all times			
012	Support Lean Thinking in the Global Standardization of Engineering Processes	Provide a Standard Software Format for Engineering Product Data Management	Implement a standard software package for engineering product data management	Investigate 3rd party and interface options utilizing system data for Item Master, BOM, Routing, etc.			
013	Support Lean Thinking in the Global Standardization of Financial Processes	Implement Central Cash Management	Determine and accommodate financial requirements of Canada, Europe (EU, VAT), Asia	Bolt-on 3rd party capability in place for project use			
014	Support Lean Thinking in the Global Standardization of Financial Processes	Implement Central Cash Management	Include currency considerations	Can utilize system settings configured to example attached			
015	Support Lean Thinking in the Global Standardization of Financial Processes	Implement Centralized Integrated Processing of Period Financial Closings	Consolidate Regional Financial Statements	Reports should be hard-coded to utilize data available			
016	Support Lean Thinking in the Global Standardization of Financial Processes	Implement Centralized Integrated Processing of Period Financial Closings	Consolidate global financial statements	Reports should be hard-coded to utilize data available			

Figure 10.10 Policy Deployment and Measurements Summary — Technology Deployed (cont.)

purchase (although, all things being equal, it is generally best to go with vendor-supplied software). To effectively consider whether to bring in a new package or go forward with the existing one, an education process should occur that explores EDI/XML processing for manufacturing. If possible, benchmarking should be utilized to assess comparable processes

MANAGEMENT POLICY DEPLOYMENT AND MEASUREMENTS SUMMARY

GAP CONTROL#	LEAN BUSINESS POLICY	LEAN PROJECT STRATEGY	DEPLOYED PROJECT OBJECTIVE	TECHNOLOGY DEPLOYMENT	PROCESS IDENTIFICATION	LEAN PERFORMANCE TEAM	PERFORMANCE MEASUREMENT
017	Support Lean Thinking in the Global Standardization of Financial Processes	Implement Centralized Integrated Data Support, Processing and Monitoring of the Business Plan	Develop global standard reporting formats	Refer to Steering Committee for design of reports			
018	Support Lean Thinking in the Global Standardization of Financial Processes	Implement Centralized Integrated Data Support, Processing and Monitoring of the Business Plan	Monitor, evaluate and report product line and manufacturing site profitability	Refer to Steering Committee for design of reports			
019	Support Lean Thinking in the Global Standardization of Financial Processes	Implement Centralized Integrated Data Support, Processing and Monitoring of the Business Plan	Develop Period-To-Date reporting, including Regional Sales, Margins and Trends	Refer to Steering Committee for design of reports			
020	Support Lean Thinking in the Global Standardization of Information Systems Management	Implement Global Standard Hardware and Software	Implement unmodified software packages	Modify Open Issue approvals only			
021	Support Lean Thinking in the Global Standardization of Information Systems Management	Implement Global Standard Hardware and Software	Leverage vendor supplied software upgrades	Maintain simulation database to apply upgrades and 3rd party			
022	Support Lean Thinking in the Global Standardization of Information Systems Management	Implement Global Information Technology Processes and Organization	Implement secure data & operations processes in a system that is seamless to the users	Utilize a systems management tool for all operations changes			
023	Support Lean Thinking in the Global Standardization of Information Systems Management	Implement Global Information Technology Processes and Organization	Implement standards for systems uptime and reliability and measure and report performance	Identify all data and systems operations processes for measurement			
024							

Figure 10.10 Policy Deployment and Measurements Summary — Technology Deployed (cont.)

in other similar businesses. Team assignments are then defined during a project planning activity that is followed by the actual assessment process. Depending on the results of the assessment process, the team will either proceed with improvements to the existing system or implement a new package along with any additional improvements.

The lean commerce team then evaluates the scheduling processes in each plant in terms of overall effectiveness and efficiencies. Following this assessment, the lean commerce team should then design the lean improvements and/or new processes according to the findings of the assessments. The team develops requirements for implementing the model by concentrating on product structure, policy, development, processes, and training and recommends the necessary information system capabilities. The lean commerce team then builds the improvements, defines an implementation plan, and implements the plan. This process could be performed one plant at a time but would probably be more efficient if all plants were included as one project, particularly when the plants are interdependent or building the same or similar products. This is especially true from the standpoints of material planning and the desirability of developing new information systems capabilities from a uniform and complete design.

The lean commerce team then concentrates on shopfloor improvements, primarily pull systems. The initial team goal should be to define a specific area of a specific plant and build an effective model. The requirements for implementing the model can then be identified with operations, material, and system implications defined. When the lean commerce team builds an implementation plan and implements it, members of the team should include the process area coordinators and appropriate support from all process areas including finance, engineering, materials, operations, and information teams. The final activities for the lean commerce team are to establish the usage of system codes and develop the final control file configuration for the system. These activities are best performed during the process test later in the project when all process owners have had the opportunity to work with the software.

Performing Lean Performance Analysis

The Lean Performance Analysis tasks are the heart of the Lean Performance project. It would be reasonable to state that every task prior to this one has been a preparation for this task. Prior to the session, each team submits their selected Lean Performance Analysis masters for team distribution (Figure 10.11). The project manager should also distribute the summary status at this time (Figure 10.12). Completing the Lean Performance Analysis throughout the enterprise means that the teams improve all processes, produce process workflow, and work instruction standards; identify all process or system GAPs; document solutions to those GAPs; document the benefit to be obtained by implementing the new process or solution; and define a performance measurement for the new process solution. This is a fairly tall order. Before we describe the Lean Performance practices to accomplish that tall order, let's step back a bit.

190 ■ Lean Performance ERP Project Management

Lean Business Policy:	Support Lean Manufacturing	Control Number
Lean Project Strategy:	Reduce Storage of WIP/Stage Mat'l	001-001-001-001
Project Objective:	Eliminate Returned Goods Room	
Technology Deployment:	Implement Online Credit Capability	
Process Identification:	Fuel Pump Returns	
Lean Performance Team:	Aftermarket Operations Team	

| Gap | Solution | Benefit | Performance Measurement |

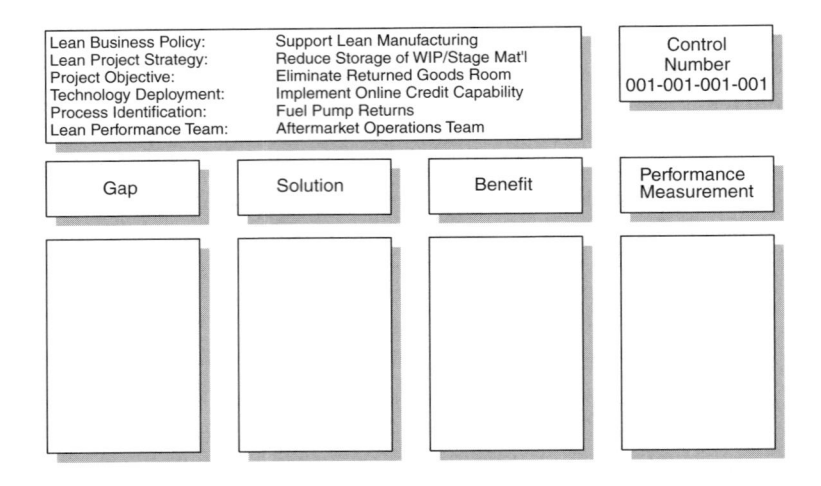

Figure 10.11 Lean Performance Analysis: Process and Team Identified

A process must be identified and diagnosed (analyzed) before it can be improved. Often, this is not done systematically for several reasons. Perhaps the most prevalent reason is the denial of the existence of process problems, often in defense of process owners or the owning departments. There is also a tendency to move directly to a solution, even if it is inappropriate or at best a quick fix. Lack of knowledge about operations, problem areas, or systematic problem identification and diagnosis techniques can also lead to spirited defense of the process *status quo*. Power politics can sometimes play a defeating role as well. In technical innovation projects, the tendency to jump to the solution is great because of fascination with the possibilities of the technology itself. The Lean Performance Analysis approach assumes that all lean improvements to a process must provide added customer value or else they are not lean improvements and the activity has been a waste of time and money. Adding *muda* to a process is not an improvement because there is no customer value in waste.

Lean Performance Analysis uses the lean principles, lean diagnostic tools, and Lean Performance practices to identify process problems and opportunities. The analysis begins with defining specific elements of the problems and opportunities during completion of the process workflow. During this task, we make observations and gather data and owner/customer input that provide the basis for an analysis of data to determine the root causes of process problems. The general guidelines of Lean Performance Analysis are:

- Lean cultural principles govern.
- Challenge power players and those who work to subvert the open process of discussion and solution.

MANAGEMENT POLICY DEPLOYMENT AND MEASUREMENTS SUMMARY

GAP CONTROL#	LEAN BUSINESS POLICY	LEAN PROJECT STRATEGY	DEPLOYED PROJECT OBJECTIVE	TECHNOLOGY DEPLOYMENT	PROCESS IDENTIFICATION	LEAN PERFORMANCE TEAM	PERFORMANCE MEASUREMENT
001	Support Lean Manufacturing	Reduce Manufacturing Lead Time	Implement 24 hour turnaround of customer orders	Use system capability to generates pick/pack lists throughout the day	Customer Order Processing	Materials Team	
002	Support Lean Manufacturing	Reduce Manufacturing Inventory	Implement iPull supplier management practices	Set the item master to create commodity order recommendations at quantity/price break chosen	Vendor Order Management	Materials Team	
003	Support Lean Manufacturing	Reduce Manufacturing Inventory	Eliminate returned goods storeroom	Utilize online credit capability of software	Fuel Pump Returns	Aftermarket Operations Team	
004	Support Lean Manufacturing	Implement Flexibility for Low Volume Products	Implement manufacturing line sequencing	Utilize system capability to sequence models and variations within a model on all lines	Injector Line Management	Injector Operations Team	
005	Support Lean Manufacturing	Implement Flexibility for Low Volume Products	Implement multi-plant sourcing of finished goods	Implement multi-plant MPS capability, including capacity simulations	Advanced Production Placement	Materials Team	
006	Support Lean Manufacturing	Implement Flexibility for Low Volume Products	Implement EDI/XML or other E-Commerce solution for interplant orders	Use messaging feature to notify placement of multiplant requirements immediately	Advanced Production Placement	Materials Team	
007	Support Lean Manufacturing	Implement Supplier Partnerships And Certification	Implement a pay-on-receipt process for vendors	Allow vendors access into delivery and schedule screens to manage JIT deliveries	Vendor Order Management	Materials Team	
008	Support Lean Manufacturing	Implement Activity Based Costing	Establish Product Target Costing/MUDA Free Product Target Costs	Establish simulation costing database for development of additional cost data	Customer Order Quoting	Materials Team	

Figure 10.12 Policy Deployment and Measurements Summary — Process and Team Identified

- Observe the workplace; only here will you be able to make the observations, collect the data, and elicit the process owner and customer insights that will provide the basis for Lean Performance.
- Focus as soon as possible on a specific process problem or opportunity.

MANAGEMENT POLICY DEPLOYMENT AND MEASUREMENTS SUMMARY

GAP CONTROL#	LEAN BUSINESS POLICY	LEAN PROJECT STRATEGY	DEPLOYED PROJECT OBJECTIVE	TECHNOLOGY DEPLOYMENT	PROCESS IDENTIFICATION	LEAN PERFORMANCE TEAM	PERFORMANCE MEASUREMENT
009	Support Lean Manufacturing	Implement Process Integrated Document Tools	Implement Bar Coding for Plant Documents	System can be set up to print readable part#'s on orders and pick lists	Manufacturing Order Management	Operations Team	
010	Support Lean Manufacturing	Implement Process Integrated Bar Coding	Implement Bar Coding for Customer Requirements:	Use system capability to scan confirm shipment, scan shipping charges, and produce labels	Customer Order Management	Materials Management	
011	Support Lean Thinking in the Global Standardization of Engineering Processes	Design and Utilize Concurrent Engineering Processes	Provide access to engineering product data at the manufacturing sites.	Use system capability to support online real-time access at all sites, at all times	New Product Introduction	Engineering Team	
012	Support Lean Thinking in the Global Standardization of Engineering Processes	Provide a Standard Software Format For Engineering Product Data Management	Implement a standard software package for engineering product data management	Investigate 3rd party and interface options utilizing system data for Item Master, BOM, Routing etc.	New Product Introduction	Engineering Team	
013	Support Lean Thinking in the Global Standardization of Financial Processes	Implement Central Cash Management	Determine and accommodate financial requirements of Canada, Europe (EU, VAT), Asia.	Bolt-on 3rd party capability in place for project use	Accounts Receivable	Finance Team	
014	Support Lean Thinking in the Global Standardization of Financial Processes	Implement Central Cash Management	Include currency considerations	Can utilize system settings configured to example attached.	Accounts Receivable	Finance Team	
015	Support Lean Thinking in the Global Standardization of Financial Processes	Implement Centralized Integrated Processing of Period Financial Closings	Consolidate Regional Financial Statements	Reports should be hard-coded to utilize data available.	Financial Statement Reports Processing	Finance Team	
016	Support Lean Thinking in the Global Standardization of Financial Processes	Implement Centralized Integrated Processing of Period Financial Closings	Consolidate global financial statements	Reports should be hard-coded to utilize data available.	Financial Statement Reports Processing	Finance Team	

Figure 10.12 Policy Deployment and Measurements Summary — Process and Team Identified (cont.)

- Use the Lean Performance Analysis steps systematically.
- Make a thorough diagnosis of the process.
- Always work in teams (be sure there are no "Lone Rangers," especially those with personal agendas masquerading as processes or solutions).

MANAGEMENT POLICY DEPLOYMENT AND MEASUREMENTS SUMMARY

GAP CONTROL#	LEAN BUSINESS POLICY	LEAN PROJECT STRATEGY	DEPLOYED PROJECT OBJECTIVE	TECHNOLOGY DEPLOYMENT	PROCESS IDENTIFICATION	LEAN PERFORMANCE TEAM	PERFORMANCE MEASUREMENT
017	Support Lean Thinking in the Global Standardization of Financial Processes	Implement Centralized Integrated Data Support, Processing and Monitoring of the Business Plan	Develop global standard reporting formats	Refer to Steering Committee for design of reports	Business Plan Performance Status	Finance Team	
018	Support Lean Thinking in the Global Standardization of Financial Processes	Implement Centralized Integrated Data Support, Processing and Monitoring of the Business Plan	Monitor, evaluate and report product line and manufacturing site profitability	Refer to Steering Committee for design of reports	Business Plan Performance Status	Finance Team	
019	Support Lean Thinking in the Global Standardization of Financial Processes	Implement Centralized Integrated Data Support, Processing and Monitoring of the Business Plan	Develop Period-To-Date reporting, including Regional Sales, Margins and Trends	Refer to Steering Committee for design of reports	Business Plan Performance Status	Finance Team	
020	Support Lean Thinking in the Global Standardization of Information Systems Management	Implement Global Standard Hardware and Software	Implement unmodified software packages	Modify Open Issue approvals only	Change Management Process	Information Team	
021	Support Lean Thinking in the Global Standardization of Information Systems Management	Implement Global Standard Hardware and Software	Leverage vendor supplied software upgrades	Maintain simulation database to apply upgrades and 3rd party	Change Management Process	Information Team	
022	Support Lean Thinking in the Global Standardization of Information Systems Management	Implement Global Information Technology Processes and Organization	Implement secure data & operations processes in a system that is seamless to the users.	Utilize a systems management tool for all operations changes	Change Management Process	Information Team	
023	Support Lean Thinking in the Global Standardization of Information Systems Management	Implement Global Information Technology Processes and Organization	Implement standards for systems uptime and reliability and measure and report performance	Identify all data and systems operations processes for measurement	Systems Operations Processes	Information Team	
024							

Figure 10.12 Policy Deployment and Measurements Summary — Process and Team Identified (cont.)

- Produce a process workflow standard for documentation; process documentation provides the vehicle for further understanding, suggestions, and improvements.
- Do not jump ahead to a favorite solution; gather complete data on each process *what* first.

- Distinguish between process analysis and solution; use any relevant lean diagnostic tool as a basically open-ended checklist to focus and trigger observation, analysis, and improvement, including:
  - SDCA (standardize/do/check/act) and PDCA (plan/do/check/act)
  - 3MUs (*muda, mura, muri*)
  - 5Ss (sort, straighten, scrub, systematize, sustain)
  - 5Ws–1H (who, what, where, when, why, and how)
  - 4Ms (man, machine, material, and method)

Lean Performance Analysis utilizes the SDCA cycle, in which the process is:

- Standardized (identified and mapped): Process tasks are designed or identified with the process owners or customers at the *what* level, value-added tasks are confirmed, and current necessary tasks are challenged.
- Done (measured and improved): Measurements are identified at process checkpoints, tasks are mapped to process enablers (including new technologies) by the process owners, the process is improved to leverage new technology, unmodified software is applied, and the process workflow or other standard is produced.
- Checked (tested): Processes outputs are produced to the new standards in a test mode, GAPs are identified and solved, and measurements are confirmed at process checkpoints.
- Acted upon (implemented): Process owner acceptance is confirmed, process customer accepts output, process control and checkpoints are accepted, and process work instructions are completed.

After the project is completed, a PDCA cycle will be employed to continuously improve enterprise Lean Performance. Continuous Lean Performance allows lean enterprise environments that maintain process standards to plan process improvements by utilizing the Lean Performance Analysis cycle. In the ongoing PDCA cycle, proposed changes are documented on the process standard, process changes are done in test mode, results are checked, and new process designs are acted upon (implemented).

The Lean Performance Analysis SDCA/PDCA cycle develops process standards to ensure that your best practices are being followed. Following process standards results in processes that deliver high quality. Errors are prevented. Communication is possible. Successful application of the various lean diagnostic tools checklists usually precedes any attempt at a Lean Performance project in the information/support and management decision processes. Existing checklists already in use or the checklists presented in Chapter 6 can be adapted to the information/support and management decision process areas. Imagine using the 5S checklist in the computer room! Great results can follow if the tools are used with uniformity and humor. Finally, the Lean Performance Analysis improves processes. An improved process necessarily changes how work moves through the process. An improved process changes organizational responsibility assignments in that it changes how work is done. Inevitably, when the process work is completed, organizational structuring work will be necessary. This restructuring will be addressed in the third phase of the project, continuous Lean Performance.

In order to complete the Lean Performance Analysis, we first must complete the process workflow task, which is begun by making sure that all information/support processes have been identified, by verifying process owners and customers, and by confirming the identification of these processes with the process owners and customers. The process workflow is developed by these process owners and customers, all of whom should agree to a process purpose statement. Existing documents and drawings or secondhand sources should not be used to develop the diagram. The project facilitator should create a spreadsheet or other management tool to schedule process definition meetings for process owners and customers (Figure 10.13). To complete this analysis,

- Follow one unit of work — an item, lot, order, or batch — through the entire process as it is currently performed.
- Define and map the steps or tasks of the process at a detailed input/output level to identify process requirements.
- Document every step in the process, including disruptions in the flow.
- Identify what *really* happens, not what is supposed to happen.
- Illustrate the *what* portion of the process (e.g., what tasks must be done to produce the desired output).

It is essential to begin to ask ourselves why we perform each task during the requirements definition activity so we retain only the value-added tasks in the process to produce outputs that our customers value. Figure 10.14 shows an example of a process at the requirements definition or task level. Process owners then prepare a draft process workflow of their processes with on the task section (process requirements) completed.

Project result: "before" process diagram

Now the process owners use each lean principle to examine the "before" process workflow diagram. They are looking for any deviation from lean principles and any non-value-added tasks and interruptions. We said earlier that the Lean Performance project would be governed by applying the lean cultural and lean transformational principles to the information/sup-

196 ■ Lean Performance ERP Project Management

Level														
1	Business Planning				Sales			Customer Service						
2	Analyze Sales History	Analyze Open Orders	Analyze Seasonal Trends	Analyze Other Business Trends	Generate Forecast	Pricing	Analysis	Order Entry						
3								Customer Profile Management	Establish Part Cross References	Receive Order				
										Receive EDI Order	Receive Mail Order	Receive FAX Order	Receive Telephone Order
4 ID NUMBER	1100	1200	1300	1400	1500	2100	2200	3110	3120		3131	3132	3133	3134
PRIORITY														
C/S	A	0	0	0	0	0	0	0	0		0	0	0	0
STATUS OPEN	1	1	1	1	1	1	1	1	1		1	1	1	1
ACTIVE	1													
CLOSED TOTAL	1	1	1	1	1	1	1	1	1		1	1	1	1
RESOURCE														
List All Process Owners and Customers														
		1	1	1	1	1	1	1	1		1	1	1	1
	1	1	1	1	1	1	1	3	5		3	3	3	3

Figure 10.13 Process Requirements Definition: Interview and Status Listing

Level														
1														
2													Customer Returns	
3	Receive Internal Order	Verify Pricing / Terms / Credit	Determine Delivery Date	Allocate Available Inventory	Determine Production Lead Time	Maintain Credit Data	Enter Order	Notify Production	Customer Order Change Management	Receive Request	Return Authorization	Approve Return	Assign Control Number
4 ID NUMBER	3135	3140	3151	3152	3153	3160	3170	3180	3190	3211		322	3213
PRIORITY C/S													
STATUS OPEN	O 1	O 1	O 1	O 1	O 1	O 1	O 1	O 1	O 1	O 1		O 1	O 1
ACTIVE													
CLOSED													
TOTAL	1	1	1	1	1	1	1	1	1	1		1	1
RESOURCE List All Process	1	1	1	1	1		1 1			1		1	1
Owners and Customers	1	1	1	1	1	1	1		1	1		1	
TOTAL	3	3	5	5	5	1	3	3	3	2		2	2

Figure 10.13 Process Requirements Definition: Interview and Status Listing (cont.)

Level				Receive Material	Material Disposition Determine Cause/Fault	Document Conclusion	Decide Final Disposition	Move Material	Issue Credit	Customer Billing Print Invoice	Mail Invoice	Notify Finance	Resolve Problems	Operations Management Capacity Planning Capacity Data Management Determine Machine Capacities	Monitor For Accuracy
1															
2															
3				3220	3231	3232	3233	3234	3240	3310	3320	3330	3340	4111	4112
4															
ID NUMBER															
PRIORITY															
C/S															
STATUS															
OPEN				0	0	0	0	0	0	0	0	0	0	0	0
				1	1	1	1	1	1	1	1	1	1	1	1
ACTIVE				1	1	1	1	1	1	1	1	1	1	1	1
CLOSED															
TOTAL															
RESOURCE															
List All Process				1	1	1	1	1		1	1	1	1		
Owners and Customers										1	1	1	1		
						1	1	1						1	
					1										
									1	1	1	1	1	1	1
				1	3	3	3	3	2	3	3	3	3	1	1

Figure 10.13 Process Requirements Definition: Interview and Status Listing (cont.)

Figure 10.13 Process Requirements Definition: Interview and Status Listing (cont.)

200 ■ Lean Performance ERP Project Management

Level											
1		Supplier Management									
2	Maintain BOM Data	Purchase Plan Preparation	Quotations					Purchase Order Processing			
3			Receive Production Demand	Receive Non-Production Demand	Request Quotes	Analyze Bids	Select Suppliers	Generate Purchase Order	Receive Demand Data	Review/ Revise	Generate Spot Buys
4											
ID NUMBER	5300	6100	6210	6220	6230	6240	6250	6260	6310	6320	6330
PRIORITY											
C/S											
STATUS											
OPEN	0	0	0	0	0	0	0	0	0	0	0
ACTIVE	1	1	1	1	1	1	1	1	1	1	1
CLOSED											
TOTAL	1	1	1	1	1	1	1	1	1	1	1
RESOURCE											
List All Process	1										
Owners and Customers	1	1			1		1	1	1	1	1
			1	1	1	1	1	1	1	1	1
			1	1	2	1	1	2	1	1	2
	2										

Figure 10.13 Process Requirements Definition: Interview and Status Listing (cont.)

Level					Inventory Management						
1											
2			Supplier Data Maintenance	Supplier Follow-Up	Receiving	Receiving Inspection	Warehousing	Store Finished Product	Cycle Counting	Annual Physical Inventory	Shipping Receive Ship Requests
3		Release Blanket Orders					Store Components				
4											
ID NUMBER	6340	6400	6500	7100	7200	7310	7320	7330	7340	7410
PRIORITY C/S											
STATUS OPEN	O 1	O 1	O 1	O 1	O 1	O 1	O 1	O 1	O 1	O 1
ACTIVE											
CLOSED											
TOTAL	1	1	1	1	1	1	1	1	1	1
RESOURCE											
List All Process					1						
Owners and Customers									1		
				1				1			
		1				1	1			1	1
	1	1	2	1							2

Figure 10.13 Process Requirements Definition: Interview and Status Listing (cont.)

202 ■ Lean Performance ERP Project Management

Level												
1												Quality Management
2									Inventory Planning			Supplier Quality Monitoring
3	Prepare Shipments	Select Carrier	Prepare Shipping Documents	Load Carrier	Shop Floor Reporting	Report Production	Report Discrepancies	Prepare Customs Documents		Determine Lead Times	Determine Lot Sizes	Determine Time Fences	
4													
ID NUMBER	7420	7430	7440	7450		7510	7520	7600	7710	7720	7730	8100
PRIORITY												
C/S												
STATUS	O	O	O	O		O	O	O	O	O	O	O
OPEN	1	1	1	1		1	1	1	1	1	1	1
ACTIVE												
CLOSED												
TOTAL	1	1	1	1		1	1	1	1	1	1	1
RESOURCE												
List All Process	1	1	1			1						
Owners and Customers							1	1				
							1		1	1	1	1
				1			1					
	1	1	1	1		1		1	1	1	1	1
	2	2	3	1		2	2	2	1	2	2	3

Figure 10.13 Process Requirements Definition: Interview and Status Listing (cont.)

	Level 1	2	3	4		Financial					
		Material Deviation Control	Product Certifications		Receivables	Payables	General Ledger	Budgeting	Costing		
ID NUMBER		8200	8300		9100	9200	9300	9400	9500		
PRIORITY											
C/S											
STATUS											
OPEN		0	0		0	0	0	0	0		87
ACTIVE		1	1		1	1	1	1	1		1
CLOSED											0
TOTAL		1	1		1	1	1	1	1		88
RESOURCE											22
List All Process											13
Owners and Customers											22
											5
					1		1		1		5
		1	1								4
											3
		1	1								2
							2	1	1		27
											5
											1
											18
											1
											4
											1
		1	1		1						18
											16
											11
		3	3		2	1	1	2	2		179

Figure 10.13 Process Requirements Definition: Interview and Status Listing (cont.)

Customer Profile Management (1.3.1.1)	Customer Order Change Management (1.3.1.2)	Receive Order (1.3.1.3)	Verify Pricing (1.3.1.4)	Verify Terms (1.3.1.5)	Determine Delivery Date (1.3.1.6)	Maintain Credit Data (1.3.1.7)	Enter Order (1.3.1.8)	Notify Production (1.3.1.9)
Record Transit Times		Receive EDI Order			Determine Availability			
Record Ship Via		Receive Mail Order			Allocate Available Inventory			
Record Ship Days		Receive Fax Order			Determine Production Lead time			
Record Part Cross Refs		Receive Telephone Order			Verify Credit			
Record Customer Contacts		Receive Internal Order						

Figure 10.14 Process Requirements Definition: Order Entry

port and management decision processes. The Lean Performance Analysis is brought into sharper focus by applying the lean transformational principles to the emerging process workflow (Womack, J., and Jones, D., *Lean Thinking: Banish Waste and Create Wealth in Your Corporation,* Simon & Schuster, 1996):

- Precisely specify the value by product or family.
- Identify the value stream for each product.
- Make the value flow without interruption.
- Let the customer pull value from the process owner.
- Pursue perfection.

*Precisely Specify the Value by Product or Family**

Value is that product or service that process customers would specify as being what they need as the output from a given process. It is measured by what the customer is willing to pay. It can be discovered by taking the role of the customer and asking, "If I was the customer of this process, would I be willing to pay for it?"

Another way to think about value is

Customer value = what the customer got ÷ what it cost the customer

(Source: Adair, C.B., and Murray, B.A., *Breakthrough Process Redesign: New Pathways to Customer Value,* AMACOM, New York, 1994, p. 56.)

To precisely specify value by product or family is a broader concept than what we are attempting to address here. It is more to our purpose to target this activity as *precisely specify value by process and/or within process.* To do so, the process owners and customers ask and answer the following questions about their processes:

- Can you clearly identify the process?
- Is there an up-to-date process standard (BOM, routing, procedure, work instruction) with all the process tasks or steps identified?
- Could anyone in the company perform the process after some training, based on the process standards?

*Identify the Value Stream for Each Product**

We are going to need to start with a slight modification of this principle in that we are dealing with processes, and in a typical company many of these processes may involve one or more products. It would be more to

---

* Adapted from Womack, J., and Jones, D., *Lean Thinking: Banish Waste and Create Wealth in Your Corporation,* Simon & Schuster, 1996.

Table 10.1 Value-Added and Non-Value-Added Processes

Value-Added	Non-Value-Added
Ordering	Waiting
Fabricating	Counting
Assembling	Inspecting
Packing	Checking
Shipping	Copying
Filing a claim	Filing

Source: Adair, C.B. and Murray, B.A., *Breakthrough Process Redesign: New Pathways to Customer Value*, AMACOM, New York, 1994, p. 119. With permission.

our purpose to identify the value stream for each process. The process owners and customers should be looking for value-added tasks to retain in their process (see Table 10.1) and should try to eliminate such non-value-added activities as:

- Expediting
- Temporary processes
- Workarounds
- Supplemental processes
- Extra systems
- Formal vs. informal systems

Next, the teams should determine if they have identified any additional tasks performed in the process that are not yet included on the process workflow standard and should ask if those tasks provide customer value (i.e., would customers pay for them if they knew we were doing them?). The teams should analyze each task on the process workflow diagram for value-added process time, using measurements such as dates and time stamps. Usually, value-added time will be measured in minutes and non-value-added time in hours or days. The teams then complete an improved process workflow diagram that does not include the non-value-added steps/tasks. Unfortunately, many process tasks are necessary for legal, regulatory, or business reasons, tasks such as auditing or invoicing. Before deciding to eliminate a non-value-added task, the teams should determine whether the task is required by regulation or law or is otherwise necessary for business survival and should decide where non-value-added steps must remain for now because they are required by management or are cost trade-offs or space trade-offs.

Make Value Flow without Interruption*

Flow is the uninterrupted movement of a product through the steps in a process and between processes. A definition of process flow would also be useful, because in the information/support process improvement arena we are dealing with a type of flow: "Flow is what changes the process from a static entity consisting of the work progressing through the inputs, tasks, and outputs into a dynamic concept. ...Flow varies from hour to hour and day to day. Flow is affected by volume, mix, new customer requirements, changes in people, environment and a host of other factors" (Source: Adair, C.B., and Murray, B.A., *Breakthrough Process Redesign: New Pathways to Customer Value*, AMACOM, New York, 1994, pp. 111–112). Because we are going to be working with process flow, it might also be useful to know what the characteristics of flow actually are and how to identify and measure those characteristics. To measure key flow characteristics, we start by documenting the time required and distance traveled for each unit of work using measurements such as dates, time stamps, feet, or yards. We want to find out if the process has any built-in interruptions or delays or any side journeys for the work in process (including paper). We can also chart the flow by measuring the distance that the unit of work moves. This process, much like the development of the material flow diagram, will bring to light any disconnected flow in the process. It should be clear that longer distances result in longer move times, longer move times result in bigger batches, bigger batches result in longer waits, longer waits result in more work in process, more work in process requires more space, more space results in longer distances, and on and on.

Measuring and documenting the time and distance characteristics of process flow also highlights other process characteristics — for instance, process interruptions. Process interruptions occur when tasks produce outputs at different rates. When tasks are mismatched, movement of work occurs in batches instead of flowing in small units, or the optimum small unit of one. Movement of process work units in batches always produces higher work in process. Again, think of paper in an information/support process as being the work in process. All interruptions to flow result in waiting time and longer process cycles. Just as in the physical product processes, variations in the task input rate lead to variations in the task output rate, set-up and changeover time expansion, quality problems, and

---

* Adapted from Womack, J., and Jones, D., *Lean Thinking: Banish Waste and Create Wealth in Your Corporation*, Simon & Schuster, 1996.

process breakdowns. Characteristics of intermittent flow include batches of more than one, task activity separation, unnecessary movement, and queues of work waiting for processing. With continuous flow, on the other hand, work is consistent and regular and is balanced, with stable capacity utilization (no one is over- or underloaded).

When work and the flow of work, including information work, are balanced, processes are synchronized with customer needs. How many instances can we think of where a downstream process is waiting for work but the upstream process is running a "batch" report? The generation of customer requirements to feed a shop schedule is perhaps the best example to use here. Timing the release of customer-order-based schedules by grouping the orders into processing batches defeats the very mechanics of pull and flow on the manufacturing floor that we have worked so diligently to obtain. The lean commerce model shown in Figure 4.1 provides for the delivery of customer requirements as they are received as rapidly as possible to the end fabrication area of shipping or assembly. The quicker the folks making products get the order, the quicker the order can be filled. A batch size of one is optimal for physical processes, and a batch size of one is also the goal of information/support processes in the lean enterprise.

The results of balanced flow include less work in process (and less paper) and the fastest throughput to downstream customers. Especially with the advent of workflow messaging technology, the capability to achieve balanced flow, to reduce batch quantity to one, and to increase the move frequency to one at a time creates the opportunity to link tasks from the information/support processes to the physical product processes and to enhance the capability of an already lean production environment to produce at the same (output) rate of the customer pull, thus achieving *takt* time implementation throughout the physical and supporting information processes.

*Let the Customer Pull Value from the Process Owner**

Pull occurs when the signal to initiate a process comes from downstream processes and ultimately the customer. Is the process directly connected to the customer? Does the process owner deal directly with the end customer? If so, does the process owner review the process with the customer regularly to ensure customer satisfaction? Is the process customer internal? If so, does the process owner review the process with the customer regularly to ensure customer satisfaction?

---

* Adapted from Womack, J., and Jones, D., *Lean Thinking: Banish Waste and Create Wealth in Your Corporation,* Simon & Schuster, 1996.

Pursuit of Perfection*

The pursuit of perfection relies upon the maintenance and continuous improvement of the four preceding principles. To pursue process perfection, ask if there is a regular review of the performance metrics (cost, quality, delivery) of the process.

Completing Lean Performance Analysis

During the Lean Performance Analysis, we will suggest a process measurement for each process analyzed in the policy deployment Lean Performance Analysis stream. Process owners have invited customers to suggest improvements to the process and have determined whether or not recent improvements to the processes meet the goals of the lean transformational principles. They have analyzed and challenged the root causes of all the remaining process tasks, especially challenging non-value-added but apparently necessary tasks. Team members have utilized their knowledge of the traditional lean diagnostic tools to pursue perfection in their processes:

- 3MUs (*muda, mura, muri*)
- 5Ss (sort, straighten, scrub, systematize, sustain)
- 5Ws–1H (who, what, where, when, why, and how)
- 4Ms (man, machine, material, and method)

Process owners now complete the process workflow standard to find out *how* the software will perform the processes. This is the most appropriate time for the teams to attend software education. Armed with their process workflow drafts specifying the process requirements, the process owners can enlist the assistance of the software vendors' trainers and consultants in answering the *how* questions. When applying a manufacturing software package, the team should:

- Obtain complete documentation from the vendor for each application.
- Evaluate standard software screens and reports for completeness and ease-of-use.
- Map and evaluate the standard software to the process requirements, highlighting any task not enabled properly by the software.
- Investigate the possibility of workaround solutions for any missing software features and capability.

---

* Adapted from Womack, J., and Jones, D., *Lean Thinking: Banish Waste and Create Wealth in Your Corporation*, Simon & Schuster, 1996.

We will revisit these issues during the GAP analysis that follows next. While most software for ERP and other manufacturing applications from solid vendors are packed with more process-enabling features than any implementation can reasonably use, occasionally application of the software creates additional tasks. Some of these software-required tasks may even appear to be *muda*. When applying new software, it is paramount to keep in mind that a value-added improvement is a change to a process task that increases value by reducing cost, improving quality, or speeding delivery, and any task added to the process by the enabler that does not increase value should be questioned, although we may have to live with some of them (the Lean Performance Analysis contains a vehicle for questioning process or system GAPs), below.

While documenting their processes, owners should assemble examples of key forms, documents, and computer reports and screens involved. This documentation is used to verify that the new system will accomplish the full range of process requirements, and it will be useful later in completing the process work instructions. The draft process workflow diagrams should be revised to include all necessary system supports at an input–output level (at the same time identifying any input and output problems and symptoms).

Trial and error team activity should take place while the software package capability is being investigated and applied. A willingness to ask *why* a task is performed and *what* value is provided to the customer is essential. A process workflow standard is complete when necessary and value-added tasks (*what*) are defined and agreed upon and the software package or other enabler is applied to demonstrate *how* the process will be done. The *who*, *when*, and *where* decisions are then agreed upon to confirm the definitions of process owners, customers, and process boundaries (see Figure 10.15).

While the process workflows are being completed, the project manager collects the Lean Performance Analysis masters with process and team identified and distributes the results to the team as well as the steering committee to keep them informed of developments. With the process workflow standard in hand, the process owners and customers are now ready for lean process improvement, during which they employ a question-and-investigate type of discourse to develop potential plans for improving the processes. Analyzing a process workflow standard is the single most effective technique for identifying opportunities for process improvement. Before the discussion gets more complicated, it is important to remember that examining the boundary tasks of two consecutive processes can result in the harvesting of low-hanging fruit (i.e., obvious improvements). Often, these improvements can be made by eliminating or reducing travel time and distance, duplicate counting and checking, or inspection of work being handed off from one "silo" to another.

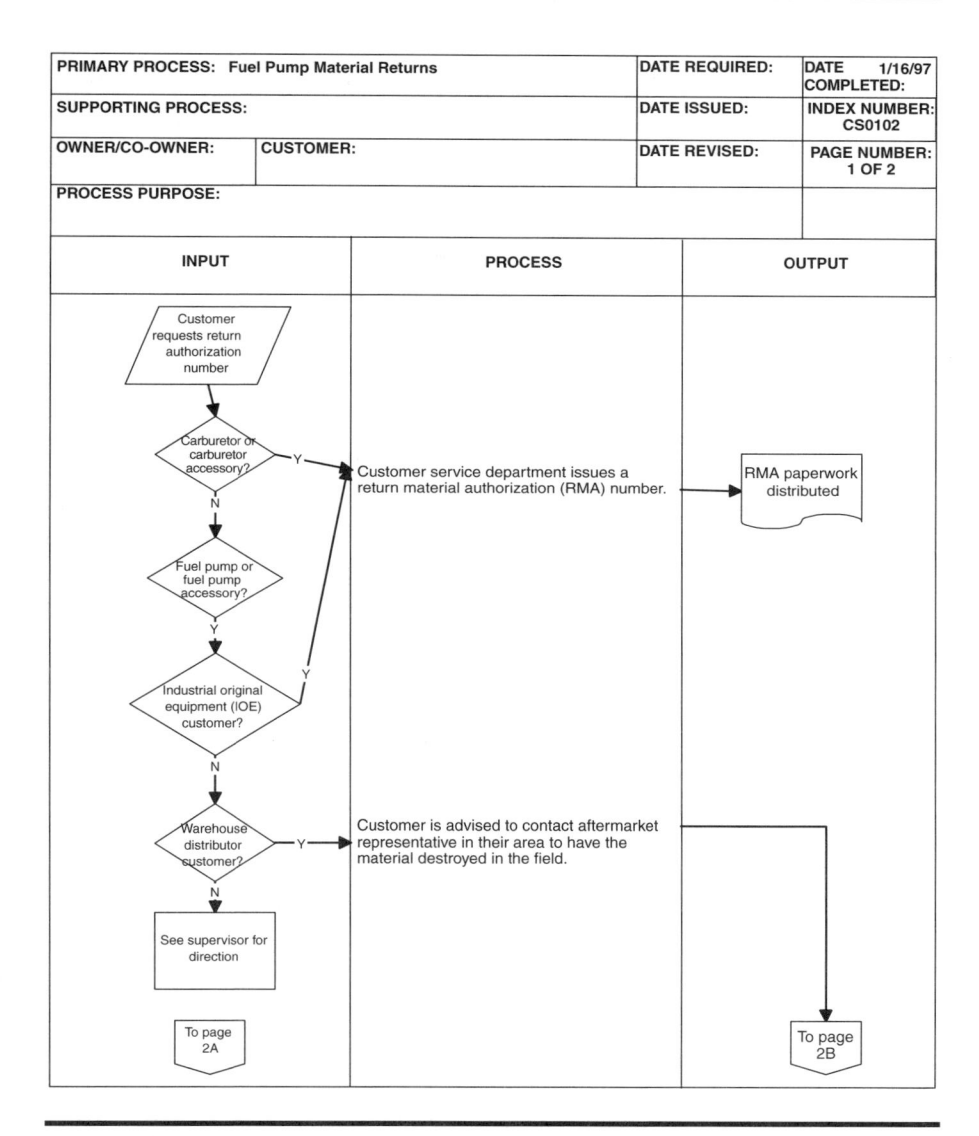

PRIMARY PROCESS: Fuel Pump Material Returns		DATE REQUIRED:	DATE COMPLETED: 1/16/97
SUPPORTING PROCESS:		DATE ISSUED:	INDEX NUMBER: CS0102
OWNER/CO-OWNER:	CUSTOMER:	DATE REVISED:	PAGE NUMBER: 1 OF 2
PROCESS PURPOSE:			

INPUT	PROCESS	OUTPUT
Customer requests return authorization number → Carburetor or carburetor accessory? (Y/N) → Fuel pump or fuel pump accessory? (Y/N) → Industrial original equipment (IOE) customer? (Y/N) → Warehouse distributor customer? (Y/N) → See supervisor for direction → To page 2A	Customer service department issues a return material authorization (RMA) number. Customer is advised to contact aftermarket representative in their area to have the material destroyed in the field.	RMA paperwork distributed To page 2B

Figure 10.15   Fuel Pump Returns Process Workflow Standard

As the process workflow standards near completion, process owners and customers should meet in cross-functional and cross-enterprise team meetings to challenge and improve their processes by evaluating and measuring process performance characteristics and measurements. Team members should meet with the project facilitator to examine their processes and ask critical Lean Performance questions regarding:

212 ■ Lean Performance ERP Project Management

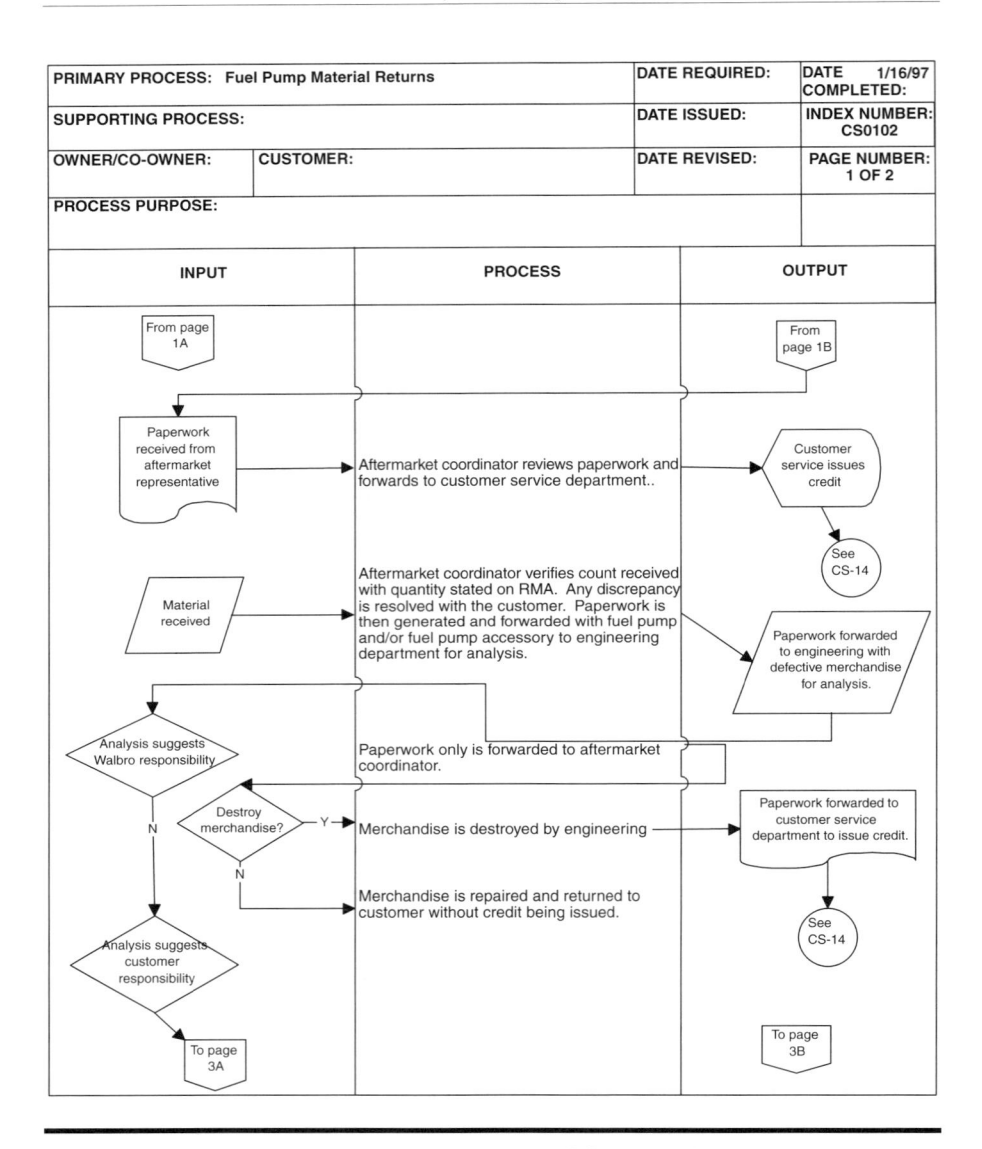

PRIMARY PROCESS: Fuel Pump Material Returns		DATE REQUIRED:	DATE 1/16/97 COMPLETED:
SUPPORTING PROCESS:		DATE ISSUED:	INDEX NUMBER: CS0102
OWNER/CO-OWNER:	CUSTOMER:	DATE REVISED:	PAGE NUMBER: 1 OF 2
PROCESS PURPOSE:			

INPUT	PROCESS	OUTPUT
From page 1A		From page 1B
Paperwork received from aftermarket representative	Aftermarket coordinator reviews paperwork and forwards to customer service department..	Customer service issues credit
		See CS-14
Material received	Aftermarket coordinator verifies count received with quantity stated on RMA. Any discrepancy is resolved with the customer. Paperwork is then generated and forwarded with fuel pump and/or fuel pump accessory to engineering department for analysis.	Paperwork forwarded to engineering with defective merchandise for analysis.
Analysis suggests Walbro responsibility — N	Paperwork only is forwarded to aftermarket coordinator.	
Destroy merchandise? — Y	Merchandise is destroyed by engineering	Paperwork forwarded to customer service department to issue credit.
N	Merchandise is repaired and returned to customer without credit being issued.	See CS-14
Analysis suggests customer responsibility		
To page 3A		To page 3B

Figure 10.15 Fuel Pump Returns Process Workflow Standard (cont.)

- *Process integration/total system focus:* Are any opportunities or requirements presented by new software capabilities?
- *Process waste and strain:* Does the process utilize more resources than necessary or require additional or redundant tasks? Do any process tasks cause a strain on the operating resources of the system? Do any process tasks cause waiting time or queues?

PRIMARY PROCESS: Fuel Pump Material Returns		DATE REQUIRED:	DATE COMPLETED: 1/16/97
SUPPORTING PROCESS:		DATE ISSUED:	INDEX NUMBER: CS0102
OWNER/CO-OWNER:	CUSTOMER:	DATE REVISED:	PAGE NUMBER: 1 OF 2
PROCESS PURPOSE:			

INPUT	PROCESS	OUTPUT

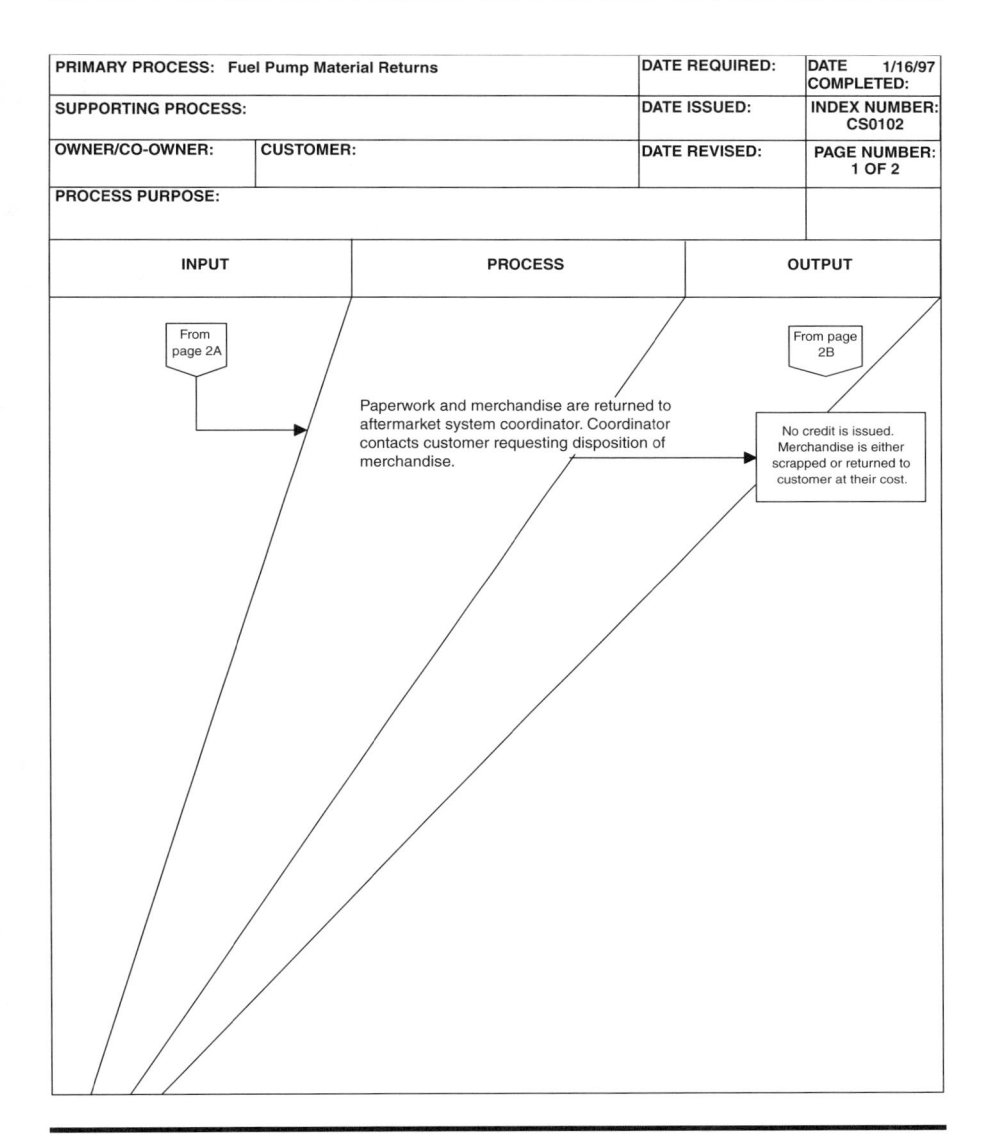

From page 2A

Paperwork and merchandise are returned to aftermarket system coordinator. Coordinator contacts customer requesting disposition of merchandise.

From page 2B

No credit is issued. Merchandise is either scrapped or returned to customer at their cost.

Figure 10.15 Fuel Pump Returns Process Workflow Standard (cont.)

- *Process discrepancy:* Who owns the process? Does the process have a co-owner? What is the process output? Where is the process performed? When is the process performed? How often is the process performed? Why is the process performed? Are the process owners and customers in agreement about process tasks and the need to perform them? Is the process based on a common data source?

- *Process empowerment:* Have we eliminated process barriers and redundant counting, checking, and verifying tasks? Can we find any interdepartmental transfers and interfaces? Are handoffs and duplicate efforts involved in transferring paper, documents, data, or other process elements between or within departments or other process dividers? Are process owners closely linked to their process customers? Do any layers have to be removed? Do any barriers remain between the customer input and the decision makers, task doers, and process owners? Can the process be improved by local decision making or other empowerment? Are all employees involved in the process empowered to fulfill their tasks?
- *Process effectiveness:* Does the process fulfill its purpose? Does the process reduce business risk? Does the process increase control over cost elements or causes, quality of output, and speed of output?
- *Process efficiency and timeliness:* Is the process efficient? Does the process have any bottlenecks? How can these bottlenecks be eliminated?
- *Process cost:* Does the process have a measurable cost? Are the measurements at a task (manageable) level? Are all cost drivers identified? If measurable cost is not possible, can a cost be estimated? Have we applied a vendor-supplied and -maintained software wherever possible? Have we minimized or eliminated the need to customize the software wherever possible?
- *Process quality:* Are any of the process tasks based on (or produce) data or information not commonly accepted to be accurate? What is the root cause? How is process quality assured? What is the measured quality of the process? How often do we have to reprocess the work performed in this process because of an inaccurate result?
- *Process speed:* Is process speed or throughput time being measured? Are these measurements at a task level? Does this process have any waiting periods, transfer time, or other queues, including batch processes? Can they be eliminated?
- *Process complexity:* Can the process be simplified? Are any interdepartmental transfers or interfaces in evidence? Can they be reduced or eliminated? Is the process supported on a single CPU or server? If not, why not? Are all process data provided by a common central source (database)? Are the data dependent on the PC database?
- *Process concurrence:* Are all tasks on the process performed in one process area and by one process owner? Where tasks are performed in more than one process area or by more than one process owner or co-owner, do any opportunities exist to provide a concurrent flow?

The completed process workflow standard is now ready for wider analysis. The teams meet to critique the processes using a practice called the GAP analysis. We are especially interested in those processes that have a system enhancement recommended or contain a critical realization of project objectives. GAPs, also known as problems or opportunities, are found at two levels in an organization. At the organization strategy level, products, services, and markets are the focus. In a Lean Performance project, processes and the GAPs found in them are the focus. In a reengineering project, the team would already have tackled the organization's strategic GAPs and attempted to redesign or redefine the products, services, mission, and markets.

The Lean Performance Analysis identifies process and system GAPs at the action or process level, so teams should refer any findings at the organization strategy level to the steering committee for new lean strategy development and management policy deployment during phase three. The Lean Performance project starts with developing lean business policies to be deployed at the action or process level, and process tasks, inputs, and outputs are the focus of these efforts.

Process and system GAPs are the identifiable impediments to better process performance. A process GAP is the difference between what the process provides and the process customer's minimum acceptable standard. A system GAP is the difference between what the enabling information technology system provides and the process owner's minimum acceptable standard. Process and system GAPs state system functionality sought or needed by process owners and customers to achieve project objectives derived from the lean business policies and lean project strategies. Solutions to process GAPs are proposed by process owners and customers when GAPs in the processes or system block attainment of project objectives. A cost/benefit estimate must be completed for each GAP identified. Site teams are empowered to act within the project scope to meet the project objectives. In the Lean Performance Analysis, the Lean Performance teams identify potential system GAPs when the manufacturing software is mapped to the process tasks. The GAPs are provided to the information systems team members, utilizing the open issue format, for preliminary analysis. Lean Performance teams also evaluate the workaround solutions for missing software features and capability highlighted by the process owners during development of the process workflow standards. The teams develop solutions that support full realization of lean project objectives at the process level. They select, prioritize, and submit solutions for system integration development to the steering committee through the use of the open issue process.

The information team has a number of important responsibilities to perform during the GAP analysis, the most important of which are evaluating the effectiveness of the current use of PCs and identifying process tasks that occur on PCs but which may be candidates for central database and CPU support. The information team should evaluate processor utilization and effectiveness where more than one CPU is used in a process. The team should highlight process tasks that require support from multiple processors or servers, considering multimachine file support wherever necessary, and should suggest process improvements so that each process can occur on a single CPU where possible. The information team should analyze the process workflows for location handoffs and system data implications and confirm the effective application of unmodified standard vendor software, especially where use of standard software capability can possibly solve those GAPs identified by process owners. The team should also consider requirements and/or opportunities for process integration presented by new software. On another front, the information team should ensure that every process workflow is seamless to the users, suggest revisions where necessary, and confirm that the data process sequencing is optimal and that all new data elements are available for processing on the appropriate screens.

Prior to recommending any modifications to support proposed GAP solutions, the information team should determine where GAPs are only interim or phased requirements resulting from current system interfaces and limitations already being corrected. Information team members should also examine each process workflow using their knowledge of the enabling software to verify that the teams have taken full advantage of the opportunities presented. The information team should make sure that full benefit has been attained from the capacity of the data processes to automate the information/support processes or any tasks in the information/support processes, as well as integrating or linking information/support processes or individual tasks within information/support processes. The information team should look to resequence process tasks where possible in order to reduce *muda* in a process. This may involve linking more than one location together to share or process information or data, as in a cross-functional or cross-enterprise process. The information team should examine and report on all opportunities to inform, distribute, and/or share information or keep track of activities that are either within the information/support processes or outside of them but linked by task or other user dependency. Often, the information team members can see an unrealized opportunity to provide data for analysis or to perform analysis and provide data to another process. (Adapted from Davenport, T., *Process Innovation: Reengineering Work Through Information Technology,* Harvard Business School Press, Boston, MA, 1993.)

Next, the facilitator should conduct Lean Performance team cross-functional and cross-enterprise Lean Performance Analysis GAP sessions with all teams to analyze the GAPs selected at the process level by the respective teams. By beginning with the improved secondary and/or discrete processes, the cross-functional and cross-enterprise teams can eliminate a good deal of complexity and build from a solid foundation of already improved processes. The cross-functional processes can be analyzed sequentially by reviewing the discrete components and then can be presented concurrently to illustrate the full breadth of the process. Cross-functional processes depend on complex organizational (departmental) interaction due to conflicting priorities and schedules. Lean improvement of cross-functional processes may involve organizational restructuring to develop clear ownership, responsibility, and authority for a given process. The analysis of cross-enterprise processes resembles cross-functional process analysis. Again, the processes can be analyzed sequentially and then presented concurrently. The analysis also depends on complex organizational interaction across company boundaries. These lean improvements also involves organizational restructuring within and across companies. To accomplish this, it is necessary to develop a process-level case that demonstrates the benefits of utilizing the improved process and/or implementing the GAP solution.

The final element of the Lean Performance Analysis is the definition of process performance measurements. Processes are amenable to a variety of measurements, such as time to execute or cycle or the cost per cycle, as well as the variability, usefulness, and consistency of the process output. It is also possible to take "negative" measurements by concentrating on the occurrence of process input and output defects. During the Lean Performance Analysis, team members begin to define process performance measurements that will be formalized and implemented during the third phase of the project, Continuous Lean Performance. For now, it is enough to identify possible measurements and begin to monitor them for usefulness, prior to proposing them to the steering committee. At the conclusion of the GAP analysis, the teams determine candidates for modification, those processes for which a modification will demonstrate benefit. Each process owner illustrates GAPs in their own processes and recommends system enhancements to support the improved process (Figure 10.16).

The project manager should stop for a minute to evaluate current project performance compared to the established project objectives and to examine the early winners — that is, the new processes developed, processes improved, and processes made obsolete. What improvements have been gained? Where can these same lessons be applied? The project manager will want to review the Lean Performance Planning diagrams for adequacy and update and improve them where necessary. The teams should complete updating of the improved processes with process workflow standards before handing them off for development of process work instructions.

218 ■ Lean Performance ERP Project Management

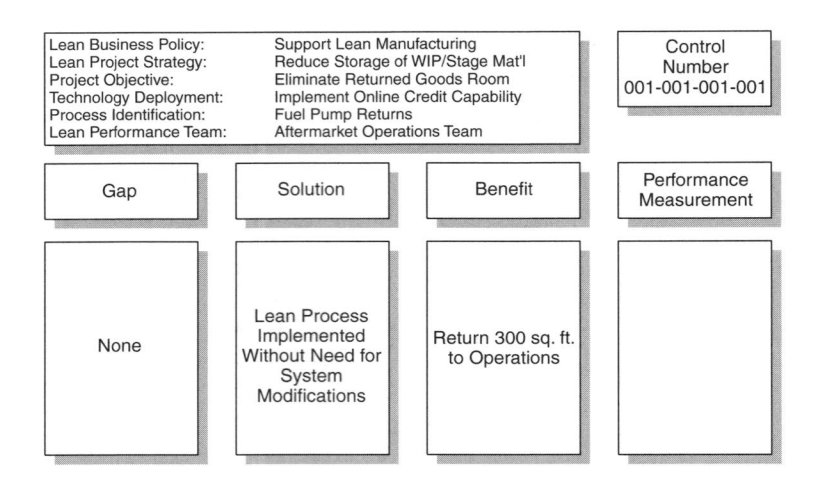

Lean Business Policy:	Support Lean Manufacturing
Lean Project Strategy:	Reduce Storage of WIP/Stage Mat'l
Project Objective:	Eliminate Returned Goods Room
Technology Deployment:	Implement Online Credit Capability
Process Identification:	Fuel Pump Returns
Lean Performance Team:	Aftermarket Operations Team

Control Number
001-001-001-001

Gap	Solution	Benefit	Performance Measurement
None	Lean Process Implemented Without Need for System Modifications	Return 300 sq. ft. to Operations	

Figure 10.16 Lean Performance Analysis: GAP Solution and Benefit

Producing Work Instructions

The teams are now ready to develop process work instructions for the completed process workflows by utilizing the approved project format. This is also the point in the project at which forms and other documentation are revised as required, with preliminary drafts being reviewed with supervisory and lead personnel for their revisions and approvals. The forms are then evaluated for completeness and order quantity, and beginning quantities of forms are ordered where needed. The work instructions are drafted in ISO 9000, QS, or other applicable format that identifies document and transaction flows and responsibilities (see sample work instruction in Figure 10.17). The process workflows are examined to determine where any manual procedures will be necessary for implementation, especially for the workarounds. The support for interim and/or phased implementation should be included in this assessment, as should references to all process work instructions in the process master index (Figure 10.18). The project quality assurance review should encompass all project diagrams completed thus far, and any diagrams for modified project deliverables should be updated, including:

- Process workflow standards
- Process work instructions
- Material flow diagrams
- BOMs and routings

SCREEN NAME: Online Return Credit		REV. LEVEL 0	SITE CODE: 001	INDEX NUMBER: 0713
	PAGE: 1 OF 1	DATE ISSUED:	DATE REVISED:	DATE PRINTED: 9/19/2001

    COPY 1ST SCREEN REFERRED TO IN INSTRUCTION

ORDER: SYSTEM ASSIGNED, (CAN ASSIGN MANUALLY)
    Press the enter key for the next field

SOLD TO: ENTER THE CUSTOMER CODE
    Press the enter key for the next field

BILL TO: CODE DEFAULTS TO SOLD-TO CODE, UNLESS OVERRIDDEN
    Press the enter key for the next field

SHIP TO: DEFAULTS TO THE SOLD-TO CODE
    Press the enter key for the next field

ORDER DATE: THE DATE THIS ORDER WAS ENTERED
    Press the enter key for the next field

REQUIRED DATE: DEFAULTS TO DUE DATE
    Press the enter key for the next field

PROMISE DATE: DEFAULTS TO DUE DATE
    Press the enter key for the next field

DUE DATE: CUSTOMER REQUIRED DATE MINUS SHIPPING LEAD TIME (PLANNING USES THIS DATE)
    Press the enter key for the next field

PURCHASE ORDER: ENTER THE CUSTOMER PO
    Press the enter key for the next field

REMARKS: CAN ENTER GENERAL REMARKS ABOUT THIS CUSTOMER
    Press the enter key for the next field

PRICE TBL: IF SET UP A PRICE WILL DISPLAY
    Press the enter key for the next field

DISC TBL: IDENTIFIES A PRICING STRUCTURE (BASED ON SHIP-TO ADDRESS)
    Press the enter key for the next field

Figure 10.17   Online Return Credit Work Instruction

Conduct a quality assurance review with the outside reviewer to validate the project results to date. Be sure to present the updated diagrams and other documents to report to the Lean Performance teams for approval before presenting them to the steering committee. Obtain approval to proceed with the implementation of improved processes from the steering committee. Then, begin the integrate systems module.

Lean Performance Project

Process Workflow Listing	Date Issued	Index Number
Master Index	Date Revised: 12/5/2000	

Document cross reference
Document retrieval instructions
Management summary

	Index No.
Business planning	
Business planning	BP-01
Labor requirements	BP-01.01
Material requirements	BP-01.02
Purchase plan	BP-01.02.01
Customer service	
Quality reporting — customer returns	CS-01
Invoicing	CS-02.01
Cumulative shipped reconciliation	CS-02.02
Pricing	CS-03
Sales forecasting	CS-04.01
Quoting	CS-04.02
Order processing	CS-05.01
Purchase order maintenance	CS-05.02
Aftermarket order process	CS-05.03
Production and operations management	
Production line scheduling	PO-01
Production line scheduling — pilot runs	PO-01.01
Work in process — machining castings	PO-02.01
Work in process — machining covers	PO-02.02
Machining department material flow — castings/covers	PO-02.02.01
Work in process — preassembly	PO-03.01
Work in process — final 1 assembly	PO-03.02
Work in process — final 2 assembly	PO-03.03
Material flow map for preassembly, final 1, final 2	PO-03.03.01
Manufacturing	PO-04.01
Manufacturing flow for series	PO-04.01.01
Manufacturing flow for series	PO-04.01.02
Diecasting	PO-05.01
Diecasting material flow	PO-05.01.01
Shopfloor reporting — production reporting	PO-06.01
Shopfloor reporting — labor reporting	PO-06.02
Work order releases	PO-07.01
Work order releases — component requisitioning	PO-07.02

Figure 10.18 Process Master Index

Lean Performance Project

Process Workflow Listing	Date Issued	Index Number
Master Index	Date Revised: 12/5/2000	

Plant maintenance — preventive maintenance	PO-08.01
Quality reporting and analysis — deficiency reporting	PO-09.01
Quality reporting and analysis — sort/rework/scrap	PO-09.02
Quality reporting and analysis — component sampling	PO-09.03
Quality reporting and analysis — small-parts inspection	PO-09.04
Quality reporting and analysis — machine-line inspection	PO-09.05
Quality reporting and analysis — preassembly inspection	PO-09.06
Quality reporting and analysis — final 1 inspection	PO-09.07
Quality reporting and analysis — final 2 inspection	PO-09.08
Quality reporting and analysis — final teardown	PO-09.09
Quality reporting and analysis — final visual	PO-09.10
Quality reporting and analysis — scrap accounting	PO-09.11
Tool and gauge control	PO-10

Supplier management

MRP[g] reports — MRP review	SM-01
Contract management — purchase order process — requisitioning	SM-02.01
Contract management — purchase order process — purchase order generation	SM-02.02
Contract management — purchase order process — spot buys	SM-02.03
Contract management — purchase order process — expediting (domestic)	SM-02.04
Contract management — purchase order process — expediting (foreign)	SM-02.05
Contract management — purchase order process — reschedules	SM-02.06
Contract management — purchase order process — tooling orders	SM-02.07
Contract management — purchase order process — mailing purchase orders	SM-02.08
Contract management — purchase order process — MRO[h] purchase orders	SM-02.09
Supplier evaluations — sourcing/quotations — selection	SM-03.01
Supplier evaluations — sourcing/quotations — approved vendor list	SM-03.02
Supplier evaluations — sourcing/quotations — supplier setup	SM-03.03
Supplier evaluations — sourcing/quotations — RFQ[i]	SM-03.04
Supplier evaluations — sourcing/quotations — performance rating	SM-03.05

Inventory management and logistics

Master scheduling — demand determination	IL-01.01
Master scheduling — production mix/quantity	IL-01.02
Receiving — Arizona warehouse	IL-02.01
Receiving — incoming at plant	IL-02.02
Receiving — stockroom	IL-02.03
Receiving — incoming inspection	IL-02.04
Receiving — MRO supplies	IL-02.05
Receiving — sample parts	IL-02.06

Figure 10.18 Process Master Index (cont.)

Lean Performance Project

Process Workflow Listing	Date Issued	Index Number
Master Index	Date Revised: 12/5/2000	

Traffic — foreign exportation	IL-03.01
Traffic — exportation of HAZMAT	IL-03.02
Traffic — foreign warehousing	IL-03.03
Traffic — Arizona warehouse	IL-03.04
Traffic — returnable containers	IL-03.05
Traffic — bar-code labeling	IL-03.06
Inventory control — cycle count	IL-04.01
Inventory control — production report	IL-04.02
Inventory control — lot control	IL-04.03
Inventory control — parts recovery	IL-04.04
Inventory control — piece-count verification	IL-04.05
Inventory control — bulk issues	IL-04.06
Inventory control — physical inventory	IL-04.07
Work order release — designation	IL-05.01
Warehousing — warehousing configuration	IL-06

Financial management

Customs — importation of production material	FM-01.01
Customs — MRO importation	FM-01.02
Customs — exportation invoicing	FM-01.03
NAFTA — certificates of origin	FM-02.01
NAFTA — assembly descriptions	FM-02.02
Product costing	FM-03.01
Product costing — standard costs	FM-03.02
Product costing — CRNs[j]	FM-03.03
Product costing — quality cost reporting	FM-03.04
Cash management — petty cash disbursement	FM-04
Payroll — distribution	FM-05
Accounts payable	FM-06
General ledger — financial statements	FM-07.01
General ledger	FM-07.02
General ledger — government reporting	FM-07.03
General ledger — taxes	FM-07.04
General ledger — month-end closing	FM-07.05
Inventory accounting — valuation	FM-08

Product engineering

ECN[i] — setup	PE-01.01
ECN — change notice	PE-01.02
ECN — change coordination	PE-01.03

Figure 10.18 Process Master Index (cont.)

Lean Performance Project

Process Workflow Listing	Date Issued	Index Number
Master Index	Date Revised: 12/5/2000	

Bill of material — parts list maintenance   PE-02
Research and development — development   PE-03.01
Research and development — new product releases   PE-03.02
Product masters — where first used list   PE-04.01
Product masters — data maintenance   PE-04.02
Engineering drawing — print distribution   PE-05.01
Engineering drawing — drawing maintenance   PE-05.02

Performance measurements
Bill of materials accuracy   PM-01
Routings accuracy   PM-02
Inventory accuracy   PM-03
Shop delivery performance   PM-04
Invoicing accuracy   PM-05
Product quality   PM-06

Control file setups
Sales quote control file
Sales order control file
Customer schedules control file

[a] WMX = **DEFINE**.
[b] WED = **DEFINE**.
[c] MA = **DEFINE**
[d] MB = **DEFINE**
[e] TPP = **DEFINE**
[f] RTV = **DEFINE**.
[g] MRP = material requirements planning.
[h] MRO = **DEFINE**.
[i] RFQ = **DEFINE**.
[j] CRN = **DEFINE**.
[k] ECN = **DEFINE**.

Figure 10.18   Process Master Index (cont.)

11

INTEGRATING SYSTEMS MODULE

PROJECT TEAM TASKS

Installing Hardware and Software

The information team should begin to install system hardware and software, including printers. Although every system installation is different, some basic tasks are usually found in the installation of the hardware and software for every system. While a template covering the usual basic tasks is provided, the discussion here is more of a general review of the tasks that the hardware and software vendors most probably have outlined in great detail in their installation manuals. It should be noted that the information team technical support people have already attended hardware and software technical support training and should be thoroughly familiar with the manuals and other instructions prior to beginning installation of the software. This discussion is not intended to supersede those manuals; rather, it is intended as a guide for the project manager and to aid in constructing the overall project plan.

After installation of the system CPU (not discussed here), the next step is not always installing the application software, be it enterprise resource planning (ERP), manufacturing execution system (MES), customer relationship management (CRM), supply chain management (SCM), or other such applications. Usually the database and utility software must be installed first, after which the application software can be installed. A process should be established for verifying disk space, determining directory structures, and conducting periodic reviews of the error reporting to uncover hardware failures. The information team should also frequently review the system error reporting for operating system and application software errors. The information team should be especially careful to document the processes they will employ to correct error situations, as suggested by system manuals or the error reporting itself.

Project result: system recovery log

Initiating the System

Any number of tasks are involved in initiating the system, including:

- Create user help fields
- Create startup scripts
- Set up generalized codes
- Set up function keys
- Set up batch identifiers
- Set up general ledger entities
- Define the system/account control file
- Set up language codes and default language codes for users
- Set up company addresses
- Set up taxes, with only one tax system supported per database
- Set up currencies and exchange rates
- Finalize address coding methods
- Define address control file

Setting Up System Security

System security is set up next, and most systems will include such requirements as:

- User IDs
- Passwords
- Menus

A list of users and the functions they will use is based on the process ownership from the process master index. A system menu report is run, and initial user menus for each system user are put in place.

Creating Test and Training Environments

Separate environments should be created as soon as possible for testing purposes, for training, and for the development of work instructions. Data files for the testing and training environments should be developed and loaded with real data, utilizing conversion programs for loading data where possible. When the testing and training environments are stabilized, a baseline copy is kept for periodic refresh in the testing environment only. In the training environment, the project trainer has the final say on when (if at all) to refresh the data. No formal testing is provided in the training environment, as the process owners will provide plenty of that during the process test. The testing and training environments must be kept current as far as program changes, upgrades, and system setting decisions released to the production environment.

Creating Production Databases

The production database(s) are created only after completing all project testing and decisions at the conclusion of the process tests. Database connections are established for multiple sites and/or entities, and system users receive a listing or menu of the available databases.

Testing System Setup

Prior to the initial lean commerce team testing activity, all facets of the system setup are tested to uncover any hardware glitches and to verify that terminals communicate with servers and all communications software is functioning properly. Any emulation software is also tested, as are all modem, DSL, and T1 connections, as well as all printers and other peripherals. Network management software (on multiple databases, if installed) is also tested.

Managing the Data Conversion Process

Management of the data conversion process includes the following actions:

- Review the results and recommendations of the Lean Performance teams.
- Identify related files of both the new system and the current system.
- Evaluate the field-to-field correlation between the two systems.
- Determine record sizes and numbers.
- Determine the capability to automate data load for engineering and financial data.
- Verify the database transfer capability.
- Finalize the method of data load (manual, automated, or some combination).
- Use the testing and training environments to test conversion routines and programs.

- Be sure that process owners and customers validate data during all testing activities.

Project result: data management/data conversion strategy

- Plan the conversion itself, being sure to include confirmation that supporting systems have been converted and are successfully running.
- Include cutover timing and its implication (e.g., before or after material requirements planning [MRP]).
- Finalize interface issues and testing requirements.
- Specify requirements for preparation of data and the impact of any fields that must be manually converted or conditioned.
- Determine procedures for converting data.
- Develop a contingency plan for errors.
- Complete the conversion plan, being sure to include dates, tasks, and work steps.
- Publish the data conversion workplan so project team members can review and comment.

Project result: final conversion and cutover work plans

Evaluating Additional Software Packages and Interfaces

Evaluating additional software packages and/or interfaces that have been proposed by the Lean Performance teams includes the following steps:

- Identify related factory systems for quality, shipping, engineering, shopfloor, inventory, scheduling, etc., based on input of the lean commerce team.
- Determine use of system FAX capability for supplier management or any other processes suggested by the teams.
- Verify the customer EDI/XML strategy.
- Identify necessary interfaces to accounting, order entry, forecasting, and shipping, including:
  - EDI/XML
  - Payroll
  - Pitney Bowes Freight Management
  - UPS or Federal Express
  - U.S. Postal Service
- Document the use of appropriate systems technology to support processes, projects, and strategies with identified enablers.
- Establish contacts and help-desk support for third-party applications.

- Assign process owner responsibility for all but the system-level setup technical issues.

Process owners are responsible for operating their own process applications and should be able to provide process workflow and work instruction documentation for operation of the third-party process support. The next important task for the information team to complete is to overlay the overview diagrams of the process areas with the system supports for the process areas. The team then closes the loop on all system process support decisions and presents the visual results to the project manager, project team, and steering committee (Figure 11.1). The team ensures that all project team members' applications and processes are included.

Conducting Process-Oriented System Design

Evaluating and planning the modifications programming begins when the process/system architecture is finalized. The first task in conducting process-oriented system design is to establish standard forms and templates for project documents, including screen and report samples. They should be based on the layout of the standard system software screens and reports wherever possible to ensure a uniform look and ease of functionality when mapping fields to screens and reports. It is always easier to insert fields into "clones" of existing system screens, especially when attempting to maintain system upgradeability using vendor upgrades, but doing so is not always possible. Sometimes a screen contains field references that occupy what might otherwise be available space. Rather than using space reserved by the vendor for a field that your process owners and customers may want to utilize in a future release, a new screen can be built that is based on the existing screen, and the unmodified screen is reserved for future use.

Next, forms and methods for documenting technical specifications are determined and examples of the following elements are developed based on the process workflow:

- Conceptual design specifications document
- External design specifications document
- Internal design specifications document
- Detail design specifications document

This step is followed by organizing a system design team that includes members of the existing Lean Performance information team, as well as temporary hires, contractors, consultants, and vendors who are providing services. Information systems design team training covers process workflows

230 ■ Lean Performance ERP Project Management

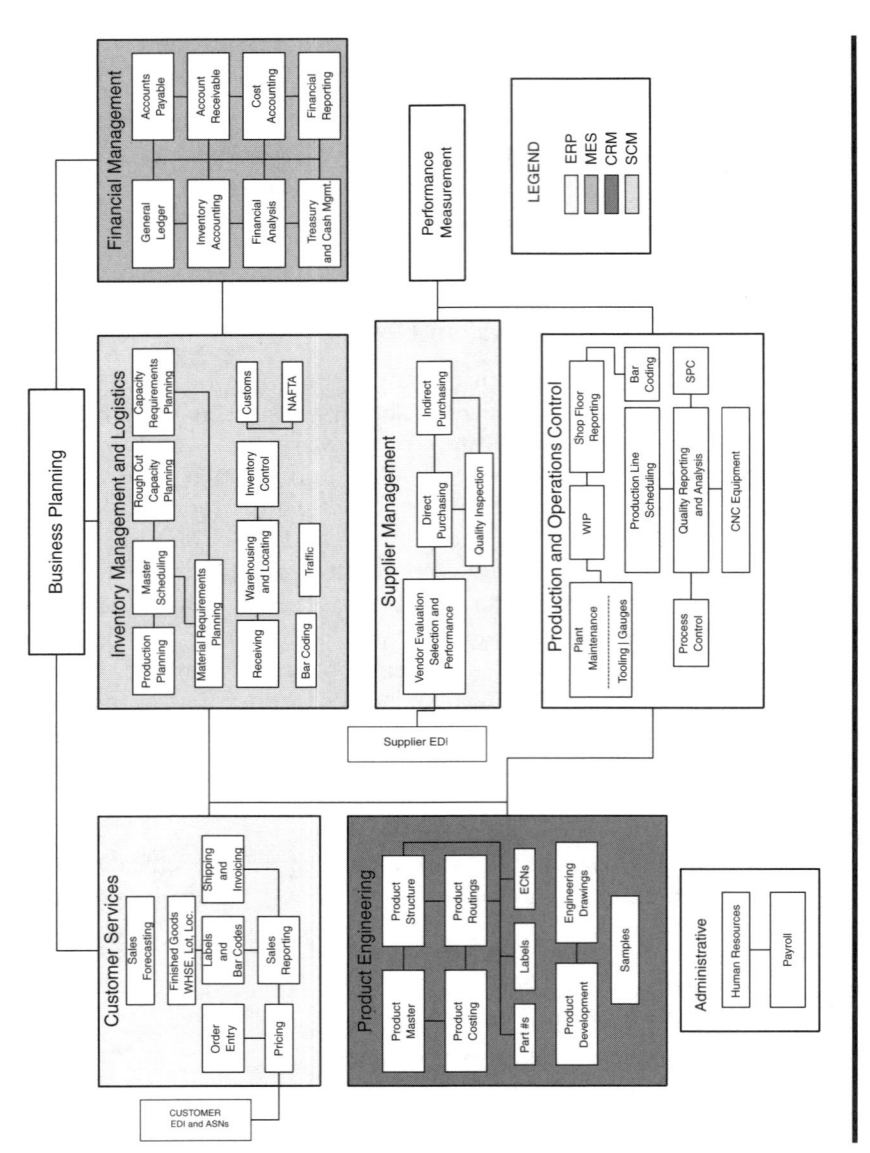

Figure 11.1 Process/System Overview Diagram

and work instructions. Team members should become familiar with the design policies regarding wraparounds or outside program calls for insertion of logic so as not to intrude into system source code (a standard screen and report design example can be provided). Any report that extracts, processes, and presents data is not a modification.

Project result: design team organization chart

Summarizing Proposed Modifications

To summarize the proposed modifications:

- Review completed process workflow documents and verify that GAPs cannot be solved by standard or known third-party available software.
- Prepare a list of reports, screens, and forms needed to support required process outputs.
- Prepare samples of all new (cloned) screens, reports, and forms using representative process data.
- Verify field-level correlations of all forms, including purchase orders, invoices, customer order acknowledgments, shop paper, shippers, and bills of lading.
- Review samples of forms with appropriate users and determine the number of copies of each form that will be needed to perform the improved process.
- Reduce the number of forms as much as possible and modify forms as required to follow the flow of data input.
- Perform a review of proposed modifications with software vendors.
- Verify that the proposed modifications are actually necessary by researching vendor-supplied solutions already available in current or pending releases of software and user-group and third-party offerings.
- Confirm the potential modifications and estimate time and cost.
- List any and all proposed modifications to the standard package, including new and revised data elements, records, screens, and reports; also list all new programs and processes.

Project result: preliminary program modification listing

- Review the results with the process owners and customers, then revise estimates to include the timing, cost, and criticality of each modification and enhancement.

Project result: revised program modification listing

- Determine high-priority items.
- Develop a programming schedule.
- Specify those that will and will not be ready before the system "go-live" date.
- Review all planned modifications with steering committee and obtain approval to proceed.
- Finalize a design team workplan that includes time and resource estimates for all tasks to be performed by the team.

Project result: design team workplan

- Prepare a short description of any modifications to standard programs and develop a brief narrative summary of the purpose of any new programs needed.

The conceptual design documents can and should be brief, as they are only meant to convey the purpose of the modification. The team should refer to and include the Lean Performance Analysis that demonstrates and supports the proposed modifications. The results of their work should then be presented to the project team.

Project result: conceptual design documents

Completing Hardware and Communications Analysis

To complete this stage of analysis:

- Review hardware requirements.
- Review processes and the technical designs for possible changes to the hardware strategy.
- Redefine hardware requirements considering throughput issues and storage and communication requirements, including printer, terminal, and PC requirements identified during the process workflow development.
- Perform an initial load analysis on the hardware, preferably during the lean commerce team testing process.

The initial load analysis is the time to shake things down without a lot of time lost. Hardware and communications problems encountered during the wider process and stress tests will cost more in terms of lost time and jeopardizing confidence in the project.

To complete the hardware and communications analysis:

- Review and resolve all open technical issues.
- Verify the location of each data entry and processing function.
- Verify all new communication capability and install data and video communications lines where needed.
- Review documentation of all updates and changes to current communications capability necessary to support the new system.
- Review and revise the budgeted equipment requirements, including bar codes, fiberoptics, DSL, T1, etc.
- Determine all site-preparation requirements, including buildout, air conditioning, and power.
- Update the site configuration diagrams to present to the steering committee.

At this stage of the project, documentation is helpful to close issues, especially those nasty budget issues that may surface when actual project hardware requirements are fully known.

Project result: revised site configuration diagrams

- Review and resolve any and all remaining system integration issues.
- Schedule and attend any additional hardware training necessary to resolve these issues.
- Bring in experts, if necessary.
- Finalize hardware installation budgets and schedules and update and review the hardware strategy changes with the steering committee to obtain approval to proceed.
- Complete the installation of hardware and software at all sites.

Preparing Detailed Design Specifications

System technical design is performed only after process workflow is complete and only if a GAP is demonstrated and if closing the GAP will result in a sufficient benefit. The external design specifications describe any new and revised system processing functions, including definition of modular processing logic, as necessary, to document key design points. The purpose of the document is to provide for a visual handoff to the next team members involved in the modification, often third-party partners.

Project result: external design specifications

Working with the third party or internal resource, the team then develops the database design, specifies the necessary processing logic and new data elements, and identifies any new logical views or alternative indexes of the data required. The proposed modified physical database is then reviewed with software vendors. Often, software vendors can help save time and money when applying modifications to their software, and they may even be interested in adding these modifications to their packages as standard code. If they do so, then obviously the burden of carrying the modifications forward to future versions is transferred to the vendor. The contents of any temporary files or interfaces or other system tricks should be recorded to provide for setup, test, or run issues that might occur when the modifications are in production.

Project result: internal design specifications

When the modification documentation is in hand, then:

- Review the results of the modifications with the process owners requesting them.
- Use updated process workflow and work instruction standards.
- Be sure that the technical personnel assigned are present at the run-through but design it from the process owners' perspective to cut down on the "but I thought you said" problems later; verifying the usefulness of a design is a lot of work up front but makes more sense than trying to do the work later when management is observing a live environment full of bugs or process GAPs that are based on poor communication.
- Finalize user-approved samples of new screens and reports.
- Complete forms design for any forms called for in the process, if needed.

In the Lean Performance project, system technical design completes development of software improvements to close documented system GAPs, completion of site configuration schematic and hardware listing to reflect final project configurations, planning, programming, and testing of data conversion and interface programs, and the installation and testing of software and communications capabilities.

Managing Outsourced Programming

Unless the enterprise intends to enter the software business, the temptation to start hacking away at the software should be resisted, especially when trying to adhere to the project schedule. The better path is to determine vendor outsourcing requirements and establish a vendor selection and control process. Packets prepared for potential vendors should include conceptual, external, and internal design specifications. When vendors have been selected, then a revised internal design analysis for any proposed modification can be outsourced. The team should be prepared to pay for the analysis and should make no promises of follow-up work to the vendors. All estimates should be accompanied by documentation and will provide the basis for determining who will do the programming. Every step of the programming process should be documented, and vendor development of design and program specifications should be supervised closely.

Project result: detail design specifications

Vendor unit tests are simple demonstrations that the individual program performs as specified in isolation from any other functionality, and these tests should be monitored closely.

Project result: unit-tested programs

Defining Interface and Database Testing

- Determine the testing requirements for the new system, interfaces, and conversion programs.
- Evaluate sources of data required for database input or conversion.
- Identify manual procedures required for data input.
- Identify site preparation requirements (if any) associated with data input to the system.
- Identify resource requirements for data input and conversion.

Project result: final software specifications, documents, and testing requirements

- Gather all project documents and updated diagrams for a Quality Assurance Review.
- Review results to date with the project team and conduct a review with the steering committee after the quality assurance review.

12

TESTING IMPROVED PROCESSES MODULE

PROJECT TEAM TASKS

Objectives of Testing

When the Lean Performance improvement tasks of the project are being completed and when modifications that will be included in the live system have been received and preliminary tests conducted, no further modifications should be performed until after 90 days of live, stable system operation. The system as it will be used live is now available for further testing. While the lean commerce team has conducted some tests on customer-facing processes, the testing cycle is now expanded to include users at the manufacturing plants and at corporate headquarters. Plant and corporate teams will participate in testing the software during the prototype/pilot, process, and stress tests. Successful completion of these tests will confirm that the processes performing the work are understood, that these processes have been improved and can be successfully accomplished with the new software, and that the manual workarounds that have been developed in lieu of modifications will work.

The three primary objectives for testing are (1) to move testing from the Lean Performance teams to the wider user base of the manufacturing sites, (2) to ensure that the data, programs, processes, and hardware can support the daily business of the enterprise, and (3) to expose any odd or exceptional circumstances now rather than during live operations by conducting final testing of the improved processes with the fully involved users. This last objective is achieved utilizing actual plant data to exercise the software by entering transactions in the manner in which they will ordinarily be performed. In this way, testing involves the process owners, process customers, and system users.

A number of secondary goals are accomplished by this testing, including data validation and on-site testing of all programs, hardware, and networks. Team members also validate process workflows and work instructions and provide initial hands-on training. The information team attempts to ensure system stability and verify system control settings while developing audit procedures for critical data and establishing tolerances where necessary for data calculations, such as unit-of-measure conversions and standard cost calculation variances.

Prototype and Pilot Test

The prototype and pilot test is conducted at the conclusion of the Lean Performance Analysis, prior to the process and stress tests, to ensure that the system is functioning adequately for the more involved testing. The prototype and pilot test is performed using a controlled script, a roadmap, that ensures that all system functions are tested in a sequence reasonably mirroring the live configuration (Figure 12.1). Often, such a roadmap is available from the software vendor or a third-party source. If not, it can be developed by reviewing the system menus and tracing a path through the essential system transactions. The test should be performed by the Lean Performance team leaders. All the process owners will be involved later on in the full process testing, but for now the team leaders are attempting to validate software system functionality, not software process applicability.

To conduct the prototype and pilot test utilizing a prepared roadmap:

- Load data using test data conversions or process data conversions in the same way they will be utilized at the system cutover.
- Confirm the usability and integrity of individual screens and functions using a single-level assembly BOM.
- Expand the test to include a subassembly BOM level after the initial single-level test is successful.
- Run the test cycle with a full product structure.
- Present the test results to the full project team in a team presentation.

Project result: prototype and pilot test results

Establishing the Test Team

Plant test teams conduct much of the testing. Project management should provide overall test coordination of test cycles, assist with problem resolution, and deploy the resources necessary to support plant teams. All

DATA-BASE REVIEW ACTIVITIES

Organization ____
Plants ___ and ____

Print and verify completeness and accuracy of system data for assemblies selected for testing activities:

    Assembly Selected :

XXXXXXXX-XXX

Print	Screen
Multi Level Bill Of Material Report	AAAA
Routing Master Listing	BBBB
Inventory Planning Data Listing	CCCC
Inventory Master Listing	DDDD
Work Center Listing	EEEE

    Verify

Completeness of Items on BOM

Accuracy of Items on BOM

Update BOM as necessary

Completeness of Routing Operations

Accuracy of Routing Operations

Update Routings as necessary

Completeness of Inventory Planning Data

Accuracy of Inventory Planning Data

Completeness of Inventory Master

Accuracy of Inventory Master

Completeness of Work Center Data

Accuracy of Work Center Data

User Tables

Figure 12.1 Pilot Prototype Test Roadmap

team members should be involved in the final review of the testing activity prior to going live with the new manufacturing software. An announcement should be sent to all test participants outlining the pilot/prototype process and stress test activities and schedules. Plant team leaders and coordinators should be selected to prepare for the kick-off session and assume the responsibility for determining or confirming plant process owner assignments. Plant team leaders should also be responsible for gathering one day of data for the initial test cycle. Plant teams should include:

- Plant team leaders
- Plant team process test coordinators

SYSTEM SET UP ACTIVITIES

Review current system planning status	FFFF
Print a Planning/Scheduling Report	GGGG
Review current system production plan	HHHH
For each product	
Set up Planning Forecasts Through December	IIII
For each product	
Enter a very low month forecast that we can consume using same month customer orders as we enter them	
Review Customer Master Data for Customer _____	JJJJ
Update Where Necessary	KKKK
Review Customer Credit Maintenance	LLLL
Update Where Necessary	
Review Price/Contracts for Customer _____	MMMM
Update Where Necessary	NNNN
Set up Safety Stock/Beginning Inventory	OOOO
Set MRP control fences at Zero by plant	PPPP
Review Multi-Plant Setup/Correct Where Necessary	QQQQ
Multi-Plant Plant Definitions	RRRR
Multi-Plant Trading Definition	SSSS
Multi-Plant Control Maintenance	TTTT
Multi-Plant Location Type Maintenance	UUUU
Review Product Costing	
Run Incremental Cost Calculation	VVVV
Run Accumulated Cost Rollup	WWWW
Review Labor/Machine Rate Code Maintenance	XXXX
Review Product Cost Listings	YYYY
Single Level Product Cost Report	ZZZZ
Multi Level Product Cost Report	aaaa

Figure 12.1   Pilot Prototype Test Roadmap (cont.)

- Plant process owners
- Lean Performance team leaders from all teams
- Test support resources, including consultants
- Information systems support resources

At least one information systems resource person should be assigned to each scheduled session and should be on-call. An information systems test leader should be assigned to coordinate rosters, schedules, and activities with the information team and to report results of the tests to all information team members. The test leader should be at each session in the initial cycle. Developers (including vendors) responsible for modified programs should be on-call for any reasonably scheduled session dealing with their programs.

TEST CYCLE 1

Load Sales Forecasts for Month_____
    Week _1___
    Week _2___
    Week _3___
    Week _4___
    Week _5___
	bbbb

Enter Customer orders for each product	cccc
Enter Only for weeks __1__ and __2__	
Customer ____	

Each part/for each week
        Use quantities both less than
        and greater than forecasted (mix them up)	

Be sure that order is not on hold or at incomplete status	
Review impact of orders entered on planning inquirie	dddd
Review impact of orders entered on Planning/Scheduling Report	eeee
Review impact of orders entered on planning maintenance	ffff
Review impact of orders on customer inquiries and listings	gggg hhhh iiii
Run Low Level Code	jjjj
Correct system demand data as necessary. Set up and run MRP	kkkk
Review system planning status	llll
Print a Planning/Scheduling Report	mmmm
Review impact of orders entered on planning inquiries for each product	nnnn
Review impact of orders entered on Planning/Scheduling Report	oooo
Review impact of orders entered on planning maintenance	pppp
Review Multi-Plant Requirements Inquiry	qqqq
Review Multi-Plant Shipments Inquiry	rrrr
Review/Revise Multi-Plant Order Print Flag Maintenance	sss

Figure 12.1   Pilot Prototype Test Roadmap (cont.)

Test Team Kick-Off Meeting

At the kick-off meeting, all attendees are introduced to the process and stress testing, including the objectives and goals and the structure and schedules of test activity. Plant team members review and confirm initial plant operating cycles, such as start–end, MPS generation, or material resource planning (MRP) generation. They should be prepared to review and finalize rosters and assignments, test setup activities, and the process groups that will be used in the initial test cycles. Team members also review and confirm the schedule for the initial test, as well as the forms and procedures to be used in the tests. Team leaders issue instructions to plant process owners and customers to identify and collect documents before

TEST CYCLE 1 cont.

Review Production Planning Maintenance for Global Orders	
Production Planning Maintenance (FG)	ttttt
Production Planning Maintenance (Component)	uuuu
Item (FG) Inquiry	vvvv
Item Component Inquiry	wwww
Review Planning/Scheduling Inquiry by Department	xxxx
Perform Production Planning Maintenance for Global Orders	
Release Week __1__ - __2__ orders	
Production Planning Maintenance (FG)	yyyy
Production Planning Maintenance (Component)	zzzz
Item (FG) Inquiry	1111
Item Component Inquiry	2222
Review Production Planning/Scheduling Inquiry by Department	3333
Print a Planning/Scheduling Report	4444
Submit Requisition for Spot Buy	5555
Approve Purchase Requisitions	6666
Process Requisitions to P.O. Line Release	7777
Receive Purchased Material	8888
Simulate and report pay for production for each motor.	
Report Week __1__ orders	
Labor/Production Entry	9999
Finished Goods Receipts	1010
Review Journal Entries	1212
Reverse several transactions	
Operation Backflush Transaction Reversal	1313
Labor Transaction Reversal	1414
Material Transaction Reversal	1515
Review Journal Entries	1616

Figure 12.1 Pilot Prototype Test Roadmap (cont.)

initial test cycle. Each plant selects its own documents/data for each test cycle. A progress reporting procedure is discussed that includes a daily conference call among plant test teams. Tests are conducted in the plants at user workstations as if the processes were "live." The people who will be participating in the system stress test are specified, and dates and times are established. Any necessary clarification of the test procedure is provided, including making it clear that each team member should select a transaction for repeated, continuous data entry to "stress" the system.

Process Test

The process test utilizes the process workflow standards developed by the team members. The primary activities of the process test are the testing of process workflow standards and finalization of the process work instructions. The test teams will review progress on a daily basis by plant and

TEST CYCLE 1 cont

Process Scrap Transactions	1717
Process Disposition Entries	18118
Process Material Issues	1919
Perform Multi-Plant Requirements Maintenance	2020
Perform Multi-Plant Order Consolidation	2121
Perform Multi-Plant Shipments	2323
Perform Multi-Plant Order Print	2424
Perform Multi-Plant Receipts	2525
Review Multi-Plant Requirements Inquiry	2626
Review Multi-Plant Shipments Inquiry	2727
Set Pick List Print Flags	2828
Set Packing Slip Print Flags	2929
Set BOL Print Flags	3030
Perform Ship List Maintenance for Week __1__ Order s	3131
Print Shipping List	3232
Perform Telzon Upload	3434
Perform Pick List Maintenance for Week __1__ Order s	3535
Print Pick List	3636
Perform Ship by Pick List for Week __1__ Order s	3737
Print Packing List	3838
Print Bill of Lading	3939
Perform Telzon Download	4040
Review ASN processing.	

Figure 12.1 Pilot Prototype Test Roadmap (cont.)

post and resolve open issues. They also schedule the nightly supporting batch processes. Setup and information support activities might include the loading of data from the preproduction environments, if utilized, into the test environment. Responsibility for the test setup tasks (including data loading, setup tables and validation, and security) is established. Data in the test environment is managed with the backup/restore procedures defined in the information systems daily operations schedule, as though the system were "live," in order to test those processes. All end-of-day processes, interfaces, backups, and batch processes are added to the operating schedule of information systems and performed to that schedule throughout the test cycle. Data setup testing includes a full EDI/XML data

TEST CYCLE 1 cont

Review impact of orders shipped on planning inquiries	4141
Review impact of orders shipped on Planning/Scheduling Report	4242
Review impact of orders shipped on planning maintenance	4343
Review impact of orders shipped on customer inquiries and listings	4545 4646 4747

Simulate and report pay for production for each motor.
  Report Week __2__ orders
    Labor/Production Entry
    Finished Goods Receipts
	
	4848
	4949

Review Journal Entries	5050

Reverse several transactions
  Operation Backflush Transaction Reversal
  Labor Transaction Reversal
  Material Transaction Reversal
	
	5151
	5252
	5353

Process Scrap Transactions	5454
Process Disposition Entries	5656
Process Material Issues	5757
Perform Ship List Maintenance for Week __2__ Orders	5858
Print Shipping List	5959
Perform Telzon Upload	6060
Perform Pick List Maintenance for Week __2__ Orders	6161
Print Pick List	6262
Perform Ship by Pick List for Week __2__ Orders	6363
Print Packing List	6464
Print Bill of Lading	6565
Perform Telzon Download	6767
Review ASN processing	6868

Figure 12.1   Pilot Prototype Test Roadmap (cont.)

load and MRP generation. All users are verified, and all information systems processes and documentation are fully tested, with information systems personnel assigned to all system operations as though they were "live." Completion of all setup activities are verified prior to the start of testing, and a "go/no-go" procedure should be followed. A final project team meeting ensures that preparations are complete, and equipment and data readiness are verified. The entire company should be notified of the testing activities and schedules.

Management of MRP processing is a critical issue for the testing process, in that data expectations for material planning, the use of bills of materials (BOMs), and work center and cost information are all dependent on system generations. During the test, MRP full generations should be run only after the day's testing ends and only as approved during the daily afternoon review session. MRP partial generations on new or items with new demand activity may be run between testing cycles (e.g., 12:00 p.m. and 4:00 p.m.) when continued testing is required and only with full team agreement. The concern here is not to disrupt or penalize those testers who are proceeding through a cycle involving data validation.

Each test session should have specific goals, and a checklist should identify the percentage of goals completed. A daily morning conference call among plant test teams is used to coordinate activities, and a daily afternoon conference call is used to report results. Tests are conducted at user workstations in the plants involved. The test team enters actual transactions that simulate a day's business, and various reports and queries can validate the results during and after the entry of these transactions. Data collected at each plant include all documents that can be used to recreate a day's business. Any or all of the following may be utilized:

- EDI order report
- Returned materials
- Credit memos
- Debit memos
- Shipping lists
- Inventory reports
- Bills of lading
- Scrap tickets
- Pick lists
- Packing slips
- Invoices
- Pay tickets
- Weekly production plans
- Production schedules
- Sales and operating plans
- Consigned material shippers
- Consigned material receivers

The open issue log should be maintained centrally and reviewed before each session, with categories or types of open issues and problems categorized as:

- System operations
- Bug
- Modification needed
- Modification not working

- Business decision/policy needed
- Additional headcount required by workaround
- Process workflow/work instruction update needed
- Training needed

The regular daily cycle for order entry through shipping is defined by each plant team, with the activities that occur at regular (e.g., weekly or monthly) intervals being noted where or when they occur within the regular daily cycle, as are the differences in cycle lengths within the overall business cycle (e.g., quarterly, semiannually, or yearly). The plant teams gather the supporting documents utilized to generate the transactions and retain those documents throughout the first 30 days of live system processing. Initially, these documents include copies of all data-input documents utilized to process a day's worth of business and eventually will represent one week's normal business. During the test, teams resolve any differences among plants in their global system processes. Issues such as how often to run MRP and any others that arise should be resolved.

During the test, teams determine requirements for future information system support. The information support schedule is refined from these activities, and any conflicts between information support capabilities and plant requirements are resolved. Each plant submits its own documents and data (e.g., parts, customers) for each test cycle. Each plant also should have a full set of process workflows and work instructions available at the start of the tests.

The test cycles begin with an initial system demonstration test cycle that consists of limited, selected data (one or two selected processes, several customer orders, etc.) entered by each plant team and processed according to the schedule established for this exercise. When one plant has successfully completed one cycle, the next plant begins. When all of the plants have successfully completed the first cycle, they begin to process the second cycle in the same order. When all of the plants have completed all of the cycles, the initial test ends and the results are reviewed.

The second test expands the activity by having all plants enter data simultaneously. At the conclusion of each cycle, the results should be reviewed. The third test consists of all users of one plant entering all data for all cycles throughout the period simultaneously. That plant is followed by each successive plant. The fourth and subsequent tests consist of all users at all plants entering all data for all activities for all cycles simultaneously on each business day remaining before cutover.

Process groups are suggested as a starting point for the development of logical test cycles. Test teams determine their cycles according to the daily and weekly operating cycles in their facilities. A process group should consist of all the processes governed by a Lean Performance team.

Cycle one processes could consist of:

- EDI/XML order load
- Order entry
- Shipment initiation
- Production reporting

Cycle two could build on the first cycle to include:

- EDI/XML order load
- Order entry
- Scheduling
- Component scheduling
- Build and pay with bar code (production reporting)
- Shipment initiation
- Process shipment

Cycle three could build further to include:

- EDI/XML order load
- Scheduling
- Vendor scheduling and releasing
- Receiving
- Build and pay with bar code
- Shipment initiation
- Process shipment

Additional cycles should test all processes on the process master index, and the cross-functional teams can have specific cycles. The testing process for the finance team could include:

- An order with multiplant demand on the manufacturing plants
- Cross-plant routing with a part coming back to the original plant
- Outside operation of service at a vendor
- EDI or XML invoice

The testing process for the materials team could include:

- Bar-code incoming and outgoing
- Physical inventory

The following processes could be included in the testing process for the operations team:

- Departmental schedules
- Outside operation departmental schedule
- Scrap and re-op tickets, including reversals
- Interplant moves without MRP-driven action or order records
- Overriding traffic routing to split shipments (air/truck)
- Corrections of shipping documents
- Shipment of multiple item numbers
- Ship interface testing where applicable
- Print documents on equipment to be used live
- ASNs
- Customer/vendor return material process
- Quality on-hold and off-hold process

The testing process for the materials team could include:

- Daily pricing process
- Sales analysis process
- ASNs
- Automatic order pull
- Test of firm and forecast orders
- Purchasing EDI/XML

The testing process for the engineering team could include:

- Coordinating the engineering change process
- Testing multiple material changes using effectivity on same BOM revision level
- Testing master assembly drawings as phantoms

Constant information change should occur throughout the test cycles, with processes being performed in nonsequential order. Additionally, any special cases that could impact system operations should be tested.

Project result: process test results

Stress Test

Participation in the stress test should include all members of the user community. In the stress test, each user selects a transaction for repeated and continuous data entry to "stress" the system. Prior to the actual stress test, the stress test procedure should specify that all process owners and customers, as well as all other system users, will participate in the system stress test on assigned dates and times. The system environment security should be reset to put the participants into the proper environment upon sign-in. The initial daily information systems operating cycle is determined during the test process, as are the off-line programs, batch, backup, restore, and interface download timing. One full process test cycle in at least one plant must be completed before the stress test can be performed. The stress test plan documents how, when, where, and who will confirm the hardware load analysis and test all downloads, interfaces, conversion programs, and data transfers at expected system operational load volumes and beyond. Responsibility for testing all system operations procedures and scenarios (e.g., back-up, recovery, security, daily/weekly or other batches, off-line system programs and/or generations) should be assigned. Response times and operational problems for all test scenarios and conditions are noted, and corrections and repeat testing are carried out until satisfactory results are obtained.

Project result: stress test results

Process Workflow and Work Instruction Update

All process workflow and work instructions must be available for review on and printing from a system drive accessible to all Lean Performance team members. Process workflow and work instructions that are distributed with the training agendas and packages are at "pre-issue" levels. They are subject to change during the test process being conducted by team leaders and process owners and customers and may be revised and improved. Before the process test, each plant team participating should designate a member as document coordinator. This person notes and collects changes, revisions, updates, and improvements to process workflows and work instructions. Changes determined during testing and training sessions are noted by team leaders and given to the document coordinators for input. Document coordinators ensure that appropriate changes are managed properly. If an individual plant proposes that a separate process be developed for that plant only, the document coordinator reviews the request with the project manager for a decision. Where the task structure of a process must be changed, the document coordinators must communicate with all the affected plants to determine if the change dictates that a separate process workflow be developed for that plant only. Document coordinators make changes to process workflows (changes to work instructions should be done by technical writers, if available). System user comments collected during the user training program and change requests generated during process testing are reviewed prior to formal issuance of process workflows and work instructions to identify process changes required and make any necessary process documentation changes.

Project result: network-resident process workflow and work instruction standards

Conducting the User Training Program

The four important steps to take in preparing for and conducting an effective user training program are:

1. Plan the user training program thoroughly to assure that all departments, process owners, process customers, and system users are adequately trained to successfully operate and support the new system. It may be necessary to repeat some of the earlier classes held for new hires, replacements, and stragglers.
2. Utilize the process workflow work instruction standards for all training sessions to ensure that the training is appropriate for the system and to help the company trainer monitor updates of the training material.
3. Prepare an agenda for each training session that includes instructor information, process standards to be utilized, major topics, and scheduling and location information.
4. Publish the user training plan on the project web page (the training assignments spreadsheet can be reworked for this purpose). The project chat room can be utilized to expand access to user training program information.

Project result: user training plan

A focus of the training sessions should be to record comments and issues from the system users, who serve as the most credible basis for declaring the system ready to go live. Once again, all project documents and updated diagrams should be gathered for a quality assurance review. The updated documents are then distributed to the project team, and the project results to date are reviewed with the steering committee.

WHAT FOLLOWS LEAN PERFORMANCE IMPROVEMENT?

Phase three, Continuous Lean Performance, follows phase two Lean Performance Improvement activities. In this third and final project phase, all project implementation tasks remaining are identified and prioritized, process and system GAPs are closed, and process measurements are implemented. At the conclusion of the project, Lean Performance Management is implemented, and process continuous improvement activities are a reality in all processes.

IV

CONTINUOUS LEAN PERFORMANCE MODULES

The third and final project phase, Continuous Lean Performance, begins as phase two Lean Performance Improvement activities are being completed. By this time, improved processes are operating in and across the enterprise. The project manager and team are confident that they have initiated a continuous Lean Performance culture, not just a few isolated, obvious successes. The key indicator that continuous Lean Performance is ongoing in a given process area is the existence of formal (written) process standards. When process workflow and work instruction standards are formalized, they can be analyzed and maintained as the basis for managing and continually improving processes. The current standard is always the interim target to be used for further improvement.

As continuous improvement becomes a way of life in the company, the transition to continuous top-down policy deployment and a bottom-up continuous improvement cycle should begin. As Lean Performance expands across the cross-functional and cross-enterprise processes, layers of management can be stripped away. Managers become coaches and problem solvers for proactive physical and information/support process workers. New management positions result, some emerging on a product-line-management basis, others on a process-area basis. We will explore various lean enterprise management positions in this section.

Another indicator that continuous Lean Performance has become a part of a firm's culture is verified by the prevalence of workers employing continuous improvement practices to initiate improvements without management intervention or direction. Yet another sign of a continuous improvement culture is that all continuous improvements are being recognized and rewarded as a key employee attribute incorporated in employee evaluations and compensation. To be sustained, continuous improvement recognition and reward must be organized and managed as a permanent set of corporate human resource management activities. It is essential to establish these lean human resource practices to sustain the momentum of Lean Performance, and a minimum continuous improvement effort is necessary just to maintain processes and systems in place as they are at project end.

In this final project phase, general management-level decision processes become the important focus. Previously existing departmental reporting structures must be subordinated to newly emerging cross-functional and cross-enterprise processes and the necessity to manage and support them. The implementation of these lean processes has changed the organizational structure and management reporting requirements, and these management changes must be formalized to be sustained. As the lean processes become operational, they must be organized and managed by the ongoing management decision processes of the company. These management processes must also be lean, meaning that standardization of management decision processes must take place, including development of process standards and documentation.

As in the case of developing physical and information/support process standards (workflows, work instructions), methods of measurement and data collection must be incorporated in the management decision process standards as well. Management reports should be formatted to document lean evaluation criteria and review procedures, including criteria to relate pay and other compensation to firm performance (lean human resources management). Lean organization and management methods must now become the dominant way of structuring and operating. For example, lean education and training must be integrated into the existing education and training function. Another example is the development of lean accounting methods (e.g., *muda* free costing) to be used as the basis for periodic management reports.

13

IMPLEMENTING IMPROVED PROCESSES MODULE

MANAGEMENT TASKS

Maintaining Lean Performance Teams

Many emerging lean firms reorganize by product family when the initial lean processes are formalized, implemented, and being managed on an ongoing basis. While various personnel decisions may have been made during the life of the project, at this stage implementing additional personnel reductions or removing any remaining anchor-draggers can destroy the emerging lean teamwork in the enterprise. Maintaining commitment to the lean cultural principles is essential to sustaining the lean enterprise, chief among which is the maxim that no one loses his or her job for implementing an improvement. At this stage, everyone is viewed as having implemented improvements, and normal attrition and team-based evaluations are the vehicle of choice for eliminating those who are not team players. The teams will weed these folks out in a hurry. Formal process teams, organized by product family where feasible, have by now become the norm. Excess personnel can be assigned variously, until company growth and normal attrition can absorb them. For example, additional Lean Performance teams may need to be redefined for system implementation of the enterprise resource planning (ERP), operations planning system (OPS), manufacturing execution system (MES), customer relationship management (CRM), supply chain management (SCM), or other system enablers driving the project or recently deployed. Additional Lean Performance teams that can be defined for improved process implementation might include a team to manage the accuracy and usefulness of bills of materials (BOMs) and routings or a team to monitor inventory accuracy.

These implementation Lean Performance teams can provide system stability for the entire implementation. Recommendations for additional Lean Performance teams that might be needed are developed during the first implementation readiness assessment. Membership is determined by considering skill levels required to perform tasks documented in the implementation work plan and the new tasks defined in the improved processes. We will examine the objectives and tasks of several possible implementation Lean Performance teams next, including:

- Bill of materials team
- Financial data team
- Material requirements planning (MRP) data team
- System user team
- Process documentation team
- Steering committee policy team
- Data accuracy team

An initial meeting should be held with each Lean Performance team to review each team's implementation work plan, the tasks for which are derived from the open tasks identified in the readiness assessments. Each Lean Performance team should estimate the work days required to complete the team's tasks and confirm the expected completion dates for each task on their work plan. The Lean Performance teams should also define team objectives. A weekly team meeting is scheduled to report status and identify open issues. Before the weekly meetings, each Lean Performance team identifies, records, and resolves implementation issues utilizing the open issue format and Lean Performance analysis. Team leaders meet cross-functionally to review the status of open issues and provide resolution to them or seek resolution through the newly emerging cross-functional and cross-enterprise process managers (we will discuss these positions in detail below). Weekly team reviews with project management are also held to report status and identify open issues requiring further attention. The teams determine the methods and reports to be used to audit data. All teams should use central data, with no exceptions. If necessary, new reports can be developed for team use. Teams should also revise or prepare process workflow standards and work instructions to assure ongoing continuous Lean Performance.

The objectives of the BOMs team are to determine the methods and data necessary to audit BOMs, coordinate with affected process owners, assign audit responsibility, train the assigned personnel, and implement the BOM audit process. The team also identifies and corrects problems in the process as required and measures and reports BOM accuracy as part of the performance measurement process. BOM team members include representatives from engineering, operations, materials, and accounting.

The objectives of the financial data team are to determine the validity of critical transactions and financial data as currently processed by the system and develop and perform data and logic testing where necessary. The financial data team also designs, develops, tests, and implements additional information/support processes and system capabilities where required to produce valid financial data and reports. The financial data team includes representatives from materials and plant-level accounting as well as finance and audit.

The objectives of the MRP data team are to determine validity of critical system transactions affecting MRP processing, validate MRP results as produced by the system, and develop and perform data and logic testing where necessary. The MRP data team also designs, develops, tests, and implements additional information/support processes and system capabilities where required to realize valid MRP data. Members of the MRP data team should include representatives from materials and plant-level accounting as well as finance.

The primary objective of the system user team is to survey initial system implementation results by performing user surveys focusing on two categories: winners and concerns. Winners should be reflected in the process performance measurements. An initial recognition of winners should be published for the entire firm to see and recognize. Concerns are really more the ongoing focus of this team. Any concern about system viability should be formalized by developing and initiate an open issue, especially for any concerns requiring further action. This should include critical system improvements. The system user team also assists the project manager in analyzing open implementation issues and determining the priorities of issues that do not affect the going-live process. Team members attend software vendor user group conferences and research available software offerings, current releases, future planned releases, etc. The system user team also determines the regular daily operating cycle for each plant from order entry through the shipping processes. The members of the system user team are best positioned to note differences in activities that occur at regular (weekly, monthly) intervals and to use this analysis to determine requirements for offline processing and establish the daily operating requirements necessary for information systems to support plant activities. The system user team also determines and supports all reporting requirements for plant-level management reports as well as performance measurements. The team determines the information system operating cycles for daily, weekly, monthly, and yearly activities, including all interfaces, downloads, backups, and batch processes. The team publishes guidelines and a change management process to manage all system changes and manage those proposed changes with the approved change management process (discussed below). Finally, the system user team provides input to the trainer to assist in the development and maintenance of the ongoing system. Members of the system user team should include a system user team leader and process area representatives.

The objectives of the process documentation team are to finalize system documentation so all process workflows and work instructions are up to date for the final implemented system, format and complete all system documentation to meet QS 9000 or ISO standards, and determine effective use of system documentation to assist in ongoing training activities. Members of the process documentation team should include the project trainer, facilitator, information systems analysts, quality assurance, and a representative from the steering or Lean Performance management committee.

The objectives of the steering committee policy team are threefold. The steering committee policy team formalizes the necessary business policies to manage the system, coordinates documentation of those activities with the process documentation team to ensure that formats and standards are met, and certifies completion of the project to the steering committee so the transition to Lean Performance management can be recognized and the project concluded. The members of the steering committee policy team should include representatives of all process areas or their process cross-functional or cross-enterprise managers, including those from sales and marketing, engineering, customer relationship management, information systems, materials, purchasing, and finance.

The objective of the data accuracy team is to develop and implement data accuracy activities and measurements for critical system operating data, including routing accuracy and inventory accuracy. Members should include representatives from engineering, materials, and finance, as well as operating-level system users and supervisors.

Immediately after implementation, the project manager should hold an implementation review in each project site. During the implementation review, a winners/concerns survey should be distributed and all implementation Lean Performance teams announced. The system user team should be designated to follow up and begin to monitor ongoing system results and open issue priorities. Each team should begin to develop their workplan with the assistance of the project manager and facilitator.

Implementing Lean Performance Management

As the lean processes are implemented, the Lean Performance project focuses on the ongoing activities of the firm. Process changes have impacted ongoing operations in both anticipated and unanticipated ways, including some negative and/or dysfunctional ways. Management is the key player at this point in the transformation because organizational issues must be addressed. As the Lean Performance project ends, management must maintain the momentum toward the lean enterprise by disbanding the project steering committee and implementing Lean Performance management. The first tasks for the Lean Performance management team are to develop and publish the company policy for employee retention in a continuously improving lean enterprise and to devise a growth strategy that incorporates vendors and customers into the lean enterprise. A company approach to monitoring lean process performance measurements; staying current on new lean strategies, practices, and technologies; and continuously deploying management policy must be initiated in order to drive new lean strategies, practices, and technologies into the organization at a process level.

The project structure should be replaced by a new Lean Performance management configuration as soon as it becomes clear that the characteristics of continuous Lean Performance have taken hold, with the steering committee transitioning into the Lean Performance management team. Process area coordinators should still have the responsibility of monitoring and evaluating progress in their respective areas. They may become process managers or cross-functional or cross-enterprise process managers, positions that are described in some detail below. Lean Performance management is based on the expectation of sustained continuous improvement in all processes in the organization, particularly administrative and operational processes, management processes, and processes delivering any aspect of products and services.

Lean Performance management in the lean enterprise must also be identified and performed within a set of processes: "Of all the processes in an organization, management processes are the most poorly defined and least likely to be viewed in process terms. Indeed, some would argue that the term 'management processes' is an oxymoron" (Davenport, T.H., *Process Innovation,* Harvard Business School Press, Boston, MA, 1993, p. 275). Three popular views of the art of management are (1) management is a personal activity that cannot be described in a process definition; (2) some tasks performed by management personnel can be identified as a process or processes, but not all of them; and (3) management in a lean environment is not possible if management is not willing to subject its responsibilities and roles to the scrutiny of process orientation. In regard to the last point, a lean enterprise operates on the principle of reciprocal obligations; that is, *all* members of a lean enterprise have responsibilities and roles that they must fulfill, and all members of the firm have a right to assume that others will fulfill their responsibilities and roles. The conclusion here is that the effort to standardize management processes in the lean environment must be undertaken by a committed management, even if it seems that the results will never be perfect.

As stated in the lean principles, pursue perfection. The degree of process orientation in defining management in a firm is determined by the management of that firm, keeping in mind that a process orientation to management is a requirement for efficient and effective lean transformation and lean operations. Management in a lean enterprise is freer than management in a traditional organization because the more a firm operates as a set of integrated lean processes, the less a firm's activities require management intervention; the leaner the enterprise, the greater the scope of activities of employees and the leaner the enterprise, the greater the proportion of management activities that have been defined in process terms, which results in more time available for non-process activities (as defined by each firm). Examples of managerial positions in the lean enterprise include:

- *Lean coordinator:* A project manager generally becomes a lean coordinator in the lean enterprise, especially in the transitional period when the Lean Performance project is turning into Lean Performance management, the transition to lean processes is gaining momentum, and the rate and scope of change are increasing. This position is designated when the steering committee begins to formalize Lean Performance management at the conclusion of the project.
- *Process manager:* Because the basic building block in a lean organization is the process, it follows that process managers need the skills of the process owner. These managers are well-versed in value, value-add, flow, pull, and other lean principles, tools, and practices and are able to apply them in the processes that they own and/or manage.
- *Cross-functional process manager:* Silo management assumes functional specialization with minimal functional interaction. In a lean organization, cross-functional processes must be managed from the perspective of functional specialization coupled with a more multi-functional and organizational approach, with an eye on customer value. This type of management is fostered by functional cooperation, not competition. The cross-functional process manager points the way by developing this dual perspective.
- *Cross-enterprise process manager:* Enterprise partnerships require functional specialization with inter- and intra-enterprise functional interaction. The position of cross-enterprise process manager requires a perspective of functional specialization coupled with a multifunctional and multiorganizational approach, with an eye on enterprise customer value. The activities of this position are fostered by functional cooperation, not competition — a very difficult dual perspective to foster.

These positions may already be formalized in the organization, as they will emerge in any organization transforming into a lean enterprise. *Lean Performance management* is a term that arises as the project is ending and the positions discussed here are emerging as a management structure in the lean enterprise.

Continuously Deploying Lean Policy and Strategy

Continuous deployment of lean business strategies developed as a result of monitoring and evaluating both internal process measurements and external developments in technologies and lean techniques is the primary activity of Lean Performance management. To implement continuous deployment of lean business strategies, a series of processes similar to the initial Lean Performance planning of the project is carried out:

- Identify lean business policy.
- Identify lean process strategies.
- Deploy lean policies and strategies.
- Perform the Lean Performance analysis continuously.

Deployment of lean business strategies initiates continuous improvement on a top–down basis and has three objectives: (1) introduce into process management activities the new lean techniques and technologies that may be useful to process owners for improving the value-add of their processes, (2) ensure that process standards are reviewed on a periodic basis to determine whether they can be improved, and (3) ensure that the search continues for new avenues to investigate for process applications through Lean Performance analysis. The Lean Performance project to this point has increased the organization's responsiveness not only to customers but to all relevant change and improvement opportunities. Learning how to get lean has been the focus, but now it is possible and necessary to consider new options. Because most changes so far have been small and incremental, they have not posed major problems. It is the cumulative and continuous impact of these changes that now presents a challenge to management.

In most firms, a business plan is comprehensively evaluated, reviewed, improved, and published at least annually. In Lean Performance management, this business plan is evaluated, updated, and redeployed through identification of lean business policies and strategies and the deployment of Lean Performance analysis masters. The information and other engineers deploy new technology opportunities to the process teams for process identification and application. Management expects and receives feedback from the process teams as they apply lean improvements. In the annual business evaluation, management examines how effective they have been in deploying the lean vision, lean mission, lean business policies, and lean strategies from the previous year. Individual policy deployment Lean Performance analysis masters are then initiated as the formal handoff from management to the organization for the year's Lean Performance analysis. In this approach, management initiates the Lean Performance analysis by deploying lean policy and strategy. Process managers respond with deployment at the process level, as in the project. This activity can become a bit of a free-for-all if management allows it to. At this point, lean thinking has been integrated in the ongoing management process. There is also a mechanism providing for periodic evaluation of the lean opportunities available to the company, as new resources, opportunities, and alternative growth paths become available all the time and lean process improvements continuously free up resources with which to pursue them.

While the journey to lean in an organization is never complete, there comes a time when being lean is the dominant orientation, value set, organization mode, and management style. A constant education, training, and development program is in place for management, professionals, staff, and work force. While the Lean Performance project produces incremental process improvements, at some point ongoing process improvements do not require much management attention. At that point, new challenges should be introduced (for example, moving to administrative processes).

Auditing Lean Performance

The project process has included extensive testing, beginning with the lean commerce team test of the customer critical data interfaces and extending through the pilot/prototype, process, and stress tests. The project team should be reasonably sure that they will have a successful cutover. In order to be absolutely sure that the live system is performing properly, project management should prepare now to conduct postimplementation Lean Performance audits 1 week, 6 weeks, and 12 weeks after processes are implemented or until all audit criteria are performing to expectation. To conduct a Lean Performance audit, an outside reviewer can be called upon to review project performance with the project manager and/or lean coordinator by looking at specific issues:

- User satisfaction
- Budget performance
- User understanding
- Schedule performance
- Open issue review
- Project objectives attained

The reviewer will likely want to meet with each team. Team members will identify specific operating and system problems during the audit by exhibiting documentation and examples. The project manager or lean coordinator should be available to review issues with appropriate Lean Performance teams in order to prioritize problems for resolution and develop resolutions and corrective actions. The project manager or lean coordinator should present the audit results in outline form to the steering committee or the Lean Performance management team for action. Any unresolved issues should be the lead items at the next review. Problem resolution results should also be covered and closed at the next audit.

Audits results can be measured using three criteria or any variation of them that more adequately fits a given environment:

- Survival
- Stability
- Improving

An audit result of survival status means that the system and teams are able to perform the following:

- Recognize 100% of customer orders.
- Obtain material to produce product.
- Produce product.
- Ship all product produced.
- Fax or otherwise document shipments to customer (ASNs).
- Invoice all shipments accurately.
- Audit shipments to invoice.

When these items are satisfactory, the team can be reasonably sure that the new system and processes are having no adverse effect on the team's customers.

An audit result of stability status means that the system and teams are able to perform the following:

- Recognize 100% of customer orders.
- Load customer orders into proper schedule weeks.
- Report schedule information for customer shipment requirements.
- Generate MRP demand planning data for materials.
- Validate that material requirements are accurate.
- Obtain material to produce product.
- Report schedule information for final assembly requirements.
- Produce product.
- Ship all product produced to accurate order quantities.

- Fax or otherwise document shipments to customer (ASNs).
- Invoice all shipments accurately.
- Audit shipments to invoice.
- Generate useable financial data.

When these items are satisfactory, the team again can be reasonably sure that the new system and processes are having no adverse effect on customers or company operations. System and processes are meeting the minimum customer requirements for shipments and data.

An audit result of improving status means that the system and teams are able to perform the following:

- Load all eligible orders via EDI.
- Recognize 100% of customer orders.
- Load customer orders into proper schedule weeks.
- Schedule requirements for customer shipments with system data.
- Generate MRP demand planning data for materials.
- Validate that material requirements are accurate.
- Obtain material to produce product
- Schedule final assembly production.
- Produce product.
- Ship all product produced to accurate order quantities.
- Ship all customer orders with accurate customer information, including labels, tags, and bar codes.
- Report and document shipments to customer requirements using ASNs.
- Invoice all shipments accurately.
- Audit shipments to invoice.
- Generate auditable financial data.

As before, when these items are satisfactory, the team can be reasonably sure that the new system and processes are having no adverse effect on the team's customers or team operations and the team is meeting or exceeding customer requirements for shipments and data. The system will now support efforts at continuous improvement.

PROJECT TEAM TASKS

Completing the Implementation Readiness Assessments

After a review of the project plans for each implementation site, tasks remaining are identified and reported to the steering committee. Resource assignments are reviewed and adjusted. An implementation readiness assessment is prepared for each site. Additional workplan tasks that are

1. Process ownership must be reconciled for several financial and engineering processes between international site and corporate.
2. The bay routers were scheduled for delivery, but aren't here yet.
3. The construction of the communication building is not complete.
4. Testing of communication lines reveals problems with supplier. Also, need to look at LDDS problems.
5. System default control account files submitted for review are not yet approved for implementation.
6. New standard cost process is ready to implement. Will finalize workflow and work instructions prior to go-live.

Figure 13.1 Implementation Readiness Assessment for International Site

audited include establishing personnel requirements for the project team, identifying skill levels required to perform steps documented in the implementation work plan, monitoring work days required to complete each task of the implementation project, and monitoring target completion dates for each task. The project manager should also be sure that the installation of additional hardware is on track or completed. The entire team should prepare for cutover and startup support. The materials and data accuracy teams should verify that the system is ready for master production schedule (MPS) implementation based on item master and BOM accuracy. Team members should finalize conversion plans and schedules and obtain steering committee authorization to cutover to the new system and processes. A process should be in place for verifying data completeness and accuracy after the data are converted. All team members should monitor new system performance, and the project manager should review all open issues in preparation for the first audit. See Figure 13.1 for an illustration of the kinds of issues and tasks that are often uncovered during implementation readiness assessments. Implementation readiness assessments are performed at important project milestones. The final audit is the basis of the go/no-go decision. The implementation countdown begins with all remaining accepted items and the critical path defined.

Verifying System Integration

System integration is verified by completing a number of tasks that primarily involve the project manager, team leaders, and information systems team. A checklist for systems integration verification should include the following items:

- Identify additional hardware that might be needed.
- Prepare a detailed hardware installation schedule.
- Install additional hardware for testing prior to implementation.
- Verify that the system is ready to go live based on data accuracy.
- Evaluate information system personnel assignments.
- Identify manual tasks to run in parallel.
- Finalize conversion plans and schedules.
- Finalize cutover countdown.
- Confirm any tasks that must be maintained in parallel.
- Obtain steering committee authorization.

Counting Down to Implementation

Implementation countdown is the final component of the project workplan and includes all the tasks that must be completed before going live. The countdown must include all necessary tasks for going live, and the team must agree. All tasks must have the necessary resources available for on-time completion. Any task that appears on the final work plan that cannot be completed before going live must be investigated, and the consequences and implications of that uncompleted task should be communicated far and wide within the company, as no exceptions mean no surprises.

Implementing Improved Processes

Improved processes are implemented by area, process, or product line, depending on the Lean Performance management structure adopted. Data are converted, and completeness and accuracy are verified. The new system is cutover. Team update meetings are held to identify problems and answer questions, and audits are performed. The information team is notified of technical problems via the open issue procedure, in which system performance is monitored and the open issues are reviewed with the steering committee until the steering committee transitions into Lean Performance management.

Providing Additional Training

To provide additional training, project management must evaluate personnel assignments and revise them as necessary. New hires, transfers, and stragglers often must be rounded up and brought into the training cycle. Be sure to use process workflow and work instruction standards and real data to demonstrate new processes. Generally, the last item included in training is specifying the workaround tasks to be performed when the new system and processes go live. Any manual tasks to be maintained are determined, and those people who need to be trained in the tasks are identified.

Providing Production Startup Support

To provide production startup support, in addition to auditing the system performance, the project manager or lean coordinator should continue to identify and correct open issues and to review and formalize month-end close processes by assisting in the initial month-end close.

14

CONTINUOUSLY IMPROVING LEAN PERFORMANCE MODULE

PROJECT TEAM TASKS

Defining and Initiating Lean Performance Measurements

As we have seen, project objectives drive project performance, and measurable business objectives drive continuous Lean Performance, with a concentration in process quality, process cost and process throughput and speed measurements. Team members incorporate the Lean Performance analysis into the deployment and reporting of performance measurements. An example is provided as Figure 14.1. The three traditional reasons for measurements are:

- History
- Baseline
- Focus goal setting

The first law of performance measurements is *"All humans hate to be measured,"* the second law of performance measurements is *"If I'm going to be measured on something, I want to pick how the measurement works,"* and the third law of performance measurements is *"When the measurement shows that I'm improving, and especially if I get rewarded for improving, I like being measured."* The second corollary of the third law of performance measurements is *"Performance measurements tend to be used to make the organization look good, not to help the organization look for ways in which to improve."*

268 ■ Lean Performance ERP Project Management

Lean Business Policy:	Support Lean Manufacturing		Control Number
Lean Project Strategy:	Reduce Storage of WIP/Stage Mat'l		001-001-001-001
Project Objective:	Eliminate Returned Goods Room		
Technology Deployment:	Implement Online Credit Capability		
Process Identification:	Fuel Pump Returns		
Lean Performance Team:	Aftermarket Operations Team		

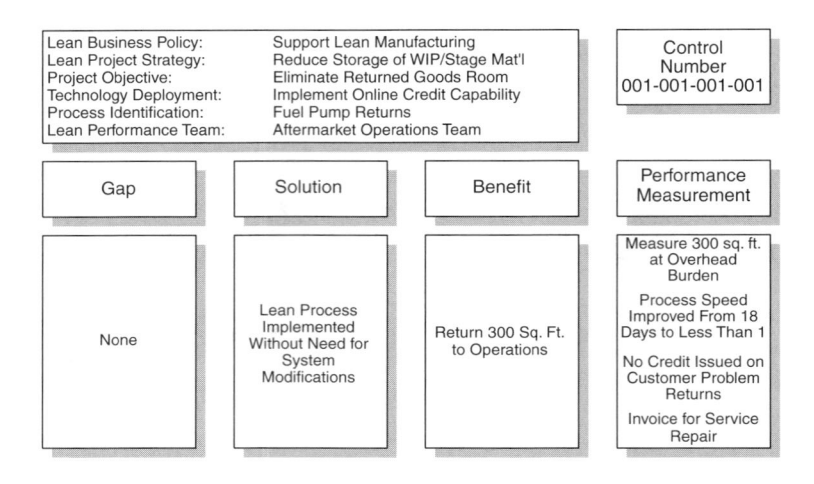

Gap	Solution	Benefit	Performance Measurement
None	Lean Process Implemented Without Need for System Modifications	Return 300 Sq. Ft. to Operations	Measure 300 sq. ft. at Overhead Burden Process Speed Improved From 18 Days to Less Than 1 No Credit Issued on Customer Problem Returns Invoice for Service Repair

Figure 14.1 Lean Performance Analysis: Process Measurement Identified

While the current performance measurements utilized to manage the business are probably going to remain in place after the project concludes, if Lean Performance is going to avoid the usual self-serving but not very useful performance measurements and also abide by the empowerment principles of the lean culture, principles for establishing new performance measurements are going to have to be established; for example:

- Performance measurements must be process oriented or based.
- Performance measurements must be visual.
- Performance measurements must be meaningful.

One important characteristic of processes is that process-cycle-focused or process-time-focused measurements tend to be more useful for continuous improvement efforts than other measurements. Reducing cycle time is generally an indicator that other measurable items are improving and usually means that non-value-add is decreasing or quality of output is increasing. In some cases, reduced cycle time can be an indicator that customer service is improving and it usually means that batches and queues are shrinking. One other benefit of focusing on cycle time is that it usually is easy to determine a measurement for it.

A Lean Performance measurements definition includes three types of measurements, as can be seen by the examples illustrated in Figure 14.2:

- Financial
- Operational
- Process

MANAGEMENT POLICY DEPLOYMENT AND MEASUREMENTS SUMMARY

GAP CONTROL#	LEAN BUSINESS POLICY	LEAN PROJECT STRATEGY	DEPLOYED PROJECT OBJECTIVE	TECHNOLOGY DEPLOYMENT	PROCESS IDENTIFICATION	LEAN PERFORMANCE TEAM	PERFORMANCE MEASUREMENT
001	Support Lean Manufacturing	Reduce Manufacturing Lead Time	Implement 24 hour turnaround of customer orders	Use system capability to generates pick/pack lists throughout the day	Customer Order Processing	Materials Team	Order Process Cycle Time
002	Support Lean Manufacturing	Reduce Manufacturing Inventory	Implement iPull supplier management practices	Set the item master to create commodity order recommendations at quantity/price break chosen	Vendor Order Management	Materials Team	Order to Price
003	Support Lean Manufacturing	Reduce Manufacturing Inventory	Eliminate returned goods storeroom	Utilize online credit capability of software	Fuel Pump Returns	Aftermarket Operations Team	Return Process Cycle Time
004	Support Lean Manufacturing	Implement Flexibility for Low Volume Products	Implement manufacturing line sequencing	Utilize system capability to sequence models and variations within a model on all lines	Injector Line Management	Injector Operations Team	Number Of Line Break and Interrupts
005	Support Lean Manufacturing	Implement Flexibility for Low Volume Products	Implement multi-plant sourcing of finished goods	Implement multi-plant MPS capability, including capacity simulations	Advanced Production Placement	Materials Team	Production Expansion Quantity
006	Support Lean Manufacturing	Implement Flexibility for Low Volume Products	Implement EDI/XML or other E-Commerce solution for interplant orders	Use messaging feature to notify placement of multiplant requirements immediately	Advanced Production Placement	Materials Team	Advanced Production Placement Order Cycle Time
007	Support Lean Manufacturing	Implement Supplier Partnerships and Certification	Implement a pay-on-receipt process for vendors	Allow vendors access into delivery and schedule screens to manage JIT deliveries	Vendor Order Management	Materials Team	% of Receipts Pay on Receipt In Period
008	Support Lean Manufacturing	Implement Activity Based Costing	Establish Product Target Costing/ MUDA Free Product Target Costs	Establish simulation costing database for development of additional cost data	Customer Order Quoting	Materials Team	Quoted Cost to Actual Cost Variation Per Period

Figure 14.2 Policy Deployment and Measurements Summary — Performance Measurement Identified

A Lean Performance measurement definition should include a review of management decision processes such as business planning to verify traditional management measurements. In most cases, these measurements will tend to be for financial performance, such as financial performance to plan. They will also include traditional operations measurements, such

MANAGEMENT POLICY DEPLOYMENT AND MEASUREMENTS SUMMARY

GAP CONTROL#	LEAN BUSINESS POLICY	LEAN PROJECT STRATEGY	DEPLOYED PROJECT OBJECTIVE	TECHNOLOGY DEPLOYMENT	PROCESS IDENTIFICATION	LEAN PERFORMANCE TEAM	PERFORMANCE MEASUREMENT
009	Support Lean Manufacturing	Implement Process Integrated Document Tools	Implement Bar Coding for Plant Documents	System can be set up to print readable part #'s on orders and pick lists	Manufactruing Order Management	Operations Team	% of Ordes Processed with Bar Codes Per Period
010	Support Lean Manufacturing	Implement Process Integrated Bar Coding	Implement Bar Coding for Customer Requirements	Use system capability to scan confirm shipment, scan shipping charges, and produce labels	Customer Order Management	Materials Management	% of Ordes Processed with Bar Codes Per Period
011	Support Lean Thinking in the Global Standardization of Engineering Processes	Design and Utilize Concurrent Engineering Processes	Provide access to engineering product data at the manufacturing sites	Use system capability to support online real-time access at all sites, at all times	New Product Introduction	Engineering Team	New Product Introduction Process Cycle Time
012	Support Lean Thinking in the Global Standardization of Engineering Processes	Provide a Standard Software Format for Engineering Product Data Management	Implement a standard software package for engineering product data management	Investigate 3rd party and interface options utilizing system data for Item Master, BOM, Routing, etc.	New Product Introduction	Engineering Team	New Product Introduction Process Cycle Time
013	Support Lean Thinking in the Global Standardization of Financial Processes	Implement Central Cash Management	Determine and accommodate financial requirements of Canada, Europe (EU, VAT), Asia	Bolt-on 3rd party capability in place for project use	Accounts Receivable	Finance Team	% Cash Available To Invest Over Total Receivables
014	Support Lean Thinking in the Global Standardization of Financial Processes	Implement Central Cash Management	Include currency considerations	Can utilize system settings configured to example attached	Accounts Receivable	Finance Team	% Cash Converted Favorably Per Period
015	Support Lean Thinking in the Global Standardization of Financial Processes	Implement Centralized Integrated Processing of Period Financial Closings	Consolidate regional financial statements	Reports should be hard-coded to utilize data available	Financial Statement Reports Processing	Finance Team	Financial Statement Reports Processing Cycle Time
016	Support Lean Thinking in the Global Standardization of Financial Processes	Implement Centralized Integrated Processing of Period Financial Closings	Consolidate global financial statements	Reports should be hard-coded to utilize data available	Financial Statement Reports Processing	Finance Team	Financial Statement Reports Processing Cycle Time

Figure 14.2 Policy Deployment and Measurements Summary — Performance Measurement Identified (cont.)

as customer results reporting and performance to schedule. We are not suggesting eliminating these measurements; rather, we are proposing only that any new performance measurements that are incorporated in the company management scheme adhere to the principles of process performance measurements illustrated above, concentrating on process

MANAGEMENT POLICY DEPLOYMENT AND MEASUREMENTS SUMMARY

GAP CONTROL#	LEAN BUSINESS POLICY	LEAN PROJECT STRATEGY	DEPLOYED PROJECT OBJECTIVE	TECHNOLOGY DEPLOYMENT	PROCESS IDENTIFICATION	LEAN PERFORMANCE TEAM	PERFORMANCE MEASUREMENT
017	Support Lean Thinking in the Global Standardization of Financial Processes	Implement Centralized Integrated Data Support, Processing and Monitoring of the Business Plan	Develop global standard reporting formats	Refer to Steering Committee for design of reports	Business Plan Performance Status	Finance Team	# of Nonstandard Reports Issued
018	Support Lean Thinking in the Global Standardization of Financial Processes	Implement Centralized Integrated Data Support, Processing and Monitoring of the Business Plan	Monitor, evaluate and report product line and manufacturing site profitability	Refer to Steering Committee for design of reports	Business Plan Performance Status	Finance Team	# of Nonstandard Reports Issued
019	Support Lean Thinking in the Global Standardization of Financial Processes	Implement Centralized Integrated Data Support, Processing and Monitoring of the Business Plan	Develop Period-To-Date reporting, including Regional Sales, Margins and Trends	Refer to Steering Committee for design of reports	Business Plan Performance Status	Finance Team	# of Nonstandard Reports Issued
020	Support Lean Thinking in the Global Standardization of Information Systems Management	Implement Global Standard Hardware and Software	Implement unmodified software packages	Modify Open Issue approvals only	Change Management Process	Information Team	% Modifications to Approvals
021	Support Lean Thinking in the Global Standardization of Information Systems Management	Implement Global Standard Hardware and Software	Leverage vendor supplied software upgrades	Maintain simulation database to apply upgrades and 3rd party	Change Management Process	Information Team	Upgrade Response to Request Cycle Time
022	Support Lean Thinking in the Global Standardization of Information Systems Management	Implement Global Information Technology Processes and Organization	Implement secure data & operations processes in a system that is seamless to the users	Utilize a systems management tool for all operations changes	Change Management Process	Information Team	# of Incidents Verified Per Period
023	Support Lean Thinking in the Global Standardization of Information Systems Management	Implement Global Information Technology Processes and Organization	Implement standards for systems uptime and reliability and measure and report performance	Identify all data and systems operations processes for measurement	Systems Operations Processes	Information Team	# of Incidents Verified Per Period
024							

Figure 14.2 Policy Deployment and Measurements Summary — Performance Measurement Identified (cont.)

throughput speed, throughput quality, and throughput cost. Other Lean Performance measurements might include:

- Setup time
- Lead time

- Cycle time
- Downtime
- Number of operators needed
- Work in process
- Finished goods inventory
- Floor space needed
- Distance traveled per part
- Cost of rejects
- Equipment needed

Process workflows are the standards and the basis of process measurement, so it stands to reason that all improved processes are reviewed by the Lean Performance teams for appropriate measurements. Standards, goals, data sources, and ownership are also determined for each measurement. Performance report cards, data collection sheets, and graph formats for steering committee and Lean Performance management presentations are designed, or existing performance scorecards are utilized. Measurements are reviewed with Lean Performance management and revised as required. A Lean Performance analysis is performed on suggestions for improvement. Implementation of the Lean Performance measurement program is planned, and procedures are prepared.

After system cutover, Lean Performance measurements are initiated by monitoring ongoing performance on data collection sheets and a Lean Performance report card. Performance measurements are presented to the Lean Performance management committee each month, and actions to be taken for improvement are suggested. A Lean Performance scorecard is used to identify the key process performance measurements proposed by the disbanding Lean Performance project team. Daily, weekly, monthly, quarterly, and yearly reporting scorecards or grids are prepared for measurement presentations.

Continuously Improving Lean Performance

Continuous improvement is not just for production processes; continuous improvement is focused on the efforts of people to accomplish processes, not on the machines or computers that support them. As we have demonstrated in the project, continuous improvement is people based. People develop the processes and are part of them; improved processes improve results. Machines, including computers, are not processes. Discrete processes are not found inside the machine, either. A computer performs a data process just as another kind of machine performs a grinding process. Machines, including computers, provide process support and may be processors of machine processes, but they are not themselves processes.

Information and management decision process standards are the foundation for management and measurement of information/support and management decision processes and their continuous Lean Performance improvement. Speaking with process performance measurements data about office processes, especially from a central database, confirms that management and supervisory work is not above process evaluation and improvement. Establishing, maintaining, and continually improving these processes is management's primary role in a workplace focused on computer-enabled processes and systems.

Continuous improvement is not simply a manufacturing/operations activity. Completion of Lean Performance planning and Lean Performance improvement activities have documented the process workflow standards for management and office processes. Lean Performance is the management process that enables an organization to continuously improve all its processes. Management's role of providing top–down leadership includes policy deployment, establishment of work standards (including process workflows and work instructions), and most importantly a demonstration of active support for Lean Performance, especially when the chips are down.

The role of staff and supervisory personnel in Lean Performance is to solve problems and assist the team members, who do the work that creates the value. The team member's role in Lean Performance is to be recognized as the process expert trained to recognize and eliminate non-value-added activities using process standards, to measure processes, to develop improvements, and to communicate ideas cross-functionally and across the enterprise.

In an unmodified implementation, process performance improvements are generally accomplished based on software capability. The new software has more capability than the software it replaced and is being used more effectively because process owners and customers have applied this new capability in a lean way. By using the software in an unmodified form, system users and process owners and customers will derive additional benefit by becoming more familiar with the full features of the software over time. However, some processes may be less efficient or effective now than the previous software, perhaps because the old software had additional features that the new software lacks or because the old software had custom programmed features or interfaces that the new software lacks.

Changing customer requirements are another reason for evaluating the performance of processes and considering improvement activities. While some modifications based on these realities may be necessary, the system as implemented should initially be frozen as is to ensure system stability during the startup period. No additional modifications should be allowed in the production environment for at least 90 days following the implementation approval date. Development will continue for modifications approved by the steering committee prior to the cutover approval date, according to a change management procedure and program testing. After appropriate testing, process changes should be implemented only when the system operations stabilize. The purpose of the change management procedure is to manage changes to the software system. The change management procedure applies to three categories of changes:

- Fixes
- Enhancements
- Design improvements

Fixes are software changes that are necessary to provide data functionality as originally planned in the system design for a particular existing screen, report, or file update. Fixes include providing proper cursor movement, consistent or standard cursor and key stroke mapping or functionality, and proper error trapping and messaging. Fixes may also be needed to ensure that a key is used in a uniform manner throughout the system or to ensure that transactions update only to design. All fixes must have issues written and submitted before they will be considered for assignment of resources. Unit tests for fixes will be performed prior to loading program changes live.

Enhancements are software changes that are necessary to provide additional functionality for data that already reside in the system, such as when these data are required to perform a necessary business process task and the needed functionality is not present in the system as originally designed. Enhancements are limited to existing screens, reports, and files or new screens and reports. Enhancements include changes necessary to provide for the viewing of data that already reside in the system, updating the data, or reporting of the data. The category of enhancement applies to the need to view, update, or present data in the proper format, sequence, or time frame. All enhancements must have issues written and submitted before they will be considered for assignment of resources. Unit tests for enhancements will be performed prior to loading program changes live.

Design improvements are software changes that are desired to provide additional functionality for the purpose of improving the performance of a business process. These changes may apply to data that may or may not already reside in the system and any functionality that is not present in the system as originally designed. Design improvements are not limited to existing screens, reports, or files. Design improvements include changes necessary to provide for the viewing of data that already reside in the system, updating the data, or reporting the data. The category of design improvement also applies to any change desired to calculate, interface, upload, download, view, update, or present data in a new format, sequence, or time frame. All design improvements must have open issues written and submitted before they will be considered for assignment of resources. All design improvements should be developed through the formal design process, including the process standards (process workflows and work instructions) and the conceptual, external, internal, and detail design specifications. It should go without saying that unit tests, volume tests, and process tests should be performed prior to loading program changes live. In all of these cases, the process workflows are the tool for measuring and determining how a process and the process input/output support should be improved.

The six steps for continuously improving management decision and information/support processes and their linkages to physical processes are:

- *Deploy management policy:* The annual business plan now includes the identification and deployment of lean business policies and strategies. Any process team member can leverage the deployment by completing a Lean Performance analysis master and distributing it for information technology deployment, whether process and team identified or not. This procedure can also be initiated by any process team member to respond to a business policy or strategy deployed for any process opportunity, be it a physical, information/support, or management decision process.
- *Deploy information technology:* The deployment of information technology initiates the response of information technologists to the opportunity or need communicated by a process team member. This action can also be initiated by an information technologist to respond to a deployed management policy or strategy or for any technology deployment for any process opportunity, be it a physical, information/support or management decision process.
- *Identify process and team:* Process team members assume the responsibility of utilizing a technology deployed or seeking a solution to any GAP they have identified.
- *Complete Lean Performance analysis:* As we have seen in the project, new opportunities result from process owner input defined and communicated through the Lean Performance analysis. Here is a summary checklist to follow in the ongoing use of the Lean Performance analysis:
    - Determine the adequacy and accuracy of the process workflow: Does it adequately depict the process? Does it accurately depict the input and output supports?

- When the process workflow is correct, demonstrate a compelling reason to proceed; rely on process results data, not opinions.
- Confirm the understanding of process purpose with process owners and customers.
- Measure the current process results at a task level to determine current process results in cost measurements, quality measurements, and speed and/or delivery measurements.
- Check for the following: Are any non-value-added tasks still in evidence? Are they necessary? Are any tasks unsupported? Are the input/output supports stable? Is any information or data missing? Can any process support deficits be found?
- Gather analysis results and utilize the 3MU (*muda, mura, muri*) and 5W–1H (who, what, where, when, why, and how) checklists to confirm.

- *Build new information system supports:* Develop a new process workflow. Resequence tasks and process input/output support where necessary. Complete prototype layouts of new information systems screens and reports demonstrating field placement. Obtain process owner and customer approval of preliminary designs. Estimate measurements for process cost, quality, and speed or delivery at a task level. Be sure to simulate process execution wherever possible. Update process workflow standards and repeat demonstrations to process owners and customers. Achieve consensus that process performance is improved. In regard to program improvements, do not modify vendor source codes. Pilot the results to reconfirm acceptance and measure results. Compare the new measurements with the baseline (before) measurements. Has the process been improved? Have all GAPs been closed? Repeat and refine until measurable improvement has been achieved, and finalize the performance measurements. If no measurable improvement can be achieved, abandon the effort. Do not alter the system for no resulting benefit.
- *Complete updated process standards:* Refine the process workflows until they adequately and accurately depict the process tasks and input/output support. Complete process work instructions for any referenced screen or report in the process.

The lean transformation is never complete; it is a process, not a destination. From this point on, the challenge for the Lean Performance management team is to work together with the process teams deploying advanced management policies on a regular basis, seeking new opportunities to further improve those processes already improved in the Lean Performance project.

INDEX

A

Advocate role, 69, 70
Analysis, hardware and communications, 232–233
APICS (Educational Society for Resource Management), xxv–xxvi
APICS Performance Advantage, 24–25
Applications opportunity assessment, 90–92
Areas overview diagrams, 125
Assessment, 73–97, see also Lean Performance assessment
readiness, 262–263
Assumptions, management, 71–73
Attitudes, within company, 94–95

B

Breakthrough Product Design (Adair and Murray), 25
Business process areas, 63
Business process listing and sequence, 66
Business process reengineering, 30

C

Capability assessment, 92–93
Champion role, 69, 70
Change agent role, 69, 71
Communications, project, 119
Communicator role, 69, 70
Company capability assessment, 92–93
Company readiness assessment, 74–90
Constraints assessment, 94–95
Continuous improvement, 267–276
  defining and initiating Lean Performance measurements, 267–272
  people loyalty and, 56–57
  process data and measurements and, 57
  sources of, 272–276
Corporate culture, 11, 55–57, see also Cultural principles
Cross-enterprise process manager, 258
Cross-enterprise process organization, 41–54
  customer relationship, 48–50
  factory flow, 53–54
  lean commerce, 41–48
  production smoothing, 51–53
  supply chain management, 50–51
Cross-functional process manager, 258
Cross-functional process organization, 13
  design and engineering, 20–21
  implementation, 15–17
  maintenance, 18–19
  new product introduction, 19–20
  quality management, 17–18
Cultural principles, 55–57
  customer as next process, 56
  loyalty to people enables continuous improvement, 56–57
  process data and measurements, 57
  process owner is process expert, 56
  process standards, 56
  product quality/process quality, 55
  what-before-how thinking, 55

Current process activity overview
  aftermarket, 136
  corporate, 135
  international, 64, 137
Customer
  as next process, 56
  in pulling value, 58, 77, 208
Customer order process comparison, 31
Customer relationship management, 48–50

D

Database financial entities, 176
Data conversion process management, 227–228
Data processing, future of, 38
Deployment
  continuous of strategy, 259–260
  management policy, 60–61, 101–118
  policy identification and deployment, 102
  project mission identification, 105–107
  project objectives identification and deployment, 110–114
  project organization, 107–110
  project scope definition, 107
  project strategy identification and deployment, 102–105
  steering committee meetings, 114–118
  steering committee organization, 101–102
  vision confirmation, 102
Design and engineering, cross-functional organization, 20–21
Design specifications preparation, 233–234
Diagnostic tools, 57–58
  4Ms, 59
  3MUs, 57–58, 209
  5Ss, 59, 79–84
  5Ws–1H, 59, 84–86

E

Education, team, 167–171
Educator/developer role, 69, 70–71
Engineering team tasks, 173–177

Enterprise resource planning (ERP), 42, 46, 49, 52

F

Facilitator/coach/catalyst role, 69, 71
Factory flow management, 53–54
Finance team tasks, 171–173
Financial entities, database, 176
5Ss, 59, 79–84
5Ws–1H, 59, 84–86
4Ms, 59, 87–97

G

GAP analysis, 210–218
Gemba Kaizen: A Commonsense Low-Cost Approach to Management (Imai), 12–13, 26–27, 58–59
General ledger accounts, 174–175
General methodology comparison, 32
Georgia Tech School of Management study, 24–25

H

Hardware/software installation, 225–226
Heijunka (production smoothing), 45, 48, 51–53

I

Implementation
  management tasks, 253–262
    auditing, 260–262
    continuous deployment of strategy, 259–260
    maintaining teams, 253–256
  project team tasks, 262–267
    completing readiness assessments, 262–263
    countdown to implementation, 264
    providing additional training, 264–265
    providing production startup support, 265
    verifying system integration, 263–264

Improved process
    implementation, see Implementation testing, 237–250
    objectives of testing, 237–238
    process test, 242–248
    process workflow and work instruction update, 249–250
    prototype and pilot test, 238
    stress test, 248–249
    test team, 238–240
    test team kick-off meeting, 240–242
    user training program, 250
Improving process performance, 165–223
    commerce team, 185–189
    Lean Performance analysis, 189–223, see also Lean Performance analysis
    management tasks
        conducting steering committee meetings, 166–167
        maintaining Lean Performance teams, 165–166
    project team tasks
        engineering team, 173–177
        finance team, 171–173
        information team, 181–185
        materials team, 177–179
        operations team, 179–181
        team education, 167–171
Index, process master, 220–223
Information/support process, 37–38
Information/support process characteristics, 133
Information team tasks, 181–185
Information technology, 29–30, 275
Integrating systems, 225–235
    completing hardware/communications analysis, 231–233
    creating production databases, 227
    creating test and training environments, 226–227
    data conversion process management, 227–228
    defining interface and database testing, 235
    design specifications preparation, 233–234

    evaluation additional software packages/interfaces, 228–229
    hardware/software installation, 225–226
    initiating system, 226
    managing outsourced programming, 234–235
    process-oriented system design, 229–231
    security setup, 226
    summarizing proposed modifications, 231–231
    testing system setup, 227
ISO 9000MIT Motor Vehicle Program, 7, 10–1110
Issue resolution process, 121–124

J

Japanese production approach, 9–11
Just-in-time concept, 41, 46

K

Kaizen: The Key to Japan's Competitive Success (Imai), 12–13, 26–27, 58–59
Kanban (production control technique), 54

L

Lean commerce, 41–48
Lean coordinator, 258
Lean diagnostic tools, 57–58
    4Ms, 59
    3MUs, 57–58, 209
    5Ss, 59, 79–84
    5Ws–1H, 59, 84–86
Lean Performance, see also individual subtopics
    as business process engineering, 26
    as compared with reengineering, 25, 27
    defined, xiii–xiv, 25–27
    importance of, xiv–xvi

mechanisms of, xv
methodology, 23–39
purpose of, xvi–xvii
as system innovation, 26
Lean Performance analysis, 63–68
    business process areas, 63
    business process listing and
        sequence, 66
    current process activity overview
        (international), 64
    GAP analysis, 210, 215–218
    in improving process performance,
        189–223
    lean business policy deployed, 61
    lean performance team
        (international), 65
    process and team identified, 67
    process improvement
        completing, 209–218
        customer in pulling value, 208
        process and team identified,
            190–193
        producing work instructions,
            218–223
        pursuit of perfection, 209
        technology deployed, 184,
            186–188
        value flow, 207–208
        value specification by product
            or family, 205
        value stream identification,
            205–207
    workflow diagram template, 67
    work instruction template, 68
Lean Performance assessment
    analysis of results, 95–96
    company capability, 92–93
    company readiness, 74–90
    opportunity to make lean
        applications, 90–92
    project constraints, 94–95
Lean Performance Foundation Blocks, 27
Lean Performance improvement,
    153–162
Lean Performance practices, 60–68
    lean performance analysis, 63–68
    lean performance teams, 61–62

management policy deployment,
    60–61
visual management, 62–63
Lean performance teams, 61–62, 65
Lean production
    as compared with mass production,
        3–5, 8
    defined, xiii–xiv, 7–9
    delayed acceptance of, 9–12
    factors necessary for success, 12–13
    origin of, 5–7
Lean progression, 35
*Lean Thinking: Banish Waste and Create
    Health in Your Corporation*
    (Womack and Jones), 23–24,
    57–58
Lean transformational principles, 57–58
Loyalty, to people, 56–57

M

(The) Machine That Changed the World
    (Womack et al.), 7–8, 10–11
Maintenance, cross-functional
    organization, 18–19
Management, 69–97
    human resources, 71–72
    Lean Performance assessment,
        73–97, see also Lean
        Performance assessment
    managerial roles, 69–71
    preliminary assessment, 72–73
    of project module, 119–128, see also
        Project team tasks
    project preparation, 97
Management assumptions, 71–73
Management policy deployment, 60–61
Managers, attitudes of, xv, 11
Mass production, 3–5, 8
    design and engineering in, 21
Master index, process, 220–223
Master production schedule (MPS)
    process, 42, 51
Material flow diagram, 180
Material flow transactions, 181
Materials team tasks, 177–179
Measurement, 267–272

Mediator/negotiator role, 69, 71
Methodology, 23-39
    comparison with other lean strategies, 29-39
    general methodology comparison, 32
    Lean Thinking (Womack and Jones), 23-24
    mechanisms of process improvement, 28-29
    project scope comparison, 33
    quality issues comparison, 34
    reasons for, 24-25
    results comparison, 34
    strategic issues comparison, 32
    tactical issues comparison, 33
Mission identification, 105-107
Motivator role, 69, 70
MRP, see Enterprise resource planning (ERP)
4Ms, 59, 87-97
3MUs, 57-58, 209

N

New product introduction, cross-functional organization, 19-20

O

Open-issue form, 122
Open issues, 121-124
Open-issue template, 123
Operations team tasks, 179-181
Opportunity assessment, 90-92
Organization, project, 124-127
Outsourced programming, 234-235
Overhead cost accumulation model, 172

P

PDCA (plan/do/check/act) process, 28, 193
Perfection, pursuit of, 58, 209
Performance practices, 60-68
    lean performance analysis, 63-68
    lean performance teams, 61-62
    management policy deployment, 60-61
    visual management, 62-63
Planning modules
    deploying management policy, 101-118
    Lean Performance improvement, 153-162
    managing project module, 119-128
    team development, 129-162
Policy identification and deployment, 102
Process and team identification, 67
Process complexity, 214
Process concurrence, 214
Process cost, 214
Process discrepancy, 213
Process effectiveness, 214
Process efficiency and timeliness, 214
Process empowerment, 214
Process GAPs, 215-218
Process identification, 131-138
Process integration/total system focus, 212
Process listing and sequence, 139-142
Process manager, 258
Process master index, 220-223
Process organization
    cross-enterprise, 13, 41-54
        customer relationship, 48-50
        factory flow, 53-54
        lean commerce, 41-48
        production smoothing, 51-53
        supply chain management, 50-51
    cross-functional, 13
        design and engineering, 20-21
        implementation of, 15-17
        maintenance, 18-19
        new product introduction, 19-20
        quality management, 17-18
Process owners, 56
Process quality, 214
Process requirements definition
    interview and status listing, 196-203
    order entry, 204
Process speed, 214

Process standards, 56
Process/system innovation, methodology compared, 30–34
Process/system overview diagram, 230
Process test, 242–248
Process waste and strain, 212
Process workflow diagram, 159
Process workflow example, 148–150
Process workflow standards, 210–213
Production databases, 227
Production smoothing (*heijunka*), 45, 48, 51–53
Progress charting, for aftermarket site
  by major business areas, 159
  by primary business areas, 160
  by secondary business areas, 160
Project constraints assessment, 94–95
Project control spreadsheet, 153–158
Project objectives, identification and deployment of, 110–114
Project organization, 107–110, 124–127
Project organization chart, 126
Project quality assurance, 127–128
Project scope, definition of, 107
Project strategy, identification and deployment of, 102–105
Project summary bar chart, 119, 120
Project team tasks, 119–128
  communications, 119
  issue resolution process, 121–124
  project organization, 124–127
  project summary bar chart, 119
  quality assurance, 127–128
  steering committee reports, 128
  workplan, 119–120
Project workplan, 119–120
Prototype and pilot test, 238, 239–244
Pull/push concept, 44
Pursuit of perfection, 209

Q

Quality, product quality/process quality principle, 55
Quality assurance, project, 127–128
Quality management, cross-functional organization, 17–18

R

RAD-JAD approach, 30
Readiness assessment, 74–90, 262–263
Reengineering, 25
  methodologies compared, 30–34

S

Sales and operations planning (SOP), 51
SDCA (standardize/do/check/act) process, 28, 193–195
Seasonal markets, 46
Security setup, systems, 226
Site configuration, 130–131
Site team development, 138
Software
  installation/evaluation, 225–226, 228–229
  outsourced, 234–235
Specifications, design, 233–234
Sponsor role, 69, 70
Spreadsheets
  project control, 153–158
  training assignments, 171
5Ss, 59, 79–84
Steering committee
  meetings, 114–118, 166–167
  organization, 101–102
  reports to, 128, 152
Strategic issues comparison, 32
Strategy, continuous deployment of, 259–260
Stress test, 248–249
Supply chain management (SCM), 41, 50–51

T

Team builder/team player role, 69, 70
Team composition
  aftermarket, 143
  corporate, 143
  international, 143
Team development, 129–162
  finalizing projects and strategies, 129–130
  process identification, 131–138

reports to steering committee, 153
site configuration, 130–131
site teams, 138
team training, 138–152
Team education, 167–171
Teams, lean performance, 61–62
Team training, 138–152
Testing, 237–250
   interface and database, 235
   objectives, 237–238
   process test, 242–248
   process workflow and work instruction update, 249–250
   prototype and pilot test, 238
   stress test, 248–249
   test team, 238–240
   test team kick-off meeting, 240–242
   user training program, 250
Test team, 238–242
3MUs, 57–58, 209
Time fences, 51
Toyota production system (TPS) model, 42–43, 48–49, 53
Training, team, 138–152
Training software, 226–227
Transformational principles, 57–58

U
User training program, 250

V
Value, precisely specifying, 57
Value-added and non-value-added processes, 206
Value flow, 58, 76, 207–208
Value identification, 76
Value stream, 58, 76
Vision, project, 102
Visual management, 62–63

W
Workflow diagram template, 67, 169
Workflow example, 148–150
Workflow standards, 210–213
Workflow update, 249–250
Work instructions, 218–223, 219
   how-to example, 151–152
   updating, 249–250
Work instruction template, 68, 170
Workplan, project, 119–120
5Ws–1H, 59, 84–86